CANADA AND THE LIBERATION OF THE NETHERLANDS, MAY 1945

CANADA AND THE LIBERATION OF THE NETHERLANDS, MAY 1945

LANCE GODDARD
FOREWORD BY MAJOR-GENERAL RICHARD ROHMER

DUNDURN PRESS
TORONTO

Editor: Barry Jowett
Copy-Editor: Andrea Pruss
Design: Jennifer Scott
Printer: University of Toronto Press

National Library of Canada Cataloguing in Publication Data

Goddard, Lance
    Canada and the liberation of the Netherlands, May 1945 / Lance Goddard.

Includes bibliographical references.
ISBN-10: 1-55002-547-3
ISBN-13: 978-1-55002-547-7

    1. Canada. Canadian Army--History--World War, 1939-1945. 2. World War, 1939-1945--Campaigns--Netherlands. 3. World War, 1939-1945--Netherlands. I. Title.

D763.N4G63 2005   940.54'21492   C2005-900172-0

1   2   3   4   5   09   08   07   06   05

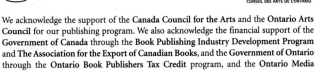

We acknowledge the support of the **Canada Council for the Arts** and the **Ontario Arts Council** for our publishing program. We also acknowledge the financial support of the **Government of Canada** through the **Book Publishing Industry Development Program** and **The Association for the Export of Canadian Books**, and the **Government of Ontario** through the **Ontario Book Publishers Tax Credit** program, and the **Ontario Media Development Corporation's Ontario Book Initiative**.

Care has been taken to trace the ownership of copyright material used in this book. The author and the publisher welcome any information enabling them to rectify any references or credits in subsequent editions.

            J. Kirk Howard, President

Printed and bound in Canada.
Printed on recycled paper.
www.dundurn.com

For my wife, Jane

Dundurn Press	Gazelle Book Services Limited	Dundurn Press
8 Market Street, Suite 200	White Cross Mills	2250 Military Road
Toronto, Ontario, Canada	Hightown, Lancaster, England	Tonawanda, NY
M5E 1M6	LA1 4X5	U.S.A. 14150

No one is as capable of gratitude as one who has emerged from the kingdom of night.

~ Elie Wiesel

The bravery and sacrifice of Canadian soldiers and airmen during the hard-fought battle for the liberation of the Netherlands is the stuff of legend and cause for eternal gratitude on the part of the people of the Netherlands.

Their never-ending affection for the liberating Canadians who freed them from the cruelly oppressive German forces has been handed down from generation to generation. It is still alive and visible in the sixtieth year since the Victory in Europe. On May 5, at the small town of Wageningen near Arnhem and Nijmegen, in the presence of my late friend, Prince Bernhard of the Netherlands, German generals signed protocols of capitulation surrendering Denmark and the Netherlands. They surrendered the rest of Europe on May 8, 1945. The Second World War in Europe was finished. The Netherlands was truly liberated. May 8 is celebrated each year as VE (Victory in Europe) Day.

It is fitting that Lance Goddard's graphic book of individual recollections and stories of Canadians and citizens of Holland be published in celebration of the sixtieth anniversary of VE Day.

These gripping accounts of fighting days among the dangerous dykes and flooded lands and in the air over Dutch terrain provide a new perspective on "how it was" in the presence of a skilled and deadly enemy. As told by veterans, Goddard's stories of death, injury, suffering, survival, and victory in the Netherlands are personal to each veteran and still alive in the memory and emotions of the speaker.

What is little known is that before D-Day, June 6, 1944, the decision had been made by the British and American senior commanders under General Eisenhower that the Canadian RCAF squadrons of the 2nd Tactical Air Force (Spitfires, Typhoons, and Mustangs) supporting the Allied armies in Europe would be dedicated to the British army. The British Royal Air Force squadrons would be there in support of the Canadian army.

So it was that when the RCAF squadrons arrived at tactical airfields in Holland in the fall of 1944 they were in support of the British army in the eastern sector of Holland. Many took part in the disastrous Montgomery operation in Arnhem and Nijmegen and in the British actions that eventually drove the German forces across the Maas River on Holland's eastern boundary.

As a result, the Canadian Army, assigned to the western reaches of the Netherlands in the most difficult and brutal territories, fought without Canadian air support.

Nevertheless, the valiant members of both the Canadian Army and the RCAF share equally in the victory, the Liberation of the Netherlands.

The people of the Netherlands even today are grateful to the people of Canada and to the Canadian veterans of the battle for the liberation of the Netherlands. This book will tell readers why the Dutch love Canadians.

Major-General Richard Rohmer, OC, CMM, DFC, O.Ont, QC
A Canadian RCAF fighter pilot
and
Veteran of the Battle for the Liberation of the Netherlands

THE DUTCH

Ted Brabers, President, Royal Netherlands Marine Corps Veterans Association

Elly Dull

Lini Grol

Liedewij Hawke

Jack Heidema, Dutch Resistance

Corrie Schogt

Henry Schogt

Martin van Denzen, President, Dutch Canadian Association of GTA

Helena van Doren

Gert van't Holt, Chairman, Welcome Again Veterans Committee

Ada Wynston

THE CANADIAN SOLDIERS AND AIRMEN

Al Armstrong, 14th Canadian Hussars

Charles Barrett, Highland Light Infantry

Doug Barrie, Highland Light Infantry

CANADA AND THE LIBERATION OF THE NETHERLANDS

Cliff Chadderton, Royal Winnipeg Rifles

Bill Clifford, RCAF

Jan de Vries, 1st Canadian Parachute Battalion

John Drummond, Regina Rifle Regiment/Saskatoon Light Infantry

Mervin Durham, Royal Canadian Engineers

Norman Edwards, 14th Canadian Hussars

Pierre Faribault, Fusiliers Mont-Royal

Charles Fosseneuve, 13th Field Artillery

Harry Fox, Hastings Prince Edward Regiment

Sydney Frost, Princess Patricia's Canadian Light Infantry

Lockhart Fulton, Royal Winnipeg Rifles

T. Garry Gould, Sherbrooke Fusiliers

John Honsberger, 4th Canadian Armoured Division

Roy Kelley, Lorne Scots

Douglas Lavoie, Fort Garry Horse

Jack Martin, Queen's Own Rifles

Gordon Mortensen, B.C. Dragoons

George Mummery, Highland Light Infantry

Ed Newman, Royal Hamilton Light Infantry

Jim Parks, Royal Winnipeg Rifles

Jack Read, Regina Rifle Regiment

Richard Rohmer, RCAF 430 Squadron

Russell Sanderson, Black Watch

Al Sellers, Governor General's Horse Guards

Doug Shaughnessy, Royal Hamilton Light Infantry

Jim Wilkinson, Black Watch

Today Canada and the Netherlands enjoy a close relationship filled with warmth and friendship. These two nations, separated by an ocean, did not always have such close ties. In fact, there had been nominal contact between the two countries prior to the Second World War. Yet a bond between them was forged in the darkest days of the twentieth century, bringing them together in a common struggle for freedom.

Freedom. Its value is precious, and unrealized until it is gone. It is essential to human existence; the loss of freedom is overshadowed only by the loss of life itself. For the people of the Netherlands, the loss of both became a grim reality in the Second World War with the brutal invasion and occupation of their homeland by the Nazis. But they struggled through those horrible years, not only to survive, but also to battle stoically for freedom.

For Canadians, the Second World War was a clash between ideologies: democracy versus totalitarianism. They faced a foe whose quest for world domination threatened everyone, and it was essential to stop them. As a member of the British Commonwealth, Canada committed itself to fighting for king and country. The outcome was uncertain, and as the tides of history changed, young men in Canadian uniforms found themselves on Dutch soil, battling for the freedom of strangers, sacrificing themselves for an oppressed people.

Canada's critical role in the liberation of the Netherlands — "De Bevrijding," as it is known in Dutch — was the key to a friendship that has blossomed between the two countries. There is no greater gift than that of freedom, and the cost was dear. Thousands of young Canadian men gave their lives in the battle for liberation and earned the gratitude of a nation.

To understand the magnitude of De Bevrijding, one must look at how the invasion took place, the level of oppression endured by the Dutch people for five years, and the monumental battles fought by the Canadian Army that led to the liberation of the Netherlands. It is the story of personal experiences, both Dutch and Canadian, of those who suffered and of those who came to their aid, creating a bond of friendship that would last for decades.

The geo-political makeup of the Netherlands played a role in the story of De Bevrijding. Located in northwestern Europe, it is the most densely populated country in Europe. At the start of the Second World War there were 9 million inhabitants in the twelve provinces that make up the Netherlands. It is bordered by Belgium to the south, Germany to the east, and the North Sea to the northwest. The country is geographically low lying, with half of it less than one metre above sea level. A great deal of land has been reclaimed from the sea through the use of dikes and sea walls, and these areas are known as *polders*. The Netherlands is divided into two parts by three rivers, the Rhine, the Waal, and the Maas, cutting across the middle of the country from east to west. Historically, the Netherlands has been renowned for its culture as well as its tulips, windmills, and wooden clogs. Progressive in its attitude, the country was the least anti-Semitic prior to the rise of the Nazis and thus became a destination for those suffering under their rule. The choice was obvious: the Netherlands was in close proximity to Germany (where the refugees were coming from in the 1930s) and it had a similar language, a long history of granting asylum to the oppressed, and, most importantly, had remained neutral in the First World War, so there was no animosity towards German refugees (as there was in Belgium and France).

In 1931, the Dutch Nazi party, Nationaal-Socialistische Beweging (NSB) was formed, but with its radical ideas, the party never gained a serious level of support in the Netherlands.

Of greater concern to the Dutch was the number of refugees coming to their border from Germany. In March 1939 alone, the Netherlands admitted eight thousand refugees, and in the end they would take in 10 percent of Germany's refugees. As much as they wished to support the oppressed, the Dutch were becoming increasingly concerned about

A familiar sight in the Netherlands, windmills originated in the Middle East, and the concept was brought to Northeastern Europe as a result of the Crusades. Today they are seen all over the Dutch countryside.

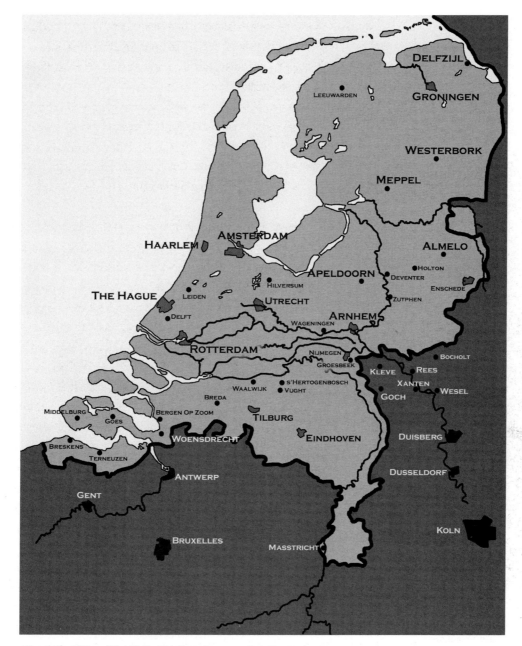

The major cities of the Netherlands and surrounding area.

The provinces of the Netherlands.

The major rivers of the Netherlands.

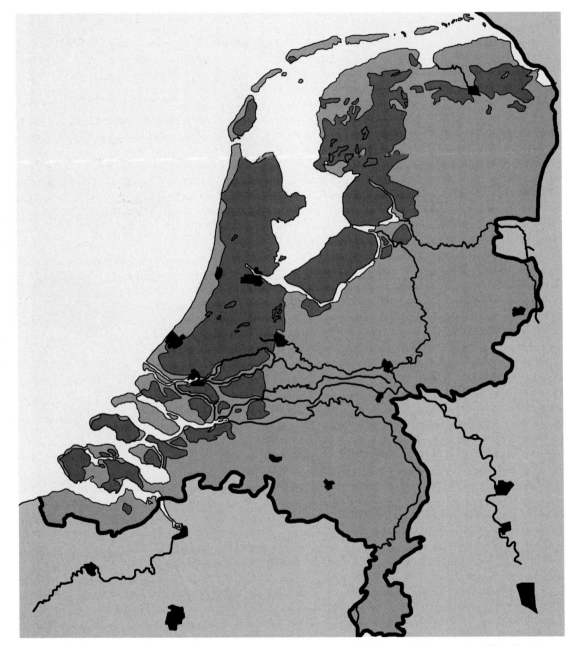

The low-lying areas of the Netherlands. The darkened areas indicate regions that are below sea level. Flooding these areas played a large role in the German defence of the occupied territories.

being overrun by refugees. The Netherlands was hit by the Depression later than other countries, and an influx of refugees didn't help the situation, but the borders remained open — at least for a while longer.

War was looming over Europe in 1939. The Netherlands had remained neutral in the First World War and had every intention of doing the same if war broke out again. In response to that stance, on August 26, 1939, Adolf Hitler guaranteed the neutrality of the Netherlands (as well as Belgium, Luxembourg, Denmark, and Switzerland).

The German army was massed along the Polish border to the east, and on September 1, 1939, the Nazis invaded Poland and began the Second World War. In the flurry of declarations of war in the next couple of days, the Dutch reiterated their neutrality on September 4. The war was in Eastern Europe, but the crushing speed and power of the German military struck fear across the continent.

With the surge of refugees leaving Germany, the Netherlands was being overwhelmed. The borders were closed in some areas, severely tightened in others. In a move that would later prove disastrous, the Dutch built a refugee camp to handle those who did get across the border. On October 9, 1939, the Westerbork Refugee Camp was opened to give them a safe haven yet keep them from the already overcrowded urban centres. The camp initially had fifty barracks erected to house eighteen hundred people comfortably.

On April 9, 1940, the Nazis invaded Norway and Denmark. Hitler's guarantee of neutrality proved to be worthless for the Danes, and concerns were raised in the Netherlands about the value of his guarantee for them. On April 19, the Dutch declared martial law, but no one could be prepared for May 10, 1940.

Without warning, without a declaration of war, and without just cause, the Nazis invaded the Netherlands as a part of Operation Gelb. They struck with devastating precision, dropping airborne units deep inside the Netherlands to seize strategic positions in advance of the ground troops. The Luftwaffe struck at the Dutch airbases and destroyed many of their aircraft. The Dutch defensive lines were easily breached in some areas, yet others provided fierce resistance. Early in the day, two Dutch Cabinet members flew to London to seek help. The cities of Limburg, Overijssel, and Achterhoek were overrun. The Dutch army was unable to match the Germans in force, speed, or equipment. To slow them down, all of the Ijssel bridges were blown up, and the Dutch opened the floodgates. As a neutral country, the Netherlands was simply not equipped to take on the Nazi war machine.

The use of the fallschirmjager spearheaded the German invasion of the Netherlands on May 10, 1940.

German *fallschirmjager* (airborne units) dropped on the airfields around Rotterdam and The Hague and captured them. Another unit dropped right in The Hague in an attempt to capture the Dutch royal family, but they were eliminated on the spot. No one in the Netherlands was safe.

Helena van Doren

We woke up early in the morning and we went outside and we saw the whole street outside, and we looked up in the air and all the airplanes went by. They were all over and we said, "Oh my gosh, the war's started." We had a little airport outside of the town for little airplanes, not for warplanes, and they came and bombed that little airfield.

Elly Dull

I was about five or six, and to us it was very sudden. On May the tenth we woke up, and my father was putting paper strips on the windows to try and keep them from shattering as the planes were droning overhead. I think it was a Sunday morning, and there were just masses of planes overhead and a very anxious broadcast. The Dutch army was passing through the streets, even with horse-drawn wagons. We lived on the coast near The Hague, and we could see the pink sky of the enormous bombardment of Rotterdam. That was a very important target for the Germans, and we could see that burning from where we were.

Lini Grol

At that time in Rotterdam I got up early in the morning and I thought, *What's going on?* People were talking in the street and carrying on, and they were talking about invasion and that the German army was coming. The patients that we had in the hospital — everybody wanted to go home, they didn't want to stay in the hospital anymore. In no time flat the wards were empty, but before long they were filled again with soldiers who had fought so hard. Some of them were in very bad condition, some of them had lost their eyes or lost their legs. Their lives were ruined.

Corrie Schogt

We lived in the countryside, and it was an absolutely beautiful spring week. My father and I were standing outside, and we heard *pang-pang-pang* over our heads — it was an air fight — there were more than one and it was very high up, and I remember my father said, "That's the end of us." We were Jewish, and my father had helped a lot of German Jews get out of Germany in the thirties. He had hoped the war wouldn't come to Holland, but it did. His remark made a tremendous impression on me. I was twelve, and my parents did not survive — they died in Auschwitz. So of course that memory is very poignant.

As the Germans crossed the river at Doesburg and Zwolle, French and British army units began to arrive to aid the Dutch. The Luftwaffe controlled the skies and proceeded to bomb the inner city of Rotterdam, killing thirty thousand people.

The German bombings exacted a terrible toll on the Dutch civilians.

Jack Heidema

I remember vividly seeing the city of Rotterdam burning. Black smoke you could see for enormous distances. I remember that very well. At age thirteen you are very impressionable.

By the end of May 10, the Dutch were reeling in shock. War was upon them, and their situation was virtually hopeless. But no one gave up the fight.

On May 11 the battle raged on for the Grebbe line. This was a defensive line set up by the Dutch using waterways and the planned flooding of polders as a means to slow down the German advance. The line was positioned to protect the major cities in the Netherlands. Confusion amongst the Dutch units was widespread; some units battled valiantly against all odds, some attempted futile counterattacks. The outcome was inevitable against the overwhelming power of the German military. By May 12 the Germans had crossed Moerdijk bridge, and the situation was getting more grim by the hour. Breda was evacuated. The crown princess and her family were evacuated to England for safety, followed by Queen Wilhelmina the very next day. The decision to leave her country in its hour of need was a tremendously difficult one for the queen, yet she would not allow herself to be captured by the Nazis and used as a puppet leader. Upon arrival in London, Queen Wilhelmina proclaimed the city the new capital of the Netherlands. This assured the Netherlands' legal existence.

Elly Dull

The royal family left for England. I remember people being initially very upset as if they were abandoned, then thinking no, because from there they could establish Radio Oranje — an Underground radio station — and have much better communication with the people.

On May 14 the Germans attacked viciously, sending the Luftwaffe to bomb the overcrowded city of Rotterdam. The number of casualties was dreadful, and the blow was devastating.

Lini Grol

Well, I was in Rotterdam at that time. I was a nurse in the hospital, and we already had lots of wounded soldiers. We thought we would stay here because there's a red cross on the roof. The alarm went off, and everybody said, "What's going to happen now?" I was fairly new in the hospital. I said to the girls, "We have to go in time for dinner," because there was a dinner at twelve o'clock and a dinner at twelve-thirty — our work had to go on. But the other ones said, "No, we don't want to go, you go." And that was my saving. Then they said, "Take the student with you." We went to the dining room, which was on the other end of the court. Lo and behold the hospital was bombed. The building was smashed and the beds were hanging on one leg and people were lying in the rubble, and we tried to save them and carry them away from the falling bricks and from the falling walls that were teetering. The roof and everything was loose, so we tried to carry the people to where it was safe. Gradually help came from the city with ambulances. We worked for five days and nights without stop, carrying patients to an emergency hospital. I don't know how many people died and how many nurses died. I was just lucky by circumstance.

Jack Heidema

The Dutch army was ill-equipped, very small. In the five days of fighting I think twelve hundred died in combat. The German army was the most powerful army in the world. Rotterdam got bombed and that was the end of the war, because the German threat was, If you don't completely surrender, we're going to do the same thing to other cities.

When the Germans threatened to bomb other Dutch cities in the same manner, General Winkelman (who had been given power by Queen Wilhelmina) ordered the Dutch army to stop fighting. On May 15, 1940, he signed the capitulation documents at Rijsoord, surrendering the majority of the Netherlands to the Germans. Excluded from the agreement was the Zeeland region, where Dutch, Belgian, and French troops continued the battle against the Nazis. Belgium had also been invaded as a part of Operation Gelb, and the French had declared war against the Germans over the invasion of Poland.

Amsterdam burns during the Nazi invasion.

Hitler's plan had been to use the blitzkrieg to overwhelm the Netherlands in just one day. The Dutch persevered for five days, but at a great cost: 2,890 were killed, 6,889 were wounded, and 29 were missing. Some Dutch pilots were able to escape in their aircraft and would return to battle the invaders of their country as members of the RAF. By 1943 these Dutch airmen would get their very own RAF squadron.

The invasion of the Netherlands by Germany. The troops march and darkness descends on the country for five years.

As the Nazis took power in the Netherlands, they took a different approach to governing the occupied territory. While other territories came under military rule, in the Netherlands the local civilian leaders were not replaced, and a German civilian authority was simply placed over the existing infrastructure. Dutch laws remained in effect. There was no instantaneous change to Nazi laws with anti-Semitic rules. The transition was gradual.

The gentle approach was by design. Hitler viewed the Dutch as "Germanic," and he had plans to annex the Netherlands into Greater Germany after the war. This long-term plan was never announced to the Dutch people: Hitler wanted to bring them around slowly. The German civilian authority allowed the Nazis to be involved in the day-to-day running of the country and allowed for subtle changes.

Lini Grol

In the beginning of the war they tried to bribe us more or less, tried to be friendly, trying to talk us into a "good thing": Hitler with one united Europe, all one big German Reich. But people didn't fall for it, except for a few. That too you can understand — if their wife was German. I was a nurse and my sisters were nurses, so we had a steady income, even as a student. You didn't get much, but it was a steady income. But there were people who didn't even have that. Hitler had promised there would be work, and indeed there was work for those who worked with the Germans. They would do that — bribe us more or less. Then gradually they took everything away. They took whatever we had: the newspapers, the radios — and then there was no communication. Everything was in Hitler's hands. So they could more or less brainwash us and make us believe everything was fine.

Henry Schogt

In the beginning the queen and the government of Holland left, but the layer immediately under the ministers stayed. They were told not to antagonize the Germans, so some people interpreted that as collaborating with them, while others didn't. There were people who immediately stepped down, while at the municipal level the Germans slowly replaced people who were obviously anti with collaborators and members of the Dutch National Socialist Party — and that was very bad. So in cities where that happened the situation was more difficult for the Resistance workers and for the Jews. For instance, one of the cities where the situation was very bad was in Groningen in the north. The Belgians had a military upper command of the Germans, and the Dutch had civilian government, and we had one of the worst war criminals at the head of the German government in Holland: Seyss-Inquart. He was Austrian; there were lots of Austrians in the Nazi higher service.

For the 1,150 legal and 650 illegal refugee German Jews at Westerbork, it was a nightmare come true. Everything that they had tried to escape from was in control of their lives again. And they were in a structure that was the very model of a concentration camp — it was no longer a safe haven. The camp was not as horrible as the German camps, with barbed wire and gun towers. That would come soon.

For the Jewish refugees, no place had seemed safer than Holland prior to the invasion. After May 15, no place could be more dangerous. The geographic conditions worked against them. The land was flat, with no mountains or large, wooded areas to hide in. The harbours were chaotic, and for the few who tried to flee by boat, it was hopeless. The German navy and U-boats controlled the English Channel. To flee by land, one had to go through Germany (which was out of the question) or head south. That was no better, since the Germans had conquered Belgium as well, and further south were the front lines of the war. Soon enough those disappeared as France fell and the Nazis came to control Western Europe. Three hundred Jews killed themselves in the first week following capitulation. They were German Jews, and they knew what was coming.

A day after taking over, Nazi censorship began in the Netherlands. While there continued to be fighting in the south, the Luftwaffe bombed Middelburg on Walcheren Island in the mouth of the Scheldt River. The city core was destroyed, and things started to fall apart. By May 19, Dutch soldiers withdrew from Zeeland, and the Nazis controlled the entire country. Just over a week later, on May 27, 1940, the Allied troops at Dunkirk were forced to evacuate to England. Over the next eight days, 350,000 men were taken across the Channel in every kind of craft that could float. The loss was devastating for the Allies.

Amsterdam 2004.

It was even worse for those who were left behind, where despair turned to hopelessness.

Arthur Seyss-Inquart was made the Reichskommissioner of the Netherlands on May 29, 1940. The position made him the highest-ranking German authority in the occupied territory. Seyss-Inquart was an Austrian veteran of Anschluss; efficient and brutal, he sought to institute and enforce Hitler's notion of "racial purity" by any means possible. Seyss-Inquart headed a civilian government, which put his focus on the population rather than on military matters. That focus made it easier for him to carry out his plans for destroying Jewish culture and commerce, with the goal of eliminating every trace of evidence that Jews had ever existed in the Netherlands. Such anti-Semitic intentions were contrary to the Dutch way of thinking. The clash of ideals would be a catalyst for the Dutch resistance.

At first the Nazi occupation appeared to be fairly liberal. Seyss-Inquart addressed the nation within the first week of becoming Reichskommissioner and stated that existing Dutch laws would remain in place and that the Germans would not impose their ideology on the Dutch. This created a false sense of security. For the Jews, the lack of Nazi ideology meant an absence of anti-Semitism. For the rest of the population it appeared that not much was going to change. As it turned out, his promises were as empty as Hitler's guarantee of the Netherlands' neutrality in 1939.

In the meantime, the gradual erosion of rights had already begun — especially for the Jews. On June 1, 1940, all Jews were removed from their positions as air raid wardens. It was a small step, and it was hardly noticed.

Henry Schogt

In the beginning it was hardly noticeable except that there were some Germans, but sneakily they started taking measures against the Jews. At the beginning they weren't allowed to be on the groups that were formed to be active when there was an air raid. Now there were no air raids immediately after the German occupation and so nobody noticed. It was slowly beginning.

When France surrendered on June 22, the Nazis controlled Europe. Darkness descended over the continent. It would be four long years before there was a glimmer of hope.

On July 2, all non-Aryan refugees in the Netherlands were ordered to register. For the Nazis, these were ones that had gotten away, and they were intent on not letting anyone slip through their fingers this time. But the occupation forces had another problem: with the

Netherlands' close proximity to England, most of the population was tuning into the BBC to get their news. The Nazis were fanatical about controlling information, and on July 4 they ordered the Dutch to stop listening to non-German radio broadcasts. The order had no effect, especially with the launch of Radio Oranje broadcasts from London, with regular addresses to the population by Queen Wilhelmina. Listening to the broadcasts had to be done in secret, but the flow of information continued.

Ted Brabers

We had the radio and we always listened to London news. So we were informed with what was going on. We never knew exactly what happened, but you got the news from London and you got the German news, and if you compared the difference, you could resolve what happened.

ID passes were mandatory, and the penalty for being without one was severe. The J denoted that the carrier was a Jew, which would often lead to greater abuse.

The erosion of rights continued through the remainder of 1940. On September 30 it was decreed that Jews could not be hired or promoted within the Dutch civil service. Government officials had to sign papers verifying that they, their spouses or fiancé(e)s, their parents, and their grandparents were not Jewish. The Nazis were starting to limit where Jews in the Netherlands could work.

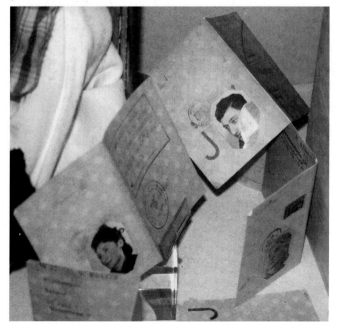

In order to control the population better, the Nazis introduced identification papers for everyone who was fifteen years of age or older. As of October 1, 1940, these papers had to be carried at all times. Failure to have one's papers resulted in a severe penalty. A large J denoted that the ID holder was a Jew.

Intent on setting an example, the Nazis retaliated against an exhibition of Dutch resistance at Noordoostpolder by sending 130 Dutch men to Buchenwald concentration camp on October 10. By November, all Jews who had worked in the civil service prior to the invasion were summarily dismissed. Included in that group were a chief justice of the Dutch Supreme Court and forty-one university professors. Students in Delft and Leiden reacted with strikes to protest the decrees against the Dutch Jews. It was the first such demonstration against the treatment of the Jews in the Netherlands, and it would not be the last.

Throughout 1941, Jews were singled out in one decree after another by Seyss-Inquart's administration. On January 10 it was decreed that all Jews had to register with the authorities. Failure to do so would result in a five-year prison term and the confiscation of all of one's property. The struggle for existence of the Jews was beginning, and not all of them were willing to go without a fight. In February, clashes between the Nazis and Jewish combat teams in Amsterdam led Himmler to order the roundup of Jews in that city. Four hundred were arrested, and the oppression was becoming intense. The Jewish population had a long history in the city of Amsterdam, and their district was a vibrant part of the city's cultural fabric. This oppression led to the February Strike on the twenty-fifth of that month. The municipal workers of Amsterdam called a general strike to protest the persecution of the Jews. The strike spread as the day wore on, including metal and shipyard workers, manual labourers, and white-collar workers. Amsterdam had been shut down. Enraged, the Nazis retaliated, yet the strike spread to Zaandam, Haarlem, Hilversum, Utrecht, Velp, and Weesp.

Henry Schogt

Well, the general strike I remember very well because that really was a strike that originated in Amsterdam. There were provocations by the Dutch Nazi police, not official police, and by the Germans. It wasn't a ghetto, but there was definitely a Jewish quarter where the not-so-well-off lived. The more well-to-do Jews lived all over the city, but there was one part where the poorer Jews lived, and it was especially in that part where there were the provocations. But also in the south where other concentrations of Jews were, there was fighting. The Jews resisted, and during one of the fights one of the Dutch Nazi people was killed, and then a reprisal: the Germans raided and arrested Jewish men in the centre of Amsterdam, and they were sent to a concentration camp, and nobody survived. When that happened, the Dutch population, the non-Jewish population, went on strike.

The measures the Nazis took against the strike were very harsh. Amsterdam had to pay a fine, and especially the Jews had to pay a lot as punishment. The measures taken by the Germans went on, they weren't slowed down. The only thing that maybe was achieved by the strike was that the barbed wire around the Jewish quarter was taken away. It didn't matter. They were raided anyway and sent to their deaths.

Volendam. Even public transportation was made off limits to the Jewish population as their rights gradually eroded until there were none left.

The strike gave the Dutch a sense of the power that they could have against the Nazis, further strengthening the resolve of many to resist the occupation. The February Strike of the Dutch people was the only protest of its kind against the persecution of Jews to occur in all of Nazi-occupied Europe. The Nazi reprisals were swift and ruthless, virtually eliminating any future public protests on the behalf of the Jews.

Once the Nazis had eliminated the public protests, they proceeded with their plans for ridding the Netherlands of all Jews. Many Dutch people felt outraged, and aid was given by underground groups to help the persecuted hide or escape. Many took this course of action at great personal risk. The Nazis established Jewish councils in the various communities across the occupied territory to accomplish their plans for the Jews in an orderly manner. These councils were used to convey German orders to the Jewish populace in a more palatable fashion, coming as they did from respected members of the community. Council members were led to believe that they were working for the benefit of their people.

The erosion of rights was not just levelled at Jews in the Netherlands (although it was more severe for them). On February 28 the Nazis declared compulsory labour for all unemployed Dutch citizens, and often workers were used as slave labour or taken away from their families for weeks or months on end.

Ted Brabers

An uncle of mine was conscripted and had to work on the bunkers at the ocean. If you were a certain age you were picked up by the Germans to work. There was fear — always fear. It was stressful on the parents because they never knew when somebody left the house if they would ever come back. The Germans could pick you

A typical maritime nation, the Netherlands had a substantial fishing fleet, but during the war it became very dangerous to venture out into the North Sea and English Channel.

Marken Island.

Volendam Harbour.

While the Nazis controlled the mainstream media, clandestine printing presses created a voice for freedom in the Netherlands.

up and you were gone. And they won't tell the parents where they took you or anything. It could tear families apart — or make them closer. And it made the neighbourhood closer, because they're protecting each other.

Jan de Vries, 1st Canadian Parachute Battalion

The only part of our family that was here [in Canada] was my mother and father, my brother, and myself. All our family was in Holland, and I know that some of them were in trouble because they were with the Underground and they also hid a Jewish family right up until the end of the war. But on the other hand it was interesting; I had one uncle who was in the German army. The Germans were good at recruiting different nationalities.

There wasn't much mail that I can recall. Mother got the odd letter, and they said that everything was okay, but the Germans censored everything so they couldn't say much, just to say that they were all alive but they couldn't say what conditions they were suffering under. We only learned that after the war.

As 1941 progressed, the Nazis made more and more attempts to control every facet of Dutch society in order to control the people. On July 5 all Dutch political parties were disbanded. Nazi Party members were put in charge of labour unions, groups, and newspapers. The reaction of the Dutch was simple: union members stopped paying their dues, groups had dwindling memberships, and newspapers were no longer read.

On July 8 all Jews were ordered to transfer all of their money to one Amsterdam bank that was essentially controlled by the German administration. The control of the Jews' money was essential to the Nazis, as their next move, starting on July 11, was to have all Jewish businesses registered and confiscated.

Ada Wynston

My mother had to close her business. She was a very famous hairdresser in Amsterdam. My father was a piano teacher, he couldn't go anymore because a Jew couldn't go to a Gentile's house, so that had a big impact on us because we were all at home. We had a nanny who was a German Jew who was with us, until she was lifted off her bed in our house and we were left behind, and that was one of the miracles of World War II. The whole thing was an unforgettable experience, although you don't even know how traumatized you are when you have to stay inside your house. This is what I remember the most, being forced to do things.

While beautiful, the Dutch countryside provided little in the way of natural protection for those who went into hiding.

The Nazis were eliminating any means of making a living for the Jews. The businesses that were confiscated were to go to non-Jews. One of the businesses affected by this decree was owned by Otto Frank. The story of the Frank family is world-famous due to the publication of *Diary Of A Young Girl* by Anne Frank after the Second World War. Their tale is reflective of what happened to so many Jewish families in the Netherlands, and the tragedy is especially poignant when it has the face of a young girl to remind the world of the innocence lost during that period. The Frank family moved from Frankfurt to the safety of Amsterdam in 1933, built a thriving business, and became contributing members of Dutch society. In anticipation of the seizure of his business, Otto Frank transferred it to two of his business associates. They ended up helping hide the Frank family for several years.

By the end of August 1941, all Jewish children were banned from schools.

Henry Schogt

In September '40 Corrie went to high school, that was her first year …

Corrie Schogt

The second year I wasn't allowed to go anymore.

Henry Schogt

For my family — we weren't Jewish — really the major problem of the war was the persecution of the Jews.

Ada Wynston

I remember being taken out of public school and being put in a Jewish school where I didn't stay very long.

Elly Dull

When it was time to start school and they were not allowed to go to the school I was supposed to go to. So I went with them to their Jewish school out of principle, and my parents let me go, and of course I insisted that that's what I wanted.

Corrie Schogt

I went to the Jewish high school after I wasn't allowed to continue at my school. We were concentrated in Amsterdam —

Henry Schogt

— slowly the Jews living outside of Amsterdam were sent to Amsterdam —

Corrie Schogt

And every day I was in the same school as Anne Frank, and every day there were fewer children. The families had been caught in raids or they went underground, as in Anne Frank's case or in my case. Or a few families committed suicide — the whole family. So that school petered out in a few months.

By late October, any Jew who was lucky enough to still have a job was required to have a special permit for that privilege. As the year wound down, orders came from Germany to commence with *Entjudung* — the ethnic cleansing of the Netherlands. Construction at Westerbork Refugee Camp added twenty-four more barracks that held an additional three hundred people per building. On December 5 all non-Dutch Jews had to register for "voluntary emigration," which in reality was a one-way ticket to a concentration camp.

The rest of the Dutch population was suffering as well. Dutch citizens were being executed for aiding Allied pilots who had been shot down over the Netherlands. One of the toughest situations was labour conscription. On December 17, Reformed Churches protested this form of slave labour, but at a cost. Many faiths lost their spiritual leaders for speaking out against injustice and inhumanity. Wearing the cloth of the Lord did not protect moral men from the reprisals of the Nazis.

On April 20, 1942, the beaches along the Dutch coast were made off limits to the populace, as the Germans were concerned with escape attempts across the Channel as well as communication and aid given to the Allies.

Restrictions on the Jews increased during the occupation of the Netherlands, placing restrictions on virtually everything they did.

Elly Dull

My mother was told to lock up the house and evacuate ten kilometres inland. The Germans thought that a target for a possible invasion by the Allies might be our coastal strip along north and south of The Hague. So we had to find another place to live, and my mother secured a flat for us in Amsterdam. The reason she was able to find that flat is because it was vacated by people who had been rounded up by the Germans in Amsterdam to be shipped off to concentration camps. In the meantime, my father's office was closed [he was a lawyer]. He was in a concentration camp, and there was no income, and my mother gradually sold paintings and traded table silver for food.

The yellow Star of David was to be worn by Jews on their clothing to make them easily distinguishable in public. It was a form of persecution that dated back to the Middle Ages in Europe.

In April 1942 the Germans began the deportation of Jews from the Netherlands. As was their habit, the Nazis eliminated the weakest first, clearing out the hospitals and deporting the Jewish patients. On April 29 more oppressive laws were passed: all Dutch Jews had to wear a yellow Star of David on their clothing. It had to be in plain sight, and the penalty for not exhibiting it while in public was six months in jail.

Ada Wynston

I became very conscious of the war as a Jew in 1942 — there was a decree that all Jews from age six on had to wear a Star of David, and as I turned six in the beginning of June I had to have the yellow star with the J on it on all of my outside clothes. So that was something I never understood, but my sister and brother didn't need it because they were younger, my mother and father did,

Jews were rounded up and transported to major cities. When the deportations began, they were transported to Westerbork, where the dreaded cattle cars would take them to the death camps.

Retaliation murders were a common occurrence under the Nazi regime. Many innocent civilians died in reprisals for Resistance activities.

and grandparents and aunts and uncles. Because they did, I never asked any questions. It had an impact because sometimes on the way to school we would be stopped by a German to see if the star was sewn on properly. If not, then you would be told make sure that the next day it was on tight. I was scared stiff.

Elly Dull

From my perspective as a child I had two very close friends, we grew up together, we did everything together, and they were Jewish, and all of a sudden they had to wear a star on their clothing, and I didn't. I was allowed to go to the beach, but they weren't.

The Dutch Resistance was becoming more organized and efficient, and the Nazis repeatedly took Dutch hostages in a vain attempt to halt the actions of clandestine groups throughout the occupied zone. On May 4, 1942, over 460 well-known Dutch citizens were seized.

Jan de Vries, 1st Canadian Parachute Battalion

The Underground was quite active in Holland, and I remember learning about one situation — there was a music teacher. The young fellow heard some noise and he went to the window, and there was a German trooper on the road down below. He opened the blind and stuck his head out, and the German said, "Come with me." He took him to a bridge not far away, there were two other youths there, and they just lined them against the railing and they shot all three. That was in retribution for the Underground doing something in the area.

Ted Brabers

All of a sudden somebody disappeared — they could be shot, they could be in a concentration camp, we didn't know. You found out later. The Underground worked in cells, and lots of time the people in the cells didn't know the other groups. There was one person that was a contact, but never by name. Nobody told you who was who unless you were a leader of the group.

Lini Grol

Of course there would be revenge from the Germans. One time a German officer was killed by a group in a small town, and the Germans lined up all the men over fifteen against the wall and killed them. Because of that one officer. So they really were very brutal in their revenge. But we were not easy, we really tried to sabotage them whenever we could.

Jack Heidema

They would take hostages, anywhere between twenty and fifty, and just line them up against the wall and then leave them there for twenty-four hours so everyone could see. In Amsterdam they had a dozen hostages that were shot, and a couple of Resistance people took a Dutch flag and draped it over top in full view of the Germans. All this stuff created more resentment and more hatred. I don't think that feeling has ever gone away. I was at my brother's grave about four years ago at Loenen — thirty-two hundred Resistance people are buried there, men and women. I found my brother's grave and put a poppy on it. I saw his name on a horizontal plaque, and I swore, "You bastards! You killed my only brother!" And I screamed. I thought the hatred was long gone, but it wasn't.

In England, those Dutch citizens who had been lucky enough to escape wanted to take an active role in the conflict with Germany. On June 2, 1942, the refugees in London got their wish and joined in the war effort through Oranjehaven for Engelandvaarders. Taking an active role would help bring De Bevrijding closer.

At the end of June a curfew was placed on all Jews prohibiting them from being outside from 8:00 p.m. until 6:00 a.m. On July 1, Westerbork Refugee Camp officially became a transit camp. The deportation of the Jews from the Netherlands began in earnest that month, with their destination being Auschwitz (in Poland), Sobibor (Poland), Theresienstadt (Czechoslovakia), and Bergen-Belsen (Germany). There was no intention to use Dutch Jews as labourers. They were all being sent to extermination camps.

Over sixty trains made the trip from Westerbork to Auschwitz. Every Tuesday a cattle train crammed full with a thousand Jews was sent directly to Birkenau (the extermination centre of

The Westerbork Camp museum. Located near the actual camp site, this museum depicts life in the transit camp, with many artifacts and presentations.

Inside the Westerbork Camp museum the story of the victims is told.

A model of the Westerbork Camp, depicting the layout of the buildings and the security perimeter.

LEFT: *Display of the bunk beds that were crammed into the barracks at Westerbork.* ABOVE: *A painting depicts the grim conditions in the large barracks at Westerbork.*

Auschwitz). Auschwitz was a massive camp, built for the efficient extermination of enemies of the Reich. Between 1940 and 1945, an estimated 1.1 to 1.5 million people died at Auschwitz.

Nineteen trains from Westerbork went to Sobibor extermination camp. Construction of Sobibor had just been completed in March 1942, and it was designed to kill as many people as possible in the shortest amount of time. Out of thirty-five thousand Dutch Jews sent to Sobibor, only nineteen escaped death.

Theresienstadt was located near Prague in Czechoslovakia. It was a Jewish ghetto run by the SS and was primarily a transit camp en route to extermination camps. The Nazis used Theresienstadt as a model Jewish settlement for Red Cross inspections, complete with authentic-looking shops, schools, and cafés. The facade was used to camouflage the mass extermination that was going on elsewhere.

Bergen-Belsen was located between Hanover and Hamburg in Germany. It was originally used as a POW camp but was handed over to the SS in April 1943 to be used as a concentration camp. The camp was notorious for starvation and deadly

LEFT: *Concrete corners and panels depict the location and size of the barracks.* RIGHT: *The latrines at Westerbork. Sanitary conditions were not a concern and diseases ran rampant at times.*

LEFT: *The fence and watchtower at Westerbork Camp.* RIGHT: *A ditch ran alongside the perimeter fence. This segment is located beside Barrack 67 (where Anne Frank was held).*

LEFT: *Once a refugee camp, the Germans transformed Westerbork into a transit camp where the destination was a death camp in Poland, Germany, or Czechoslovakia. The fence was not installed until the end of 1941.* RIGHT: *The railway tracks into Westerbork Camp. They were destroyed after the liberation, signifying the end of a very dark chapter in Dutch history.*

Statue depicting the victims at the Westerbork Camp museum.

diseases. During the Second World War, twenty thousand POWs and fifty thousand inmates died at Bergen-Belsen.

Ada Wynston

The thing is you go to a Jewish school and every day there would be some kids missing. That's what I didn't understand. I thought, *Oh wow, I just got here, made new friends, I wonder if they're sick.* You would go home and say, "I just had this new friend, but she didn't come to school today." Well, my parents wouldn't tell me what was happening; I guess you don't tell a young child.

Elly Dull

One of my little friends, Florence, disappeared. That family simply left one evening and went into hiding, I think with a fishing family in the town of Scheveningen and eventually further along in the country. They were a family of four, and they were never together all four of them, they were all placed in different houses. My friend was my age, she was five or six, and she was rarely in the same house as her parents, and they often moved. They survived. My father, being a close friend and confidant and a lawyer, he went into their house that evening and took all of their papers, all prearranged, took it into our house, and locked up their house. Then my second little friend suddenly disappeared, and that family was no longer allowed to live on our boulevard. They were all gathered together in a certain ghetto in Amsterdam, and they were grouped together with a very definite purpose in mind. So she disappeared out of my life.

Ada Wynston

It started with an afternoon when my mother wanted to go on a visit and my father said, "Please don't, it's too dangerous," and my mother was unstoppable, and she and I went out together. She wore the star on her dress, and I had a cardigan over my little shirt and skirt, and my star was under my cardigan. We were on the streetcar when we were still allowed to, and after about two stops the SS was there, or the Gestapo, and they hauled all the

Jews off the streetcar. Those whose stars were visible. I still don't know whether my mother blinked at me or made a move — I crawled around the streetcar and I went back home and just said, "Mom is gone." From that point on everything went downhill.

My mother went to Auschwitz, and she didn't stay that long. I heard some stories from two women who were with her who later lived in Toronto. They were in Auschwitz with her. They were in Mengele's experimental camp, and they were also in the so-called elite group of women because they were good-looking, and there were some camp guards who liked women and used them for other things than just talking, and my mother said no. That was a direct route to the gas chamber. With her seventy-two direct family members — her parents perished in Sobibor, but the rest of her family died in Auschwitz, and most of my father's family died in Auschwitz. The only one I ever knew was my mother's mom and one of her brothers, and herself for six years, and that's not very good. In my father's family three sisters survived and he survived, but the other sisters all died — three of them — and two brothers and their wives and children. This is how we lost almost all of our family. When you talk to people they say you're very lucky, and they are right, because four out of the five in our immediate family survived.

The front doors at 263 Prinsengracht in Amsterdam, where Anne Frank and her family hid for twenty-five months. The building is now known worldwide as the Anne Frank Huis. It is a museum maintained in remembrance of those who suffered through the Holocaust.

For Anne Frank's family, the situation had come to a head: her sister Margot had received her call-up notice, which meant that she would be deported to a "work camp." The only choices were to show up or to go into hiding. The decision to go into hiding affected the whole family. If someone did not appear for their call-up, the rest of the family would be rounded up and shipped off. The family did not want to be split up, so they did something extraordinarily rare: they went into hiding together in one location. It was almost impossible to find a hiding place that would accommodate several people and still be safe. But Otto Frank had a secret annex above his office at 263 Prinsengracht in Amsterdam, and the family was aided by Otto's business partners and friends — at great personal risk. On July 6, 1942, the Frank family went into hiding, living in fear and having to carry on without making noise or giving away their presence.

Most of the Jews who went into hiding in the Netherlands were German. Perhaps their previous experience with the Nazis filled them with well-founded distrust. For many Jews, going into hiding was not an option. They would have to lose their identities (Jews had to report any change of address; to avoid this, they would have to disappear from the face of the earth), and the loss of identity precluded getting rations. The black market would become the only source of food, and prices were skyrocketing. By that point most Jews were impoverished due to Nazi laws, and any money they had was tied up in the Nazi-controlled bank. Some families didn't go into hiding because of the fear of separation; worse, sometimes only some members had a place to hide and the rest would be abandoned to Nazi persecution. Some families preferred to face whatever was coming together.

Someone in hiding needed refuge, which meant a great imposition on a non-Jewish friend or acquaintance. The personal risks for Gentiles were great. If caught, their families faced the same fate as the Jews they were hiding. In small communities, everyone knew everyone, and it was hard to hide someone without being noticed. People were denounced by neighbours who either sympathized with the Germans or were desperate for the money paid for such information. There were Dutch citizens and underground groups that readily organized and offered safe haven. Approximately twenty-four thousand Jews were *onderduikers* (meaning "to dive under," the Dutch term for those who went into hiding), of whom eight thousand were caught.

Jewish families were being moved to the major cities and into concentrated ghettos. The homes and possessions that were left behind were sealed and would be sorted out and sent to Germany at a later date. Everything was confiscated.

The Jodenwijk in Amsterdam.

Corrie Schogt

So when we were gathered in Amsterdam the house was literally sealed, we had a little suitcase and were put on the streetcar. From there on it was difficult. We were lucky, we lived with relatives who were very kind and we had one floor of their house. My oldest sister had already gone — she was in university, and she did not want to be in hiding as to not to bring those people into danger. My little sister was still at home, and my other sister had just finished high school, but there was nothing we could do. Well, every day was one. One day my father came home and said, "We've been denounced." We think it is because he helped Jews out of Germany, and these people had gone on to other countries or stayed in Holland — but they were all registered. I think it's because of that [that he was denounced]. That night we left my relatives' house. I'm sure that my parents were not sure that they were doing the right thing because three young Germans had come to my father's office to take him away. My father, fluent in German — his mother was German — gave them a lecture, pleading, as he was able to do as a barrister, that you don't know who the criminals are, we are not criminals, and they let him go. But they said they'd come back tomorrow morning, so in other words: go! We did leave, and luckily our relatives were not taken the next morning, but the Germans did come. That night we stayed as a family, the four of us, in a friend's house, but he couldn't keep us. The next morning we were on our way to our different addresses, my parents to one, my sister to one, and I to another one. So that was the end of the family.

Henry Schogt

In the typical Dutch situation where everybody knows at least somebody, the family who Corrie stayed with in Amsterdam, the oldest son was a classmate of mine in elementary school, and in high school until he had to go to another school because he was Jewish. They survived, and we are still friends.

Corrie Schogt

But we met in the fifties in university in Amsterdam.

Liedewij Hawke

There was a Jewish family hidden on our street, all during the war, and they survived. This I didn't know, we were kept in the dark about everything. I also understand that in my area — De Bilt and Bilthoven — not as many Jewish people were taken in as in certain other parts of the country. There would be a certain cautiousness, and a lot of people did not commit themselves to take in Jewish people. They didn't really have much of a chance.

Canals criss-cross the Netherlands, creating pastoral scenes all across the nation.

Lini Grol

We had one little girl on the children's ward and we knew she was Jewish, and one evening somebody came and said, "I have to take Minka to the x-ray." In those days we didn't make forms and all that. They took Minka to the x-ray, and not a half an hour later here came a few German officers and they wanted Minka. Well, she's in x-ray. Well, where's the form? Oh we don't fill in forms. And they were mumbling about those stupid Dutch, what do they know? They don't have a record and they don't have anybody sign for that! They wanted to take Minka because she was a Jewish child, so she escaped. I'm still glad about that.

ABOVE: *Quiet Dutch towns were emptied of Jews as they were forced into the larger cities in preparation for their deportation.* FAR LEFT: *Breda street scene.* LEFT: *The Jewish district in Amsterdam circa 1942-43.*

Elly Dull

My father would have been about forty, he was a lawyer in Utrecht, and he was very involved — not immediately, but gradually — in trying to procure passports for neighbours who were trying to flee across the border into Belgium, into Switzerland. We did have children going through our house — Jewish children — not to stay with us, just for a day or two, until they could find a more permanent spot. That was usually in the south of Holland, usually in a farm, or in the far northeast — where it wasn't as densely populated, it wasn't as closely observed. That's what he did. I think he was betrayed by a live-in housekeeper, she may have been planted there.

Caught in a raid, Ada Wynston's family found themselves at the Hollandse Schouwburg, a theatre in Amsterdam that had been turned into a temporary detention area until the detainees were shipped to Westerbork. The Dutch Resistance would bribe guards to free detainees and then take them into hiding.

Ada Wynston

The grown-ups were put in the theatre in Amsterdam, in the heart of the city, and the children were taken across the street to a Jewish daycare centre. We were held there, and it was full. There were 232 kids in there, and we were looked after by the Jewish principal and Jewish nurses, and of course there were German soldiers everywhere around the outside. They focused more on the theatre where all the parents were because eventually they were transported to Westerbork. We were in there, my sister and brother and I, and more than two hundred other children, waiting to be transported to Westerbork. That was the purpose of the Nazis — keep the kids together, ship them out together, and then kill them all together in one of the camps. It was then that the Resistance in Holland was really starting to come into being. This came down from the pulpit in the churches mainly in the north of Holland, the Protestant more than the Roman Catholics. They said, "Start something, let's help the kids." We were saved by one of the larger Underground groups called the NV group, in Dutch it means "a company without name." These were young students, most of them were devout Christians — Dutch Reformed, Christian Reformed — and they took all of us, not at the same time but by bunches, out of the daycare centre. If they did have a hiding place for some kids, they would go immediately. My brother did because he was a baby, but my sister and I and a boy who later became mayor of Amsterdam were shipped in groups of thirty to the very south of Holland to what I call holding bins. It was a hiding place, in a house in the city of Brunssum, and this family Vermeer were father, mother, and ten kids — four in the Resistance — and they had a cellar. There were thirty-four kids at the same time when I was there with my sister and Ed van Thijn. From there they would try to go through the country and find hiding places for us. This is how people ended up in one place or, like myself, in two other places, and waiting until the war was over. The person who picked you up would say, "Come on, Ada, I will take you to your hiding place, you're no longer Jewish, you're going to a family that's Christian Reformed, you got to go to church if you are allowed out on the streets. You have to act as if you were one of them, if you don't it's too dangerous and you will have to be moved." You had to try to put this in your head when you're not seven years old, so you became a liar at the age of six or seven, you learn to lie to save yourself, or to save your rescuers. While I was there they were lovely people, but when there was a betrayal I had to be moved, and they just called a family not far from there, and they said, "We've got a Jewish girl, can you take her?" And this is for me something I still don't understand, when they say, "Yes, of course." That takes guts. Both families where I was had five kids, all of them were dark-haired and dark eyes so I didn't look any different than they did.

My father spent three and a half years in one room in Amsterdam, right in the heart of it all. He never went out, he was there all of the war. And then you come out and find out what happened to your family — almost understandable that you're a mental wreck. He had vibrant red hair and blue eyes and loved kids, and when I saw him again he had grey hair and his face was all sort of yellowish white, he had aged tremendously — mentally and physically.

The Germans confiscated Dutch bicycles and in some cases handed out receipts to recover them "after German Victory Day." This scene took place at Rembrandt Square in Amsterdam (near German headquarters).

Henry Schogt

In our case the Underground helped us

Corrie Schogt

The Resistance. We use that term more.

Henry Schogt

So we had ration coupons that came from them, then we had potatoes from an island, and we had coal from the Calvinists. Everybody helped.

Dutch churches responded to the deportation of the Dutch Jews with letters of protest and dissenting sermons from the pulpits. Nazi reprisals ensued, and Dutch leaders were taken hostage to control the emotions that were heating up.

On January 15, 1943, the Nazis opened the concentration camp at Vught, which was located close to den Bosch, the capital of Noord Brabant province. While Vught was smaller than Westerbork, it was far more vicious in its treatment of the inmates. The camp was primarily used for political prisoners and hostages, but it was also used as a transit camp for Jews.

Elly Dull

In the winter my father had pneumonia and he was in the hospital and he didn't come home, he was picked up by the Germans for interrogation and subsequently shipped off to a Dutch concentration camp called Vught near S'Hertogenbosch as a political prisoner. He did some Underground work, he helped people to flee. He would falsify some papers for them, we had some things hidden in our house, and he was betrayed.

The camp was very, very bad. They had guard dogs, and my father had deep scars on his legs when dogs would attack these prisoners. They were called up in the middle of the night to stand in the square while they had to give

TOP LEFT: *Monument to the over eighteen hundred Jewish children who died at Vught.* TOP CENTRE: *The list of names of Jewish children who died at Vught.* TOP RIGHT: *Poignant reminder of the loss of innocence.* MIDDLE LEFT: *Crowded sleeping quarters in the barracks.* CENTRE: *Detail of one of the crematorium ovens.* MIDDLE RIGHT: *Vught was furnished with several crematoriums for the disposal of bodies.* BOTTOM LEFT: *Museum display of inmate uniforms.* BOTTOM RIGHT: *Vught was used for political prisoners as well as for holding Jews until they were sent on to Westerbork (for deportation to the death camps in the east). It was the scene of numerous crimes against humanity. Inmates were beaten to death, some brutalized with a club wrapped with barbed wire. Often the guard dogs were set upon prisoners to inflict pain and suffering.*

their presence every day, preferably in the middle of the night and when it rained, and lift their arms up for two hours, and if you let them drop you'd get kicked on the head or you'd get shot — it was very, very bad. It was more a Dutch political prisoner camp. There was another camp like that at Amersfoort, a place of ill repute.

The Dutch royal family in Ottawa, Canada: Princess Juliana with her daughters Princesses Beatrix, Irene, and Margriet in 1943. By providing refuge, Canada began a long and rewarding friendship with the Dutch that lasts to this day.

One of the key reasons that the Netherlands and Canada developed such a close friendship was the hospitality and protection Canada provided to the Dutch royal family. While Queen Wilhelmina remained in London, Crown Princess Juliana and her family moved to Ottawa in 1942, out of the reach of the German bombers and the peril that a Nazi invasion might put them in. The future queen was warmly welcomed, and on January 19, 1943, Princess Juliana gave birth to her third daughter, Margriet, at Ottawa's Civic Hospital. The room was decreed to be Dutch territory for the occasion so that the princess would be a Dutch citizen. Princess Margriet was named after the marguerite flower, the national symbol of resistance in the Netherlands. The infant princess became a national sweetheart. For the first two and a half years of Princess Margriet's life her home was Canada. The refuge provided by Canada sowed the seeds of friendship that would blossom in the years to come.

Elly Dull

Bernhard stayed behind in England with Queen Wilhelmina. Churchill, who had his war cabinet room there in London, said at one point, "There is only one man in this room, and that's the Queen of the Netherlands," because she was so forceful and she really was a phenomenal woman.

A week after the princess's birth, terror reigned in Apeldoorn. On January 26, 1943, the Nazis rounded up twelve hundred Jews in the city and deported them. Resistance was growing, and in Haarlem an attack on a German officer on January 30 led to brutal reprisals as one hundred people were arrested and ten were executed. Not to be deterred, another Resistance group killed General Seyffardt, the commanding officer of the Dutch Volunteer Legion, on February 5. The Dutch Volunteer Legion was an army unit made up of Dutch volunteers who fought for the Nazis. Many occupied territories had a unit like it, to be used as much for propaganda as it was for military action. Some Dutch citizens did join the unit to fight the Communists (after Operation Barbarossa on June 22, 1941, when the Germans attacked the Soviet Union), and the unit wore Dutch national insignias on their uniforms. Seyffardt was an old Dutch general who believed in the fight against the Bolsheviks; he was being used by the Germans to lure more Dutch recruits, only to die at the hands of his own countrymen. The Dutch Volunteer Legion was being formed into a Waffen-SS unit, and eventually they would fight on the Eastern Front.

Rounding up Jews in the Netherlands.

Henry Schogt

In 1943 the Germans asked from the students and the university staff a declaration of loyalty. They had to sign it, and the students, with few exceptions, refused. Many of the students went underground, and others who didn't have the opportunity were sent to Germany for work in factories.

After the Germans had solidified control of the Netherlands in 1940, they freed the Dutch prisoners of war who had resisted the invasion. In April 1943, Wehrmacht General Christiansen ordered Dutch POWs to report for renewed captivity. While the decree did not include most conscripts, Christiansen had failed to make this clear in his proclamation, causing an emotional outburst across the Netherlands. Strikes ensued, which led to harsh crackdowns. The Nazis executed two hundred people, and the Resistance grew.

On May 6, Dutch men aged eighteen to thirty-five were ordered to report for work in Germany to aid in the war effort. The effect on the local economy was devastating. Even though the Germans saw the Netherlands as a member of Greater Germany in the future, their actions were ruining what future the country had.

Liedewij Hawke

There was fear and tension, enormous uncertainty and depression. My grandparents moved in with us for a while. They had my bachelor uncle with them. How were we all going to feed them? It was very stressful. I remember my mother

always being worried, and my father had to hide. The Germans were desperate for men, to defend and to dig the defences in Holland. So they would come to the door, but then we had a spot beneath the kitchen floor, under the carpeting, it was like a trap door, and Father would hide there.

Then one night somehow it had been left open — the trap door — and my mother went into the dark kitchen to get something in the middle of the night, and she fell in. Her leg — I don't think that it was broken — but there was a severe problem with her leg, and it became ulcerated. Because you didn't have any food everything became ulcerated — my legs were covered with ulcers too. I still have marks from that time. So my mother had to sit with her leg on a chair, those were the doctor's orders, so that her big wound would heal. Of course that was terribly frustrating with three young children and my sister being handicapped, so that she had to be helped with everything. My brother was lively and I was quite lively — and my mother had to cook, but there wasn't much to cook.

Lini Grol

My brother went into hiding — he thought, *My sisters are safe in the hospital,* so he went to apply for nursing in a mental hospital, and he thought, *Nobody will get me there.* But sure enough the Germans came, and the latecomers were the first ones to be thrown out. So my brother was shipped off to Germany. But he knew how to escape. He walked all the way, but

TOP: *View of the Central Station in Amsterdam from the Victoria Hotel during the occupation.* BOTTOM: *A group of Dutch men being led off into slavery. Labour conscription laws targeted men who were young and able-bodied. Later in the war the Germans would not be so choosy about whom they conscripted.*

he didn't come home. He didn't dare because he thought, *If I come home then my family will get in trouble.* My parents still thought, *Well, Gerry was taken by the Germans, he's in a camp in Germany.* He walked to the south of Holland to a village, and he hid with a farmer. Later on the farmer came in the store and she said, "You have greetings from your son Gerry, we have him at our house." Well, my mother didn't know what happened — she was laughing and crying, and at least he was safe. But he would quite often have to dig out in the garden and sleep there because the Nazis came regularly to the farms looking for people in hiding. But the farmers were very clever, they made hideouts in the field under the shrubbery.

> For several years the Nazis had banned the Dutch from listening to anything on the radio other than German broadcasts. This prohibition had never been effectively enforced. In order to control the flow of information and to manipulate the populace by eliminating outside influences, the Nazis ordered that all radios be turned in. A million radios were confiscated. But hidden radios still crackled in homes, picking up the signal of the BBC, Radio Oranje, and freedom.

Martin van Denzen

We were not allowed to have any radios. I think my dad had one hidden. We didn't have that much to begin with. Sewing machines, anything like that, they would come into the house and take all the stuff away. If you were caught with a bicycle in the street and the Germans came along it would be gone. They would just take it. Anything of value was taken by the Germans and shipped to Germany. You were not allowed to have anything.

Liedewij Hawke

My brother, who is three years older than I am, discovered the radio one day hidden in the attic. The neighbours would come and listen. It was a dangerous thing to have, they were all supposed to be handed in, but quite a few people did keep one, and they listened. And when there was no power, I understand people listened to crystal radios. I don't know quite frankly, because we were not allowed to know. My parents were always whispering, because when young children hear something they will repeat it in the streets.

> The persecution of the Jews was in full swing in mid-1943. On May 19, churches across the Netherlands spoke out passionately against the Nazi order to sterilize all Jews who were married to non-Jews. The next day Amsterdam Jews were ordered to report to Westerbork to register for deportation.

A roundup nets a large group of Dutch civilians.

Elly Dull

One of my worst memories is that one of my friends, one of the two that disappeared, moved into a ghetto in Amsterdam. By chance I ended up in Amsterdam in a different part of town, and I found her again. I went every day with a little red bicycle along the Amstel River to her ghetto. I was the only non-Jewish child who went to visit her. It was a very old apartment building. There were very steep staircases, and there was a family off in each little portal, they were crammed five and six to a flat. There was only cold water. As a non-Jewish child, I was allowed in the shops. The Jews were not allowed in until after three o'clock when there was nothing left. So I was about nine or ten and I went there every day and I went up and down the staircase, knocked at every portal, got a little shopping list, got a little bit of money, got their coupons, and I went to the store for all of the families. Nobody would get very much, I was shopping for five or six families. Then we'd have a little playtime, and I'd go back on my bicycle to our flat before dark.

Inevitably one day I came and knocked on the door and a German soldier opened the door. That night that whole block of people had been rounded up, and my friend Tilly was gone. They were all shipped off to Westerbork and onward after that. So Tilly would have been maybe ten or so. That was the end — my friends were gone.

Ada Wynston

At my first real hiding place I had a very close call, and this is why I had to leave there. My war father was the assistant to the mayor of the town, so everybody knew him, and they knew he had five kids and they must have seen me, and that was betrayed. So he told me, "If ever we tell you to go to bed at any hour of the day, don't start with your stubborn streak — you go, we will help you." In Holland they had curfews, and when it got dark, you had to draw your drapes and turn the light on, or if you didn't draw your drapes you couldn't put your light on, it had to be dark. Lucky for me this is another thing that saved my life. I was told by my war father and his eldest daughter that I had to go to bed. First they took the littlest one of the five — we slept in the same room — and this poor kid didn't know what was going on. You lay there and you don't move. They made up a handkerchief and made out that she was sick and then they put me in bed but underneath. They took everything off the bed, put a piece of wood underneath with sort of a blanket and put me there, and then the spring and another piece of wood over that and then the double mattresses and then they made up the bed perfectly. So that was my "going to bed" when it was dangerous, hiding inside the bed. Two Nazis did show up in the house and they ran through it and they came upstairs and they asked her to turn the light on, and she said, "I can't do that because my drapes are open." They looked at the one bed with the little sister and then looked at my bed and, with a bayonet, stabbed right through it. It didn't hit me because I was too little. I've been back to that house a few years ago and I stood there and I shook and I could almost not breathe. That was the closest call in that house, and of course that same night I had to be moved, and the father had to go into hiding as well. He'd be shot if he were caught.

The German presence was everywhere in the Netherlands. Here a flower seller plies his trade under the watchful eye of a German officer.

After the strikes of April and May of 1943, the Dutch Resistance hardened, growing slowly at first, in much the same manner as the Nazi oppression. The Resistance became more organized but was not operating at full scale until mid-1943.

While the early stages of resistance were characterized by passive action, tough times called for tough measures. The Dutch Resistance organized some highly motivated and successful combat units, participating in numerous daring and successful missions. The destruction of transportation and communication lines, the raiding of distribution centres (of ration coupons, papers, etc.), and the organization of prison breaks (to free political prisoners and members of the Resistance) were trademarks of the Resistance. As time progressed, they became one of the best organized and most effective Resistance operations in all of occupied Europe. An estimated fifty to sixty thousand Dutch citizens were involved in underground activities, while hundreds of thousands more provided assistance. The risks were high, though, and more than ten thousand members of the Dutch Resistance died in the battle for De Bevrijding.

The Dutch Resistance was quite sophisticated in its forgeries of German documents and passes.

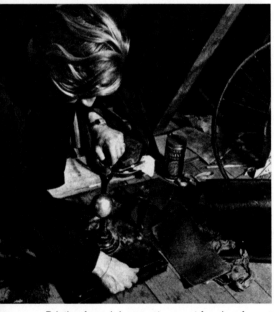

Printing forged documents meant freedom for some, survival for others.

Jack Heidema

There were two different departments. There was the L.O. — they looked after the people in hiding, we called them divers, and they also looked after getting them ration cards. The ration cards came from the fighting Resistance — two different elements altogether. My brother was in the fighting Resistance, the fighting unit — they were armed. They would do railways, bridges, German installations, and the places where the ration cards were issued. They would make raids on them and rob the cards and then pass them on to us, to the non-fighting groups. I belonged to the non-fighting group. We would then distribute those ration cards through a whole lot of cells and individuals down the line to the people that were hidden. So the Resistance was really two units — the fighting unit and the non-fighting unit. They were under a separate command.

Ted Brabers

One part I remember vividly, I found out they [the Dutch Resistance] had set up a printing press in the auction building. The auction building was for food and vegetables, and they had in the middle of the building a container to keep the eggs in there, and there was some kind of a milky substance that the eggs were kept in. Under that, the Underground had made an opening, and they had a printing press there. That's where they printed the daily bulletin and that was circulated from that place. That auction building was controlled by the Germans. They had an officer's office in there and also guards, and never ever was anyone caught.

Jack Heidema

Resistance people would meet in my mom's house. My mother was a divorcee, so she lived with my brother and myself. My mother, through my brother, got involved in the Resistance. We had meetings at our house almost from the beginning.

One of the guys was arrested, he was tortured, and he broke, and the next day seventeen people in my mother's group were arrested, including my mom. She ended up in the prison in s'Gravenhage, which is an outskirt of the city of The Hague. That was in the spring of 1944. I disappeared because they were looking for me too. I became a courier, meaning that I would take falsified papers, small arms, ammunition, from place to place. It was hazardous because if you were arrested your chances of coming back were pretty well nil.

Those willing to risk everything to be a member of the Dutch Resistance were still a minority. For many Dutch people, the day-to-day concern was to protect themselves and their families. They were forced to adapt constantly to the increasingly difficult circumstances of daily life under the brutal Nazi regime. The Germans increased the length of the workweek to seventy-two hours on August 25, 1943. Food was scarce, as were heating materials and the daily necessities of life. To live was to suffer.

Ada Wynston

I ended up in the last place until the war was over — right where all the Germans were fighting. The minute I arrived there the Germans took over the whole upstairs of the house. In that house they had thirty Germans billeted. I was sitting in the home of the enemy. No one ever betrayed me. I spent nine months in the cellar. One German came down and asked questions why I was sleeping there. I told him, "You have the whole upstairs, we're sleeping all over the house." The cellar I was in was two metres by two metres and there was no room for anybody. Every night he came down, never said a word, whether he trusted the whole thing or not, so to me you see that is a real German, he was probably called up for duty. That's how I spent my war years in hiding, I had to go to church when I could, I learned everything about being Christian Reformed — very confusing when you've been Jewish. Until the war was over I was so indoctrinated in this religion that you don't even remember what it was like to be Jewish.

Corrie Schogt

The second close call was when my parents had been caught when they were in hiding. People knew and told the Resistance, and my sister and I, who were in hiding in different places, were told to go even further underground. Because they might have found our addresses on my parents — which they didn't, because my parents knew not to have any names or addresses on them or anywhere where they were hiding. So that was a close call, and I stayed away from the family in Rotterdam who I was staying with at that point. I was with three different families, and this was the fourth that I went to, but after six weeks I was allowed to go back to the family that kept me until even after the war when my parents didn't come back. They said I could stay for a while until after high school.

We didn't find out what happened to my parents. There were a few toilet papers that were smuggled out of the detention centre in Arnhem, on which my father was very optimistic. He said, "It's very nice to be back in the world again," because he had been in hiding for a few years without books, and they were avid readers. Here they were with political prisoners, so they gave lectures to each other. The only thing was that men and women were separated, so in a few words he said, "It's okay, I'm enjoying this, unfortunately we are not together." After a few weeks they were sent to the transition camp at Westerbork.

Henry Schogt

There they met relatives.

Corrie Schogt

Other family was there, but my parents were the first to be sent to Theresienstadt because they had an S on their papers, which is punishment [*straf*, "punishment"] because they had been found in hiding. The others had gone via a raid or had gone voluntarily or had been protected temporarily but then sent on to Theresienstadt.

Henry Schogt

So we had a few testimonies about Corrie's parents in Theresienstadt, but the family is obviously reluctant to talk about it, it was very difficult for them.

Corrie Schogt

My parents of that family were the only ones not to survive. The others were liberated by Russians. It wasn't exactly filthy, but most people died from starvation and diseases, but it was not as bad as Bergen-Belsen.

Ada Wynston

The other place it was a farm, so I had to try to learn how to milk cows and kill chickens and make cheese. Once in a while I was allowed out, and I said, "Can I go play with this girl?" It was my youngest war sister's friend. "Yeah, you can go play, take the bicycle," and I took my war brother's bicycle, and I may not have been able to go one hundred metres when I got stopped. It was a one-street town — I was stopped by a German soldier with a rifle. He looked at me and he said, "Are you a Jew?" And I said, "A Jew? What's a Jew? I'm with my family, I live across the street with my mother and father and five brothers and sisters." He didn't say another word, he just shrugged his shoulders and he turned around. If he had turned back to me he would have shot me on the spot, I was shaking so hard. I tried to get on the bike and I fell into a stream next to the main street and I was covered with algae. That's how I ended back in the house green like a frog, and I was never allowed outside again until the war was over.

The Germans would often surround a block of buildings and round up all of the Jews in that area. Few would escape such raids.

DARKNESS

At the end of September 1943, the final roundup of Jews in Amsterdam took place, with ten thousand people captured. The deportations were continuous at this point in time. With sickening regularity the cattle-cars were filled with human cargo and transported across the border, most never to return. By December the Nazis began targeting mixed marriages, deporting the Jewish spouses. The Germans had run out of Jews to round up in the streets, now it was down to the last few. The existence of the Jews in the Netherlands was very near an end. Hitler's Final Solution was nearly complete.

The disregard for the Dutch labour force by the Germans had created a problem by October 1943. With the constant conscription of Dutch men into labour details, the agrarian and economic well-being of the Netherlands was laid to waste. Food was at critically low levels, and in October the German authorities reduced the Wehrmacht's demands for food locally.

The turning point in the war came on June 6, 1944. Operation Overlord and Operation Neptune combined to launch the invasion of Normandy by the Americans, the British, and the Canadians, along with members of numerous other nations' military units, in what is known as D-Day. The largest armada of ships ever assembled carried the infantry and armoured units across the English Channel while the air force and paratroopers flew overhead. In a magnificently combined effort of all branches of the military, with nations working together for one cause, the Allies invaded Europe and created the second front.

On June 8 Dutch citizens huddled anxiously around what few radios were left in the country to hear about the progress of the invasion in Normandy. That day they also heard Queen Wilhelmina calling on the Dutch Resistance to coordinate their efforts in order to create greater disruption for the Germans. While there was some increase in mutual activities, the Resistance was well-entrenched as separate entities — and it was far safer for them to remain that way.

On July 21 the Germans held the first of what would be many roundups of able-bodied men in Amsterdam and across the country. They were sent to Germany as cheap labour. The Nazis had been so effective in rounding up the Jews that they had run out, so they turned their focus to other men who could be of some help to the Reich's war effort.

In August Canadian troops battled north through France, heading in the direction of Belgium and Holland. They would not arrive soon enough to save Anne Frank's family. On August 4 an anonymous tip directed the Germans to the secret annex that hid the Frank family and a few friends. The authorities found the hidden entrance behind a bookcase, and everyone was arrested. Like one-third of all Jews who went into hiding, they had been caught. At this point the diary of Anne Frank ends, and the Frank family was moved to Westerbork camp. They would spend the next month there before finding out what bitter hand fate had dealt them.

In an effort to disrupt the German defence of northwestern Europe, the Allies sought to have the Dutch Resistance increase their armed actions behind the lines. This would force the Nazis to divert crucial military manpower from the front to the "secured" occupied zones to quell the disturbances. To ensure that the Dutch Resistance could operate at maximum efficiency in this mission, the Allies began airdropping arms and ammunition in remote areas of the Dutch countryside in coordination with the Resistance.

Jack Heidema

My brother worked at the dropping fields north of Amsterdam. I joined him. There would be contact made with the Dutch government in exile, who in turn had contact with the Royal Air Force. These dropping fields were very carefully selected — where they would drop supplies for the Resistance — Sten guns, Bren guns, carbines, hand grenades, explosives, and other things like cameras, batteries, and items that were not available. I attended nine such droppings with my brother. The field would be surrounded, usually by between thirty-five and fifty Resistance people heavily armed in case the Germans would detect this, they could defend the workers of the group; that was my part — I was a worker. The Lancasters, the Halifaxes would come in very low at about three hundred to four hundred metres. The containers would come down. We would detach the parachutes, then we would bury them. Now this is the story that most people find hard to believe: the contents of the containers were put in German army trucks. The German army trucks were driven by Dutch Resistance fighters in German uniforms, and that's how all the supplies got across Holland from north to south, from east to west.

At the beginning of September, Prince Bernhard, husband of Crown Princess Juliana, was appointed commander-in-chief of the Dutch armed forces. He immediately called on the Dutch Resistance to sabotage the railways in occupied Netherlands. The first nine days of that month saw every form of traffic blocked by Resistance actions. As well as the railways, the waterways and roads were also targeted, creating huge headaches for the Germans.

Pushing north in France.

Normandy presented the Canadians with experience in hedgerow fighting. Soon they would face a whole new obstacle with the dikes in the Netherlands.

Rails of death: the tracks from Westerbork that would end at Auschwitz, Sobibor, Theresienstadt, or Bergen-Belsen.

Sign at Westerbork indicating the ultimate destination of trains leaving the camp.

They needed to respond to the Allied advance that was swiftly moving towards the Dutch/Belgian border, and the actions of the Dutch Resistance made it difficult, if not impossible, to do.

At this time the Canadian military was moving rapidly, liberating Dieppe in northern France. By September 3 they had crossed the Somme River. The newly liberated French celebrated and greeted the soldiers warmly. The Dutch were desperately waiting for their liberation.

As the Canadians crossed the Somme, the last train from Westerbork Transit Camp left, filled with Jews heading for Auschwitz in Poland. On board were Anne Frank and her family. As liberation drew nearer, they were moved further away and closer to death.

The Nazis became more vicious as the Allies advanced closer and closer. On September 4 they executed sixty at Vught camp. The empire was collapsing. That same day Hitler ordered that the defences at Calais, Boulogne, Dunkirk, and on the island of Walcheren be shored up in preparation for a desperate battle. He wanted that line held at all costs, knowing that if the momentum was not changed, the war would soon be over.

As the Allies approached the Netherlands on September 5, Nazi collaborators took flight in what would be dubbed "Mad Tuesday." They were fearful of reprisals for the years of oppression. The Resistance wreaked havoc throughout the country, and the bulk of the German army was backing up into Dutch territory. The front line was nearing, and liberation was just on the other side.

On September 9, 1944, an American reconnaissance patrol (113th Cavalry Group Red Horse) crossed the border near Maastrich. They were the first Allies to enter the Netherlands. Three days later American troops crossed the border into South Limburg. For the Allies, the Netherlands stood before them, ready to be freed.

Lini Grol

We were hiding in a very small house, and the Germans came and pushed us all in the basement. I had to go to the washroom so I came up and the whole house was full of soldiers. When I came back two soldiers came with a big soup kettle. I was kind of pushed back with the soup kettle and it was at night, so it was dark. They didn't see me. They took two chairs and put the soup kettle on it, and I was in the corner, so I sat behind that and I thought, *I better wait until this all is over and not do anything.* I thought, *All these soldiers, they might grab a woman and rape her.* Then they started ladling soup and everybody got some. All of a sudden in came three officers, and all these soldiers got out of there. These officers had laid out a map of Holland and they started talking about how they would withdraw. I was sitting there squashed in the corner, and I thought, *Now I know where they are going.* I knew right away what they were talking about. Then they started talking about Hitler, which was not very nice what they were saying. They wanted to stop right away. They didn't want any more fighting, they said, "This is a lost cause, there have already been so many people lost, it's senseless to go on." I heard all that, and I exhaled and they heard me. All of a sudden there were three flashlights on me, and three guns. "Who are you?" I was so afraid I couldn't talk, and then one of the officers said, "She's the village idiot. She's harmless." Another one says, "Let's kill her." The third one says, "Oh, let the old woman go." They said, "Get up!" My feet were falling asleep, so I was kind of crumpled up in half and so I looked very crippled. Then the one said again, "Let's put her out of her misery, a woman like that doesn't need to live," and the other one said, "No, let her go. These people downstairs will take care of these people." They pushed me down to the cellar, and my mother said, "Where were you?" I didn't answer. I didn't dare to talk. If they found out that I could talk, I knew what they had been saying about Hitler, and I knew how they would respond. They would think me a betrayer. So I had to pretend that I was stupid, and my mother was shocked, she couldn't get over it. I didn't say a word, I just sat there with my mouth half open, I had to play this a little bit longer. Then after a few hours they started hollering that we have to get out. So out we went and we were off to the next farm. I did not stop, because if they saw me talking, not only I would be in trouble, but everybody because they would think that everybody knew what I had found out. So for several days I was stupid and mute, and finally when we were quite a distance from them and close to Arnhem I said, "We have to go north," and we walked.

Rather than wage a traditional land battle to move through the Netherlands and liberate it, Field Marshal Montgomery devised a daring plan that, if it worked, would end the war by Christmas. The plan was code-named Market Garden.

On September 17, 1944, the skies over the Netherlands were filled with aircraft and paratroopers. The British and American airborne units landed at various places, including Eindhoven, Grave, Groesbeek, Wofheze, and Arnhem. The plan was to quickly secure the river crossings at Grave, Nijmegen, and Arnhem, then the army and armoured units would sprint up a narrow corridor to relieve the paratroopers and move east towards Germany. Success would give the Allies control of the territory between the Rhine and the Ijsselmeer, cutting the Netherlands off from Germany. The German troops in the Dutch territory would be isolated and surrounded to the west, while on the east the Ruhr industrial region would be within striking distance. It was a bold plan, stabbing deep into the Netherlands, then expanding eastward towards victory. Capturing the Ruhr region would break the Germans' back; they would be unable to sustain a war machine without its vital industries supplying the Reich.

As the paratroopers dropped into the Netherlands, bitter fighting broke out. The Americans successfully captured the bridges along the Maas River, but further north at Arnhem, the British did not succeed. Intelligence had failed to place the 2nd SS Panzer Corps in Arnhem, which led to far greater resistance than expected. The British were massacred, yet they battled valiantly to accomplish their mission. The troops were stretched too thin and were seriously outgunned by the German armoured units. A dozen members of Number 2 Troop of the British 10 Commando jumped with the British 1st Airborne. Number 2 was the Dutch unit of the inter-Allied 10 Commando (other units were made up of French, Belgian, and other European troops who joined the British military to fight for the liberation of Europe). Of the dozen, one was killed and two were taken prisoner.

Operation Market Garden stalled as the advancing column from the south failed to advance as quickly as planned. The operation hinged on maintaining a tight schedule, without any contingency plans if the advance was hampered. With untested radio communications failing, the coordination of the attack fell apart. The column of men and tanks did make progress, but the plan proved to be too ambitious. The British to the north in Arnhem were isolated and without support. Their objective proved to be a "bridge too far." While there was some success in the south, the overall plan was a disaster. With the failure of Operation Market Garden, it was clear that the war would drag on into the next year. But for the Dutch in the south, liberation had finally come!

"A bridge too far" at Arnhem. Over six thousand members of the British 1st Airborne were killed in Operation Market Garden and buried near Arnhem, including many Canadians.

Lini Grol

We were between two rivers close to Arnhem where Market Garden took place. One day we looked out and here came all these planes over, and I don't know how many parachutes came down, and the Germans were standing there aiming with their guns and shot them out of the air. People started crying and praying out loud, and nobody was going to survive from that. That was terrible. We saw them in the backyard and they were climbing over the fences and then two got shot. We cried. To realize they came so far, and then they died for us, strangers.

Richard Rohmer, RCAF

The decision had been made by higher command that the Canadian Reconnaissance Wing, 39 Wing, would work with the British Army, and the British RAF Reconnaissance Wing of Mustangs would work with the Canadian Army. When we arrived in Belgium we went to a place called Diestshafen, which is to the east of Bruxelles, and we set up our base there in September.

Within three weeks or so we moved up to Eindhoven, and that is in the south sector of Holland. We operated from there, and the Canadian squadrons were in that area, either at Eindhoven itself, which was very large, or in airfields not far away. The Canadian wing in Holland operated in support of the British Army, and so we didn't get any of our work where the Canadians were doing their fighting.

We were supporting the British. We did reconnaissance for them during the big drop at Arnhem for Market Garden, and we supported the British Army in all manner of photographic reconnaissance and also reconnaissance in terms of artillery direction, and that kind of operation. So we were away from where the Canadian Army was, but we were right in the thick of things all the way through.

In an attempt to help the operation, the Dutch Resistance staged a railway strike to stymie any German attempts to transport troops to counter Market Garden. The strike was a major act of resistance, and the Resistance funded it by providing support to the strikers with stolen and counterfeit ration coupons and papers.

During Operation Market Garden, 3 Canadian Infantry Division moved up the French coast, clearing the Channel ports.

On September 19, the Germans mustered enough aircraft to bomb Eindhoven, and the next day the Allies liberated Nijmegen. That day was a proud one for the Dutch military: the Princess Irene Brigade had finally reached Dutch soil. The brigade had been formed in England and was composed of Dutch refugees who wished to return home to fight for De Bevrijding. For them, the fight had finally been brought home.

On September 21, Polish troops cleared a part of Zeeuws-Vlaanderen (west of Antwerp), and the Allies were starting to take control of the ports. Realizing that, the Germans began demolishing the harbour installations in Amsterdam and Rotterdam to render them useless if the Allies should advance that far.

Lini Grol

Around the twenty-third or twenty-fourth of September we were between two rivers — the Rhine and the Waal. It was a peninsula, and it was difficult to get off it, of course, because of the danger of the bridges. The bridges were constantly under fire. We crawled over the bridges on hand and feet with corpses on the left and right. You couldn't stop and you couldn't look — you had to go.

After we had been going from barn to barn then we saw this big building and it was solid stone, and we thought, *Now that looks really sturdy.* So I tried the back door and it was the cellar. I pushed my parents in and pushed my younger sister in, she is seven years younger than I am. My mother said, "There's already lots of people." I said, "Go in." There were so many people that they were up the stairs, so my father and mother stood on the bottom stair and my sister too, and I stood there at the top and I could see lots of action going on, a lot of fighting in the air. Planes shooting and being shot down. In the morning there were usually a few hours that were very quiet and you knew it was safe to go outside. Now the funny thing was when I looked back at them as they came out, it was a coal cellar, and everybody was black in the face. Because of the bombing you get this tremor and of course the dust comes up, and the dust was in the walls. I was sitting at the front so I was looking the other way and I was not as dirty as the rest of them. When I came outside I said, "Oh back up!" Here were rows and rows of ammunition cases piled up on top of each other. If they even threw one match even, we would all have gone sky high. We had been lucky.

On September 27 the Allied troops involved in Operation Market Garden north of Arnhem ceased fighting. For ten long days they had battled against all odds and had lost a large percentage of their men. The survivors made their way south, retreating across the Rhine during the night. Canadian engineers were involved in bringing the remnants of the British 1st Airborne back across the river. Only one in four returned.

Al Armstrong, 14th Canadian Hussars
The Canadian Army was at the left of the line as we came out of France. I guess the Brits and Americans thought that we could hold our own. Being on the flank can be difficult because you're not just fighting a frontal battle, you're fighting one on the flank as well. The Canadian Army ended up on the left flank, and they did so right up into northern Holland. The divisions were split up.

Douglas Lavoie, Fort Garry Horse
I was wounded September 17 at Boulogne, and two of our fellows were killed. C.C. Spence was our loader operator, and Ollie Johnson was our gunner. We were going in September 17 and our tank was hit and those two fellows were killed, myself and the co-driver were wounded. So I got back into England, so I really missed the winter in Holland, I didn't get back into there until February.

T. Garry Gould, Sherbrooke Fusiliers

We had to fight our way up through Belgium, and by this time I came back from being wounded the first time, and I'm recce officer, and I was doing all sorts of dumb things. Maybe I was recce officer because I was a bit reckless and I was leading the squadron up, and don't ask me why I put myself out, there was a lot of people who had gone before, and some of them previously had been taken care of, so I didn't feel like a shrinking violet and sometimes a little bold. I was going up this track, field on one side and drops on the other side, and then there was bending between two clumps of trees. We were working with the Desert Rats, and the major was with the lead section. You've got to realize that means that about six or seven functions were missing for a major to be with the lead mine-clearing section. In other words, the corporal, the sergeant, the sub-lieutenant, the lieutenant, the captain — before you get to the major, they're all gone. So we were with the Brits,

Liberation in Belgium: the Canadian soldiers got a taste of the warm welcome that they would receive as they played the role of liberator. The intensity of the reception would grow as they headed north.

A free Belgian and his young children.

Liberation found many long-lost flags resurface to be proudly flown in celebration.

A scissors bridge in action.

Canadians in Belgium.

and his men had seen tanks on both sides of the track, projecting barely above the ground, but they noticed them and they began to sweep for mines. So he held up his hand, and I screamed to a halt in the tank and did exactly what he said, radio back what the problem was, and I got told to change course. I went into an open field and we all lined up and took potshots at the church, to make sure the steeple wasn't hiding snipers. We proceeded on into the town and then I'm up against a blown bridge on the main street. It was a ground-level bridge and they dropped it twelve feet into the muddy path of the creek. The mud banks were impossible to put a Sherman tank down, in let alone come up out of it. So I said, "We're stopped" back on the radio, so the order came back to measure the distance, and I went, "Yes, sir." Of course that's the only answer you can give in the army to any order is yes, sir. So I jumped out of the tank and possibly into enemy fire, but that didn't bother me other than how to measure the distance because I didn't have any string to throw across. I had to rack my feeble brain to go back to high school geometry and used my compass, found a bearing directly across, and then paced to the left and find a forty-five-degree difference to make an Isosceles triangle, and then pace back to where I started from and send the message back, which I did, which proves that the opening was thirty-five feet, which it was. It stopped our operation because we didn't have a bridge that would stretch over that space unless the engineers came up in the night to build one. The scissors bridge on tanks was not that dimension, so that halted that particular operation that day.

62

By the end of the month we were entering Holland, I had been selected to go back to England on a course at the armoured school. I got back and said how about the British major, and he said quietly, "He's gone." He didn't make it, so the position he filled was emptied one more time by enemy fire.

The Americans and British moved north and east into Holland. But to win the war, the Allies needed supply routes to maintain the advancing armies. The ports along the French and Belgian shoreline were in Allied hands by October 1944, but they were not large enough to maintain a sufficient flow of supplies. Antwerp was a large enough port to handle the Allies' needs, and it was under their control, but there was a major problem: it was located eighty kilometres from the open sea on the Scheldt River. The wide mouth of the river was controlled by massive German fortifications, and no ships could safely enter. The plan was to capture the Scheldt and secure the supply route. That job was given to the 1st Canadian Army.

CHAPTER THREE

BATTLE OF THE SCHELDT
October 1–November 8, 1944

Antwerp was pivotal in the next phase of the war in northwestern Europe. Opening the port was absolutely necessary, so clearing the mouth of the Scheldt was the next order of business. The Scheldt posed some serious problems. It was a broad estuary controlled by the Germans on both sides. The Germans were fortified along the south shore and faced polders inland, which was an advantage for defence against land-based assaults. The land was low-lying, flat, and with no natural cover for advancing troops. Movement could be seen from miles away — eliminating the element of surprise. Assault from the river would be hazardous, and the Germans were well-fortified in that direction as well.

The northern coast of the Scheldt was made up of South Beveland Island, which was connected to the mainland by an isthmus. With formidable defences along the river, the only approach was across the isthmus. This long, narrow stretch of land provided little or no cover and allowed the Germans to concentrate their fire on one small area.

Beyond South Beveland was Walcheren Island, which had been built up into a German stronghold. The island was only accessible by a small strip of land, making it a nightmare to invade. The Germans were well-placed and were determined to hold their positions. As long as they held the sea approaches to the Scheldt River, Antwerp and its port would be of no use to the Allies. The geo-physical makeup of the Scheldt posed serious problems for the Canadians, problems that would take more than a month to overcome.

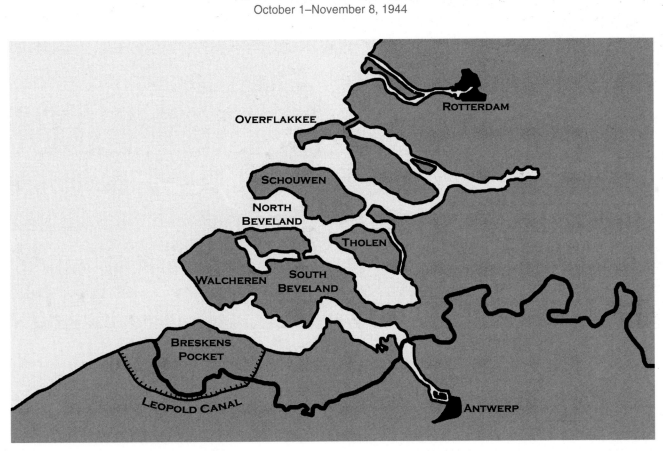

Major islands and regions of the Scheldt estuary.

A polder in the south shore of the Scheldt.

Much of Walcheren Island is made up of polders below sea level.

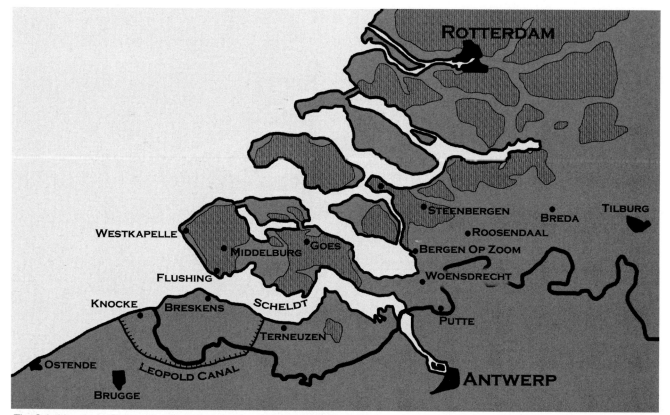

The Scheldt estuary. Darkened areas indicate regions below sea level.

Walcheren Island, 2004.

Middelburg, the capital of Walcheren Island, 2004.

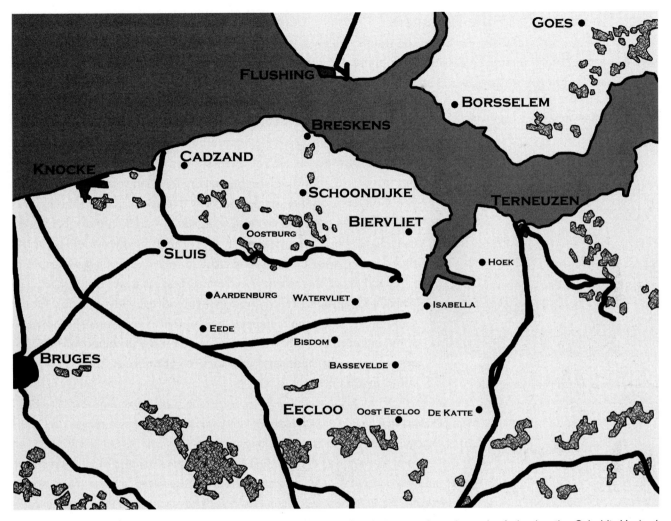

The south shore of the Scheldt.

Lieutenant-General Guy Simonds was given the task of clearing the Scheldt. He had taken command of the 1st Canadian Army from General Crerar, who was ill at the time. The command was a tough one under the circumstances. The men had been fighting for months and were fatigued. There was also a dangerous lack of trained men in the units, and places were being filled with support staff (cooks, etc.). It was the height of the conscription crisis back in Canada, and politicians were playing games while young Canadians lost their lives on the front lines. Eventually the government decided to send fifteen thousand more trained infantrymen, but the decision was made too late for the men going into the Battle of the Scheldt.

Jack Read, Regina Rifle Regiment

We had difficult times, and the morale of the troops was not the greatest because we were losing so many people and not getting many reinforcements. It was a pretty difficult situation, and we'd have less than half of what we should have had to go into any given battle.

Flooded Dutch territory. Due to the sea water the land was rendered useless for farming for many years.

Jim Parks, Royal Winnipeg Rifles

The reinforcements were getting it, a lot of them were re-mustered people from the other corps. These fellows went in and still did a good job, but that was kind of rough on them. Usually when you go into an attack you should outnumber the defenders by five to one, where I think it was the other way around with Canadians — they outnumbered the Canadians about five to one. Many times the companies would go in and they'd suffer casualties and have a tough time and not get what they're supposed to get, the orders would come down that we've got to get it, so you'd have maybe half the people that you started with and you'd try the same thing. That could happen maybe twice, and you'd be down to about eighteen or twenty-two men. Maybe some of the people had just arrived the night before and now they're gone already. You didn't get to know their names.

The plan was to have the 3rd Canadian Infantry Division clear the south bank while the 2nd Canadian Infantry Division fought along the north bank until the Scheldt was secured and the port of Antwerp was opened. The battle was to be handled in four steps: first, clear the area north of Antwerp and close the South Beveland isthmus (north shore); second, clear the Breskens pocket (south shore); third, capture the Beveland peninsula (north shore); fourth, capture Walcheren Island (middle of the river). It was not going to be easy.

The 2nd Canadian Infantry Division marched from Antwerp on October 2, heading north to the isthmus that connected South Beveland with the mainland. The Germans had flooded the area, slowing the progress of the Canadians. The men would be constantly wet and tired, battling under some of the most uncomfortable conditions imaginable.

Al Armstrong, 14th Canadian Hussars

When the German Army was retreating they blew the dikes. Now Holland has always been below sea level, so it didn't help matters any. The weather turned cold, it was wet, and some of the guys in the infantry were working up to their waists in water.

Doug Barrie, Highland Light Infantry

Fighting was pretty well restricted to the dikes that surrounded the polders. Actually, the first German counterattack that I remember coming back was German troops coming across the polder in an open order, and they were just knocked down right left and centre because they were in the open and they were slowed down because the polders were quite wet. There wasn't any real cover, so they took quite a beating, and after that the fighting pretty well remained on the dikes. You had to fight from one dike to the next, and they had their machine gun positions and they fired along the dikes. It was pretty difficult. There were trees usually along the top of the dike and there'd be a path or a roadway between the trees. So you had to try and dodge from tree to tree and get along. Often along the dikes, and especially at the junction of the dikes, there'd be machine gun holes. They could fire along even the sides of the dikes, which were maybe ten to twelve feet high, on an angle going up. It was pretty treacherous there. It was quite different from the fighting down in France.

Vast flooded areas in the Scheldt made military operations very difficult for the Canadian Army.

Most roads in the south shore are raised or are along the tops of dikes.

Jack Martin, Queen's Own Rifles

Well, that was the problem, that it relegated the infantry to one side of the dike or up on top. If you got up on top you were a dead duck. The wetness … that's where we got our name, the Water Rats, conversely to the Desert Rats of the English division in Africa. It was always wet there.

Bulldozer towing a Crocodile armoured vehicle (1st Fife and Forfar Yeomanry) out of the mud. The slippery conditions made driving treacherous in the Scheldt.

Mervin Durham Royal Canadian Engineers

We had many tanks slide off the road, and in the ditch they couldn't darn well move. They had lots of trouble with that. We would winch most of them out. They weren't that badly mired, they'd slide off the road and they couldn't control them. They were Sherman tanks, quite a mobile tank.

The Germans fought with desperation, presenting unbelievable resistance at Woensdrecht and Hoogerheide. The battles were bitter affairs, with every inch of ground being hotly contested.

Globe & Mail, October 3, 1944

Formations of the 1st Canadian Army, pounding the south flank of an estimated 200,000 Germans pinned down in western Holland by the British thrust to Nijmegen and the Neder River beyond it, drove four miles north into Holland at a point northwest of Turnhout, despite stubborn enemy resistance.

General Eisenhower broadcast a warning to the Netherlands to clear out of two islands in the Scheldt estuary which the Germans have fortified to keep the Allies from using the great port of Antwerp. He asserted massive air blows were impending.

The enemy forces are strung along the Netherlands islands of Walcheren and Zuid Beveland in the Scheldt estuary and it is estimated 15,000 are still stationed on the south bank of the estuary where Canadian formations face them.

The RAF bombed the dikes on Walcheren Island on October 3, isolating the German units there by flooding them. This would eliminate their ability to manoeuvre around the island and defend it. By stranding them in small areas, it was easy to pinpoint and bombard them. The RAF repeated the bomb runs several times in October to ensure that the island was as inundated as possible.

On the first day of bombing Walcheren Island, Radio Oranje moved its broadcast centre from London to the recently liberated city of Eindhoven. Renamed Radio Herrijzend Nederland ("Netherlands rising again"), the radio station targeted the occupied north with its programming. For the Dutch still under the heel of Nazi oppression, there was pride in the fact that the broadcasts were now from their own country and that there was more than a glimmer of hope for them.

Far from that glimmer of hope, Anne Frank and her sister Margot were sent to Bergen-Belsen concentration camp in October. The camp was horrific, devoid of food, heat, medicine, or even basic sanitary conditions. Bergen-Belsen was notorious for the thousands who died there from planned starvations and epidemics.

In occupied Netherlands, Dutch men were rounded up to work for the Germans, digging ditches and preparing fortifications. Any males from seventeen to fifty years of age were likely to be dragged off and forced into labour. For those in the north, liberation couldn't come soon enough.

On October 6, 1944, the 3rd Canadian Infantry Division and the 4th Armoured Division attacked the southern sector of the estuary by crossing the Leopold Canal under heavy fire. The battle was harrowing, and the crossing was difficult. A bridgehead was gained that night, one so slender it was barely deeper than the canal's shore. The Germans could not dislodge the Canadians, despite having a decided advantage at the top of the canal embankment, firing down on the Canadian soldiers.

Cliff Chadderton, Royal Winnipeg Rifles

The 7th Brigade [Canadian Scottish, Regina Rifles, and Royal Winnipeg Rifles] were tasked to cross the Leopold Canal on the night of October 6 and attempt to head straight north for the guns at Cadzand and possibly other objectives. We were all under strength. The Regina Rifles were given a company from the Royal Montreal Regiment, which had not seen any action. The Can-Scots crossed the canal on the east, the Regina Rifles on the western sector.

Jack Read, Regina Rifle Regiment

Because it was a fairly narrow stretch of water, we had to cross by canvas boat, and at the same time we had the flamethrowers helping. The Germans were on the other side firing on us with shells and whatnot, making it most

The Leopold Canal runs about forty kilometres from Boekhoute to Heist-aan-Zee and was built between 1846 and 1848. It created a natural defensive line for the Germans in protecting the Scheldt estuary.

difficult. As we were shielded by the sides of the canal, it didn't give us much protection. The Germans were on the other side, and we were on the near side, and at times we were throwing grenades at them and they were throwing grenades at us. Some of the people would have the nerve to take a grenade and pull the pin and they would hold it until it was nearly due to explode, because if you just let it go the Germans could pick it up and throw it back. That fight along the canal was very close to what you would call a hand-to-hand battle. There were pillboxes up and down the canal that gave them some protection and made it difficult for us. It was wet and terribly cold, with mud up to your knees and almost no sleep.

Cliff Chadderton, Royal Winnipeg Rifles

The Regina Rifles got into trouble. I was commanding Charlie Company of the Winnipeg Rifles. We were tasked to take the flimsy kapok and canvas boats, which were manned by the North Shore Regiment, and transport our troops across to the north side. In the meantime, in the Can-Scots sector, a company of the Royal Canadian Engineers was attempting to put in the kapok bridge. They did not get this bridge in until sometime just before dark. We were dug into the canal bank, which was sort of a dike. The Leopold Canal was in fact the border between Belgium and Holland at that particular location.

Lockhart "Lockie" Fulton, Royal Winnipeg Rifles

So we drove all night [returning from leave], and finally from division headquarters we were given the coordinates where our battalion headquarters was. When I went into battalion headquarters the adjutant was there, and he told me that I was to go to brigade headquarters right away, the brigadier wanted to see me. I had no idea what that was about, I was a bit late getting back, but other than that I didn't think I had committed anything that was necessary for me to make a special trip to brigade. Before I left I met with the CO, John Malcolm … and he was really concerned because we were in a very difficult position on the canal itself. They only had the one side of the opposite bank and only one kapok bridge to get back and forth. It looked like a pretty serious problem that the battalion was in, and the whole brigade for that matter. I headed for brigade, and Jock Spragge, who I really didn't know, he had just been promoted to command the brigade, and he had commanded the Queen's Own from Toronto. He said, "You are now commanding the battalion, you get back and get them going." I want them across the canal. These were my instructions and I was told I was now in command of the battalion, a job I really wasn't looking for.

Jim Parks, Royal Winnipeg Rifles

It was a small bridgehead for the first few days, and the company that was over — the Canadian Scottish company — was overrun, and one of our companies went to put in a counterattack and relieved them and regained the ground. I remember that part, and we then had trouble getting ammo. We eventually got it, it was a half a day late in getting it, before we could give them some more supporting fire.

Cliff Chadderton, Royal Winnipeg Rifles

We took a tremendous number of casualties. The unique conditions affected the battle. For the first time, we were fighting without air cover. We did have some FOOs with us, but they were knocked out of action very soon. At least in one case, a Sergeant Alex Bell of the Winnipeg Rifles was attempting to correct ranging fire from the 25-pounder guns in the rear. The unique conditions, as well, made it very difficult to evacuate the wounded. A kapok bridge was under constant fire from the Germans, and the engineers had to keep on repairing it. In our sector, we had found a small boat. This was used to try to get some of the wounded back across the canal. I was one of them. Unfortunately, because of the difficulties of evacuation, at least ten to fifteen men of the Royal Winnipeg Rifles died on the canal bank because we could not get them back to our regimental aid post [RAP].

Lockhart Fulton, Royal Winnipeg Rifles

When I got back from brigade I crossed over and talked to one of the company commanders. There was no fighting spirit whatsoever in those that were across the canal, and A Company was down probably to about fifty fighting men. The opportunities to enlarge on the ground that we had captured was just next to impossible. However, I got the pioneer officer and told him that we simply had to have another bridge across the canal to give us an opportunity to get more across so we could try to get inland. I sent the pioneer officer to get another bridge across, though he protested a little bit because it was under shellfire. Any time you crossed on the one we had across, the Germans immediately would fire onto it with mortars and machine gun fire, so you picked your time to cross, and you'd cross as fast as you could go. And hope that you could find a slit trench or something to jump into when you got across.

The battle dragged on for three hellish days as the Canadians stubbornly held onto that foothold along the shoreline. The ground was wet, and when the Canadians dug their trenches they filled with water. Artillery was constantly bombarding their positions. Large-calibre shells were being lobbed in from fifteen kilometres away. The pitched battle for the Leopold Canal was relentless.

The Royal Winnipeg Rifles War Diary, October 8, 1944

Visibility poor. At 0100 hrs 6 stretcher-bearers were sent to 1 Canadian Scottish Regiment HQ to assist in evacuating wounded. Several counterattacks involving close quarter fighting were beaten off during the night by the tired but spirited troops and high casualties were inflicted on the enemy, including several prisoners captured.

Lieutenant-Colonel J.M. Meldram held an Orders Group at 0900 hrs and issued orders for an advance to the West in an attempt to link up with Regina Rifles right flank. D and C Companies started the advance at 1400 hrs and succeeded in pressing some distance forward, but owing to high casualties and lack of ammunition were forced to retire to original positions. A Company was more successful and reached a point before concentrated enemy fire forced them to dig in along the canal. High casualties were suffered by both sides and the ground was littered with both German and Royal Winnipeg Rifles dead. Two Platoon Commanders, Lieutenant J.A.M. Currie and Lieutenant O.D. Hamilton and A Company Commander Captain W.B. Fraser were included among the wounded. Prolonged exposure to wet and cold still had to be endured in flooded slit trenches or smashed buildings as unusually bold enemy snipers and machine-gunners were on the lookout continuously and often succeeded in infiltrating between companies and platoons. Few of these lived to tell their story as the Royal Winnipeg Rifles were no less aggressive. Ammunition, cold rations and casualties still had to be carried for more than a mile.

> On October 9 the Canadians launched an amphibious assault across the Leopold Canal and shattered the German defence. Suddenly the bridgehead grew. Troops and tanks poured over the canal, and the Germans quickly retreated to their concrete emplacements.

The Royal Winnipeg Rifles War Diary, October 9, 1944

Patrol activities and beating off counterattacks occupied the four rifle companies during the night. Much needed reinforcements reached forward positions at 0330 hrs. At 0500 hrs A Company launched an attack on an enemy outpost to the West and in the face of a hail of artillery and machine gun fire succeeded in destroying the position and occupying it. This success completed the link up with the Regina Rifles and gave 7 Canadian Infantry Brigade an unbroken front. The CO attended a Brigade Orders Group at 1100 hrs and received orders to occupy the Southern approaches to the village of Grafjan. With A giving covering fire, B Company succeeded in reaching the objectives at 1500 hrs. Superior enemy forces in the village forced the company to withdraw when ammunition was getting low. Hot meals were ferried across the Canal during the evening. Wounded were evacuated by the same route.

Lockhart Fulton, Royal Winnipeg Rifles

I had one of the platoon commanders from A Company take a patrol and get across to the other side and attempt to see if there was a possibility of getting into this village. From the view that I had there seemed to be water between the other side of the canal covering any approach to that village. To make sure of it I thought I'd better send a patrol across there and see if they could determine the possibility of a larger attack to get into this village. So he crossed over and made his way with his patrol into the village without being stopped. In the meantime, my pioneer officer was just being brought back, he had been hit. He had sort of protested the job of getting another bridge across. I hadn't had any sleep, and this thing wasn't working out very well, and I was awful sorry. That pioneer officer survived the war, and he went back to teaching, which he did in Winnipeg. The officer that I sent on the patrol, he got back, and by now it was starting to get dark. He had been in water up to his neck. There had been a machine gun bullet that had gone through his helmet, and he too was pretty down. He hadn't accomplished very much; however, the patrol indicated to me that any attempt with any sizable force would be a disaster. I got onto brigade and told them the situation. The other battalion, the Canadian Scottish, was also having just as much trouble. I think that brigade and division were beginning to see that attacking from that direction appeared to be too difficult.

> The Canadians had prevailed and had taken control of the Leopold Canal. Much of the land that lay ahead was flooded. The Battle of the Scheldt would be characterized by wet, uncomfortable conditions and by some of the most severe fighting of the war.

Jim Parks, Royal Winnipeg Rifles

I always remember it being wet, always cold. Digging the mortars out of the mud all the time, and we had quite a number of casualties. They had their nests set up pretty good and they had a lot of good artillery. We couldn't get our air support in there because it was always cloudy and rainy. Tanks — they'd be silhouetted on the dikes, so they had to be careful how they moved forward. They'd pick their spots. They were always far enough back, they didn't get too close to us until we stopped, and you could hear them rumbling in somewhere — maybe the next dike back.

Al Armstrong, 14th Canadian Hussars

When we crossed from Belgium across the Dutch border, it was like crossing from daylight into darkness. We didn't expect to find the situation that we did. Being an armoured unit we came into the towns and villages before anybody else got there. The condition of the people we wouldn't believe, even today it can bring me to tears. It was bad enough to watch the adults, but to see starving children is something else. We were all young enough to have younger brothers and sisters at home, and it made a lot of us think there but for the grace of God that could be ours. Until we crossed into Holland, we had never seen starvation.

Jim Parks, Royal Winnipeg Rifles

We got over to the other side and we began to leapfrog, and you had to keep to the dikes where the roads were. Even the Germans at one position that we overtook were all dug in alongside the sides of the dikes. They'd leave their dead behind. They'd be in among the machine gun or wherever they were killed. We went into this one area on the crossroads, the house and the fence were all in one, and a courtyard in the centre where the animals could get out. We went in, and Bob Hutchings said, "Christ, there's a Jerry over there," and I said, "Where?" So I stuck a head in and I see that the Jerry's about twenty feet away and he's waving his white handkerchief. So this guy was the spitting image of Sergeant Schultz. He had a big long raincoat, he had all the pockets filled with bread and canned goods and stuff, and he pointed at this larder where all the canned food and jars and so on was. He had a cooker going. He was talking with Sergeant Enns, who could speak German, he was a Mennonite fellow. We kept in there for over half a day, he didn't want to leave, but we had orders to send him back. He wanted to stay with us and cook.

A portable stove provided hot meals for the troops, who seemed to be constantly on the move.

Al Armstrong, 14th Canadian Hussars

All our vehicles carried a camp stove, a Coleman camp stove just like you see around today, and a food break was called and somebody would hand down the Coleman stove to heat up the rations, which was hard tack, bully beef, and so on. Before the food was ready there was a couple of kids watching us. I heard one say to the other, "Canadees, soldaat Canadees." So they came over to where we were getting the food ready. By this time the guys had their mess tins out and they started eating. The kids just stood back, and they were gaunt. So one of these guys took his mess tin and he started feeding one of them. Somebody on the other side, he took his mess tin and started feeding the other. Before you know it there's a dozen kids around there, and our guys stopped eating and we were feeding the kids. We got the order to move on. We got a hold of a civilian that seemed to be in some kind of authority, and whatever food we had in the vehicle, we left it at the side of the road, and his first thought was, "We can't pay you." We're not selling.

On the same day of the breakthrough across the Leopold Canal, the 9th Brigade also launched an amphibious assault on the other side of the Breskens pocket. Alligator and Buffalo vehicles manoeuvred through the waters and landed beyond Braakman Cove near Hoofdplaat.

Doug Barrie, Highland Light Infantry

They were suffering terrific casualties trying to get across the Leopold Canal. So they decided that we'd try and speed things up and do the attack from the north and land from the Scheldt. It was a waterborne landing, and the operation was called Switchback. Really there shouldn't have been the need for Switchback if only we had been allowed to keep going after the pursuit from France and Belgium. They stopped short going into Holland because they were running out of supplies, petrol, and so on. But if we had gone a little further, we would have saved that battle and many lives.

Jack Martin, Queen's Own Rifles

Our first involvement in the Scheldt was when they loaded us onto what they called Buffaloes. They were a tracked vehicle and would take a Bren gun carrier and close the door and move into the water. There was only eight inches showing above the water, and we were quite afraid that if a wave came we were going to be swimming. We followed the Highland Light Infantry in, and we were under quite a bit of mortar fire.

Artillery shells landing in Breskens. Artillery support was key to any advances that the Canadians made in the Scheldt.

The Highland Light Infantry led the landing near Hoofdplaat, making the clearing of the south shore possible and saving many lives at the Leopold Canal.

Doug Barrie, Highland Light Infantry

We landed just after two o'clock in darkness on the lower part of the dikes. It was tough going getting off because the tide was down and the beach was large and wet, and you sank into it. Your boots sank into it, everything sank into it. So we had trouble getting off, but the main thing was that we weren't being fired upon — it was a complete surprise. The Germans weren't prepared for any landing there, so it worked out well that way.

George Mummery, Highland Light Infantry

It was quite good because there were sandbars and various other obstacles going up, but on the lead they had a Dutchman who knew the layout pretty well, so they all just followed. They carried about twenty to twenty-five guys in each Buffalo, and they took us out to the North Sea and we came in from the sea and landed on the beach. There was nobody on the beach. They never expected this to happen. They figured everything was coming from back farther on the mainland. So we get in fine, of course, once we get in our regiments were the first ones to land, and then to our right came the 8th Brigade and the 7th Brigade was in reserve. Once we got to the first dike, they were supposed to come up through us. Anyway we got in to the first dike, in fact there's a marker there now in commemoration of that. We got to the next dike, and they had all their defences set up.

Doug Barrie, Highland Light Infantry

I landed with A Company and then I went to B Company and we were on the extreme left, or the north part of the landing. We had the most trouble there because of the marshy lands on the sides. It was well-occupied by German troops, and they came alive the next morning. We were around by a farmhouse there, and we were being attacked from the north side. We sent out attacks to clear the edges and then we had to put in a full-company attack along one of the dikes to clear it. I was left out of battle. The company commander, Major King, at that time decided that he wanted to take the

A view of the beach and dike at Hoofdplaat, near where the Canadians landed.

A monument commemorating De Bevrijding and Canada's role in it at Hoofdplaat.

company in on the attack across the polders to where the Germans were entrenched. Our mortars laid down smoke, and we had the matching field regiment in support giving covering fire. I was lying down on the dike beside their OP officer, Captain Murdoch. He was directing fire. I heard a disturbance down the way, and I thought that there might be some Jerries working their way around the edge of the company. I wormed my way down to see what I could find. I couldn't find any Germans, so when I came back I noticed that Captain Murdoch's head was down, and I tapped him on the shoulder and I looked and found he had a sniper bullet right through the centre of his forehead. By that time we started to get some shelling around us, and I pulled his body back down to the bottom of the dike. He had a carrier and a driver there, and we had to take cover because the shelling was getting pretty acute. So finally we took cover in a dugout down the dike a way. It was quite well dug out, about ten feet, and we heard rustling, so I lit a match. There were three Germans there, but they weren't prepared to fight, they wanted to give up. So we took them prisoner, but we had to stay there until after the shelling had subsided. I guess it wasn't until the next day that Captain Murdoch's body was taken out and given a burial there in the dikes. Up there we had some nineteen

Canadian soldiers carrying wounded member of the North Shore Regiment.

or so killed in the next couple of days. You couldn't bury them in the polder because it was too wet, you'd go down six inches and you're into water. They had to bury them in the side of the dike. They were tended by a Dutch woman. Every day, regardless of the shelling, she'd go there and tended the graves of our dead. White crosses were put there with the names on them. So it was quite dramatic.

The element of surprise was completely in the Canadians' favour: the Germans had never considered an attack from the Scheldt side of their position, and they reacted slowly to the invasion. By the time they had mustered a response to the Canadian landing, a strong bridgehead was established, and the Germans were in trouble.

North Nova Scotia Highlanders War Diary, October 9, 1944

As we moved in on the beach ahead of us, the artillery marked the landing points with red shells. A few tracers were criss-crossing through the blackness and a haystack or barn was burning inland a few hundred yards. We touched down with B Company right, C Company centre, and D Company left. The first wave of vehicles touched down fifteen minutes after the troops. Soon the beach was a hive of industry. The great motors roaring and these huge amphibious monsters crawling like great reptiles from the sea, out over the dyke and spitting flame from their exhausts. Throughout all this noise not a shell fell in our area, although the Highland Light Infantry of Canada were being shelled a little. D Company took out 9 prisoners from a dugout on their first objective.

The companies soon got on their objectives with few casualties. The command post moved to a farm. We no sooner arrived in that area when Jerry decided it was their turn and proceeded to shell us with all he had to spare. He also practically demolished the RAP. The Stormont, Dundas and Glengarry Highlanders landed and proceeded to Hoofdplaat. A Company expanded, and occupied a farm. C Company moved up along the dike. B Company occupied a dike at the road junction.

Since we have come ashore, Jerry has made numerous small counterattacks and suffered quite a few casualties. On one occasion A Company observed about 150 enemy with two vehicles and two infantry guns proceeding up road. Artillery was brought down and one of the vehicles hit. The attack was decidedly broken up. Companies are all well dug in but shelling fairly heavy. The beach is getting quite a pasting.

Royal Winnipeg Rifles War Diary, October 10, 1944

Cloudy and cool with slight rain in the afternoon. Visibility poor. C Company night patrol to Grafjan returned at 0230 hrs without having contacted the enemy. During the morning A Company assisted the Regina Rifles in destroying an enemy held pill box. Another C Company patrol to Grafjan failed to contact the enemy but rescued a wounded B Company man who had been left when his Company withdrew on the previous day. Enemy shelling was slightly less intense. SA fire continued to make it extremely difficult and dangerous to move about. Supplies and casualties were still ferried across the Canal. Captain H.C. Chadderton of C Company and Lieutenant L. Mendels of B Company were among the numerous casualties for the day.

Cliff Chadderton, Royal Winnipeg Rifles

The world as I knew it was left behind, courtesy of the Armed Forces of Adolf Hitler. The Greenwich time was approximately 1000 hours on October 10, 1944. My new life commenced in the opening of a bunker, which had been built by the German SS defending that part of Holland. A rough road ran from the bunker north towards a Dutch town named Grafjan in Holland.

My plans for a normal life (I was twenty-five) ended in a fusillade of German artillery, helped by a German potato masher grenade dropped upon me by a leering German. My infantry company, down from 130 to 62 men due to shortage of reinforcements, occupied the remains of small bunkers on the German side of the raised canal bank.

Consciousness slowly came back. I realized that the guys that I had soldiered with were feverishly digging me out. I was alternating between excruciating pain and blissful peace, which occurred when the mud compressed the wounds. I recall yelling for a stretcher-bearer. He came with morphine and pushed the needle into the only clean spot he could find — the crevice just above my collarbone. Blessed relief as the analgesic flooded my veins! I closed my eyes. Sergeant Alex Bell took charge. I could hear him shouting. He had found a small boat — actually a punt — large enough to ferry me back across the canal to where our medical staff were waiting at the regimental aid post.

My next conscious moments might best be described as a hazy, almost boozy feeling. I was lying on a stretcher in the kitchen of a farm building. Our regimental medical officer, the much-admired Doc Caldwell from Yarmouth, Nova Scotia, was trying to revive me. He said to his medical orderlies, "Don't let him suffer." A bad omen?

Next stop: the casualty clearing station, where they applied tourniquets and gave me another shot of morphine. At the same time, they attempted to treat a serious wound in the stomach, which could prove fatal if peritonitis set in. Doc Bob Caldwell had undoubtedly saved my life. He had identified the stomach wound back at the regimental aid post and stuffed it with sulfa powder. As he was performing this procedure, he said the words which would be with me for the rest of my life. He was talking to Ernie Pash, another much-respected medic: "From now on Cliff Chadderton is living on borrowed time."

I did not think I was in very bad shape until a doctor, performing triage, stripped away the bloodstained parts of my battledress. A lot of walking wounded from the attack lined the corridor. The battlefield surgeon told them they would have to wait until he tended to this officer (me), whose wounds he classified as "probably fatal." The expression set off a jolt in the pit of my stomach.

I remember snatches of those hours: the bloodstained gurney, the fact that my shoes were gone, the anaesthetic needles, the dissipation of the pain when it reached an unbearable degree, and the nagging question, "What had happened to my men?"

A vague debate trickled through my subconscious mind. Would they take off my right leg or my left leg? The doctor told the nurse, "I think I can save one." The nurse kept finding new shrapnel wounds, thirteen in all.

The fierce fighting on the south shore of the Scheldt continued for a month. The Germans were well-fortified, but they were surrounded, and the outcome was inevitable. Control of the area by the Canadians was just a matter of time.

The Highland Light Infantry in the Scheldt.

Charles Barrett, Highland Light Infantry

Biervliet was pretty heavy going. I know we had a lot of casualties, and when we got in position, after a lot of heavy shelling, I went around to check my company positions in the middle of the night. I found that I didn't have any officers left. We had an OP sergeant or even a corporal commanding platoons, so it was pretty dicey. I called up my second-in-command, who was usually kept in reserve, and we were sitting in a wreck of a house discussing what we're going to do, and a shell hit the floor above us and shrapnel came down and doubled him up, and he was taken away. It was quite a problem in keeping up our reinforcements, they were very slow in coming, and the ones that did come had little or no infantry training, so it was quite stressful in that respect.

This photo at Hoofdplaat demonstrates the height that some dikes and barriers attained in the Scheldt.

Lockhart Fulton, Royal Winnipeg Rifles

We had no tank support because it was flooded and you could only go down the road, and a tank was a sitting duck on the roads, and at the same time if they slid off the road they were in water and almost impossible to get them out. So tank support was non-existent once we started to attack inland. The way we did it we'd float a company down the road to a village, the Germans held the villages and the farm sites. Eventually we worked out a pretty good system of attacking and overcoming opposition, and it was pretty decent opposition. Our battalion was probably no better than half strength, and we were starting to get some reinforcements. We were getting some pretty good successes, and the other battalions like the Canadian Scottish and the Reginas were using the same tactics.

In the same time frame the 2nd Canadian Infantry Division had moved north to close the isthmus to South Beveland. The action was hotly contested by highly trained German paratroopers who were positioned there. Woensdrecht, the key to controlling the isthmus, was a strategic point, and the Canadians were faced with the daunting task of making an attack over an open, flooded field. The casualties were high. The Germans counterattacked on October 8, further adding to the casualties. The Canadians were determined to control the isthmus, and on October 13 the Black Watch (the Royal Highland Regiment from Montreal) was selected to lead the attack. The unit had a long and glorious history, with a philosophy of never retreating.

The attack commenced early in the morning, with the regiment crossing the polders and cutting the rail line northwest of Woensdrecht. The Germans responded with an overwhelming show of firepower. The Nazis were well-positioned and were able to put a stop to the attack. But the Black Watch came at them again in the afternoon, with C and D companies almost attaining their objectives. The casualties sustained were severe, and the remaining men could not secure the captured territory. The remnants of D Company withdrew in the early hours of October 14, while a number of the men in C Company were taken prisoner. The Black Watch suffered 197 wounded and 85 missing in action, nearly decimating the regiment. It would be a dark day in the regiment's history, known as "Black Friday."

Jim Wilkinson, Black Watch

We took a real licking at Woensdrecht on Black Friday, the thirteenth of October. It was a mass murder, that's all it was. Of our casualties we had about sixty-five dead, so you can see how close the hand-to-hand fighting was.

Woensdrecht was the key town between the mainland and the isthmus to South Beveland.

The church at Woensdrecht. The steeple was used as an observation post due to its excellent view of the isthmus.

Russell Sanderson, Black Watch

What's referred to as Black Friday we were to make an attack on the dike that was actually part of the railroad embankment, and it was crossed by a roadway on the bend. It was called Operation Angus. We had made patrols in and saw what strength there was a couple of nights before; it was a fluid situation because they had the protection of this great high embankment and they could move around on the far side. It was decided that the attack would go in on the thirteenth, and we came up during the night to a farm. We went into there, formed up, and then we ran directly out to the point where we were going to attack, and for some reason there was a delay and the attack never went in until six-thirty in the morning instead of five-thirty, which brought on considerably more light. Trying to make our way across the flats was tragic. The flats were wide open, there wasn't a decent blade of grass to hide behind, and we suffered an awful lot of casualties, and consequently it didn't fail but it didn't succeed too well. Some elements of one or two of the rifle companies made it up to positions on the other side of the dike. That was sort of a hazardous situation when all you have to do is take and throw a hand grenade in the air and it will fall on top of the other guy on the other side of the dike. When the Germans had decided that there was going to be an attack, the German officer in charge brought in the division of paratroopers, and they didn't come any better than the Jerry paratroopers. They had the strength in there that stopped our attack, and consequently we suffered an awful lot of casualties, and a lot of the fellas had to lay out there all day wounded until dark came, and most of the next night we went out and were bringing in wounded and bodies.

Dutch civilians attending the burial of fifty-five members of the Black Watch, victims of Black Friday at Woensdrecht.

Woensdrecht, 2004.

The hill overlooking Woensdrecht, the site of the bloody assault by the Black Watch.

Private A. Bourgoulin, Sergeant A.E. Mercier, and Corporal C. Robichaud of le Régiment de Maisonneuve posing by a German 105-mm S.P. gun at Woensdrecht.

Al Armstrong, 14th Canadian Hussars

I was in the battle of South Beveland, we tried to be in a support role for the infantry. The names of the towns, Woensdrecht, Ossendrecht, there were others in between, but we followed the line of the 2nd Division and on the other side of us was the 4th Canadian Division — they were armoured.

In the armoury unit, especially reconnaissance, we couldn't do much but holding. And there wasn't too much in there that the heavy tanks could do. It was mostly infantry. The weather turned cold, which didn't make the going any easier.

The objective still had to be taken, and the mission was then given to the Royal Hamilton Light Infantry and the 10th Armoured Regiment. On October 16, under the fire of the entire division's artillery, these brave men fought their way up to Woensdrecht and pushed on to capture the hill that overlooked the village.

The hill was an important objective since it afforded the army that held it a superior vantage point overlooking the isth-

LEFT: *Statue in honour of the Canadian soldiers who fought at Woensdrecht.* TOP: *Inscription on the monument in honour of the Canadians who fought at Woensdrecht.* BOTTOM: *Monument for the Black Watch at Woensdrecht.*

mus. On that day the Canadians liberated Woensdrecht and took control of the entrance to South Beveland, completing the first of the four parts of the mission to take control of the Scheldt. The Germans attempted to counter-attack, but the Canadians held the position and repelled the Nazis. At the cost of many Canadian lives, the first stage was complete.

Jim Wilkinson, Black Watch

We were able to get to the second embankment, and then the Calgarys relieved us. We weren't responsible for capturing Woensdrecht at all. The Calgary Highlanders relieved us, and the Royal Regiment, the Rileys, they were the fellows who held the area while we were getting reinforcements. Once that was established we swung up into the Scheldt estuary.

Doug Shaughnessy, Royal Hamilton Light Infantry

Woensdrecht was pretty heavily defended. Colonel Whittaker, who was the commander, he was in charge of the RHLI, and we were in there a couple of days I guess. I think Whittaker brought down gunfire on his own positions, we were just about overrun, and we lost a lot of guys there.

Russell Sanderson, Black Watch

The Typhoons came in and rocketed the positions. They were a great life-saving thing, the Typhoons.

Bill Clifford, RCAF

143 Wing was made up of three squadrons, namely 438, 439, and 440 Typhoon fighter bomber squadrons.

Advancing troops of the Black Watch move into South Beveland near Hoogerheide.

The wing was part of 83 Group 2nd TAF [Tactical Air Force]. We flew close support. Alongside our area of operation and advancing into Holland was the Canadian Army supported by RAF 83 Group, who were also flying Typhoons, both bomber and rocket-firing Typhoons. There were many Canadian pilots in these squadrons as well, whereas 143 Wing was all Canadian.

Apart from supporting the army, attacking troop movements, dropping anti-personnel bombs on troop concentrations in hold-out areas, we were called upon to hit strategic targets and to hit areas that were being tenaciously held against our advancing army. We never ran short of designated targets, cutting rail lines to thwart the supply of troops and material, to soften things up.

Russell Sanderson, Black Watch

There was quite a fight for Woensdrecht, and I recall a large white house there. The Germans had been driven out of the area and they made it into this white house and they're all hiding in the basement. Someone noticed them from the window, and the word got back to our men. The neighbours said you should have seen it — the Canadians were coming in one side and all these Germans were coming out the cellar window trying to escape! They were all caught. That was hazardous — house clearing is one of the worst things there is, because you can hide anyplace and you have to realize that bullets can go through walls. All you have to hear is a sound on the other side and you could probably take the guy out by just shooting right through the wall. The easiest way to go house clearing is with grenades — it takes away a lot of the labour. You just pull the pin on that grenade and throw her in the door and that eliminates anybody in there — if it doesn't kill them the concussion will quiet them right down. They're quite passive when you go in.

We overcame their position, and the Germans withdrew and went north toward Bergen op Zoom, and with that movement we moved out to the neck of the peninsula toward the town of Goes.

Along the south shore of the Scheldt estuary the 3rd Division continued to pressure the Germans in the Breskens pocket.

Jack Martin, Queen's Own Rifles

Early one morning my sergeant woke me and said, "Jack, we need you on the mortar right now." So I went out, and he said, "There's a group of the enemy forming up in a little wooded area. We've got to stop that counterattack." He says to go back and throw a bomb down the barrel, and he gave me a range and direction, so I went back and threw the bomb down. I went back up onto the dike, just peered over it to watch. This group of Jerries, they all started to run to their right. One guy peeled off and turned the other way, and when the bomb landed it hit this one guy right on the chest, and of course that was the end of him. That was the only time I ever used the mortar as a sniper. That stopped the counterattack. The rest of them all disappeared into the woods, and the rifle company took over.

The Highland Light Infantry played a key role in clearing the Breskens pocket.

Douglas Lavoie, Fort Garry Horse

You wonder how some guys can come through and not a scratch on them, especially the infantry guys. Boy oh boy, that's a rough life. But some of them, they were there, right in the thick of it all, all the time, and they came out of it. They weren't shell-shocked, none of that stuff, just returned ordinary guys. But a lot of that experience they probably would never want to remember ever again.

Doug Barrie, Highland Light Infantry

I was with the regiment as second-in-command of B Company, and on the night of the sixteenth/seventeenth our company had only three officers left, and D Company had only one officer left because of the casualties taken. There was quite a gap between the two companies, and we wanted to establish a position where we could put up a machine gun and stop them from infiltrating down the dikes. So I was to look for a spot where we could put in a fighting patrol, and then I was to carry on to D Company and to help them because of their shortage, to be in charge of a couple of platoons. This was close to midnight at the time that I started out. It had been dark, but the moon came out through the clouds and it got fairly bright. I skirted along as far as I could below the dike, but I had to go over this one dike near a junction. It was a spot where I thought we could put a patrol. So I clambered up to the top of the dike and started to look at the other side. I was keeping a low profile, and all of a sudden there was a shot and I just threw myself down. I didn't feel anything at the time, but after a couple of minutes I rolled back down behind the dike for protection and I didn't know if I had just numbed my leg or what, and my hand. I started to look and saw blood going down my battledress and my hand was hurting all of a sudden. I took stock, and I found that a bullet had gone through my left hand and creased my right leg. Just cut off part of the bone, because I was down low and that's the way that it hit me. So I lay still for a short bit to get my wind and to put a dressing on, and then I had to crawl back to the company and went to the first aid detachment, and they sent me back to the hospital. I was still carrying a bullet in my thigh that I had got at Boulogne. In the hospital I had my hand treated and my leg treated and the bullet taken out of my thigh. But what I didn't know was that I still had a piece of shrapnel in my head that I had got at Buron, so it wasn't until after I got home that I got that out of my head. After that they sent me home on what they called a tri-wound scheme. "If you're wounded three times," they said, "you're out!" So I was going to be sent home, which I didn't mind at the time. I had four months, nearly four and a half months, of action, and I was ready to have a little break.

Desperately needing the supply route opened as soon as possible, Field Marshal Montgomery ordered a regrouping of all of the Allied forces. The focus was to speed up the opening of the Scheldt estuary, and in order to do so Operation Pheasant was launched on October 20. The objective was to liberate the middle and western sections of Noord Barbant province, with the Canadians advancing from the south and the British moving in from the east. The British 2nd Army moved westward from their position in southern Netherlands, attacking German positions and clearing out the territory south of the Maas River, effectively sealing off the Scheldt region. The Canadians attacked northward from

The medieval city centre of Bergen Op Zoom.

the South Beveland isthmus, squeezing the Germans into a smaller and smaller space. The Canadian 4th Division, which was fighting along the Leopold Canal, was moved north of the Scheldt River to participate in the operation. They also attacked northward, pushing towards Bergen op Zoom. The Germans who were left holding their positions at the mouth of the Scheldt River were completely isolated.

Al Armstrong, 14th Canadian Hussars

The place of Bergen op Zoom was our first major battle before the Scheldt estuary, and the orders were we would secure it in three days. Three weeks later we were still on the road to Bergen op Zoom. The German 7th Army and 15th Army — we were on their tail — and every now and then they'd turn on us and there was a major battle. The battle for Bergen op Zoom was very costly in British and Canadian lives.

Refugees in Steenbergen (north of the Scheldt) looking for shelter after being ousted from their homes by the Germans.

Lockhart Fulton, Royal Winnipeg Rifles

I think the main factor was that the Germans didn't have any backup. That once you overcame a position, there was no counterattack or no attempt by the Germans to recapture it. So it was just a straight question of being able to dominate the farmhouse positions or the village positions with smoke and artillery fire until our company could get close enough to use their weapons. The Germans that were holding the positions knew that they weren't going to be reinforced, and I think that once we got moving it was just a case of overcoming them with more power. The Germans made no effort to reinforce or counterattack in the Scheldt in all the fighting that our battalion did there.

Another key factor at this time was the role of the Royal Canadian Navy. Since D-Day, the men of the RCN had maintained a constant supply route from England, delivering food, equipment, ammunition, and reinforcements to Europe. They also ensured that the sea lanes were clear — safe from the German Navy and the dreaded U-boats. The Royal Canadian Air Force also played a major role. As was evident on D-Day, the Allies controlled the skies with superior numbers of every type of aircraft imaginable. Bomber Command would precede infantry attacks with raids that would either destroy the enemy emplacements or create enough havoc to keep the Germans from putting up a good defence. Fighter Command would provide security from attacks by the Luftwaffe and aerial support for advancing troops. The war was truly a team effort.

Bill Clifford, RCAF

I was posted to 440 Squadron when the wing moved from Bruxelles to Eindhoven in Holland early in October 1944. Our airfield was formerly a German night fighter base and had been strategically located for intercepting RAF raids on the continent. We operated out of this base through the winter of '44/'45 until the Rhine crossing in March. Usually we were shooting up trains and armoured vehicles, cutting rail lines that quite often got repaired overnight, vector bombing when the clouds were even too close to the ground for low-level attacks.

Doug Barrie, Highland Light Infantry

The air force played a great role — the Typhoons particularly. They could dive in on troops, and they played a really major part in France as well as up in Holland. It was great to know that they were there in support of us. They were often called upon because the dike fighting was very difficult.

Charles Barrett, Highland Light Infantry

We had a lot of support from the Typhoon bombers. I used them once in the Scheldt to clean out the enemy on the other side of the dike from us who were giving us some trouble. They didn't want to come in, they said it was too close to our position, but I pointed out that this particular dike had a very defining characteristic to it and there shouldn't be any problems. When they arrived they came in right over our heads, just yards above us, a wonderful sight, and the rockets fired over the top of the dike, and that was the end of the enemy there. We walked right over.

The shattered remains of a train hit by a Typhoon. Note the devastation.

As the Allies took control of the southern part of the Netherlands, the next step was to move across the Rhine. That would put the Allies in a position to take the war onto German soil. The first major crossing of the Rhine occurred on October 23, 1944, and the pressure on the Germans increased. That same day the Dutch Resistance boldly made an attempt on the life of SD-Commander Oehlschlagel, but the cost was great: the

German 105-mm and pillbox that was captured by the Canadian Scottish and the North Nova Scotia Highlanders Regiment in the Breskens pocket.

Royal Canadian Engineers.

Nazis killed twenty-nine hostages in reprisal the next day, leaving their bodies littered alongside an Amsterdam road.

On the same day as the Amsterdam massacre, the Canadians finished sealing off the isthmus to South Beveland, and they proceeded to launch an attack against the peninsula. While there was resistance, it disappeared two days later when the 52nd British Division assisted with an amphibious attack. The Germans were trying to get off the peninsula, realizing the futility of their position. For the Canadians and the British, the clearing of South Beveland proceeded fairly easily. By October 31 the peninsula had been liberated. Part three of the Scheldt mission was complete (part two of the plan was still being fought along the south shore of the Scheldt, where tough resistance would continue for several more days).

Russell Sanderson, Black Watch

There were a couple of the canals that we had to cross and then we widened out our field of attack. Some elements were moving along the shore trying to work their way along to Walcheren Island. We moved up through several little towns and took a few casualties, and in the town of Goes I recall the Bren carriers went in there and for a minute it was a case of letting everyone know we're there. They spun that old carrier around a couple of times on one track and sprayed everything with machine gun fire. Then we realized that the Jerries had just pulled out and had moved on toward the causeway that went across toward Walcheren Island.

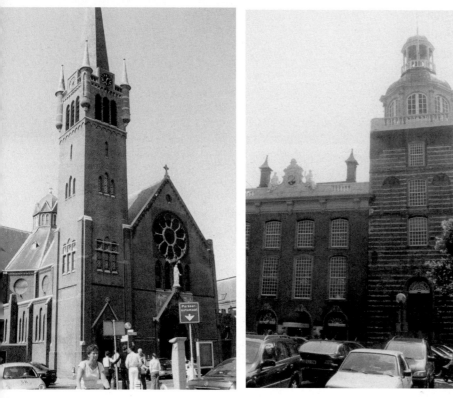

LEFT: *Church at Goes in South Beveland.* RIGHT: *The Goes stadhuis.*

Norman Edwards, 14th Canadian Hussars

We had several pushes, and we liberated the South Beveland Island. There was a point there where we captured an enemy Red Cross ship and we floated the armoured vehicles across to the island. We kind of sneaked up on them by floating vehicles across the canal and landing where they didn't expect us. The Dutch people provided barges that we floated across on. They helped any way they could.

On October 25 the Dutch Resistance boldly orchestrated a prison break, freeing forty prisoners from the Nazis. Brutal reprisals ensued, and there were several executions. To the south, the Allies were continuing to liberate more Dutch towns. On October 27, den Bosch was freed in the south, while the Princess Irene Brigade liberated its countrymen at Tilburg. On October 30 Tholen was liberated as well.

LEFT: *The Royal Canadian Engineers (7th Field) filling holes in the Beveland Causeway with bricks in late October.* BELOW LEFT: *Sergeant R.Y. Williams, Sergeant J.J. Coghill, and Sergeant W. Anaka of the Fort Garry Horse get an enthusiastic reception from some Dutch girls after the liberation of South Beveland.* BELOW RIGHT: *South Alberta Regiment gathered at a town square in Bergen op Zoom in late October 1944.*

TOP LEFT: *The waterfront at Middelburg, Walcheren Island. In the closing days of the Battle of the Scheldt, the city was isolated by flooded polders all around it.* TOP RIGHT: *Middelburg, 2004.* BOTTOM: *Flooding at Middelburg. German options for defence were limited, and there was nowhere to run.*

One of the great obstacles that faced the Canadians in the Battle of the Scheldt was Walcheren Island. Situated in the middle of the estuary, it stood in the way of shipping headed for Antwerp. The Germans had created very strong defences all along the island, and the beaches were filled with heavy artillery batteries. Early in the month the RAF had bombed the island's dikes, flooding the low-lying portions of the island. As such, the central area of Walcheren was inundated and only the highlands remained. The only approach to the island by land was a twelve-kilometre causeway from South Beveland. The causeway contained a road and a rail line, but only one track was left from bombing. The narrow strip of land to

Truck pulling ammunition truck out of a deep ditch along the Beveland causeway.

Walcheren was only forty metres wide, and it offered no protection to infantry that would dare to advance across it. The surrounding land was flat and too saturated with water for a ground assault. On the other hand, the flats were not flooded enough to sustain an amphibious assault either. The flooding of the island by the RAF did present the opportunity to use an amphibious attack from the river or the sea. With the German defences set up for the regular coastline of the island, the flooding created large breaches in the defences that could be exploited in such an attack across the water.

The Canadians had three options for attacking Walcheren Island. One: to cross the causeway from South Beveland to the east. Two: to stage an amphibious assault across the Scheldt from the south. Three: to stage an amphibious assault from the sea. The initial attack was launched on October 31 as South Beveland was finally secured. It commenced across the causeway, where the Germans could place the Canadians under a deadly barrage of bullets and bombs. With a finite amount of space available to cross, the Germans could hone right in on the advancing troops. It was a grim task, and the men of the Black Watch and le Régiment de Maisonneuve moved along slowly, leaving behind friends scattered all along the roadway. The units would leapfrog, one covering the advance of the other, then vice versa. Gradually they moved along the causeway. This frontal attack was followed up by amphibious attacks, diverting the Germans' attention to multiple defensive positions.

Jim Wilkinson, Black Watch

Leading to the causeway is a huge polder, which they had built the road on, and the Germans had these 88s right down the causeway. If you wanted to make any movement you had to go through two inches of water.

I was heading up to the causeway and I ran across this young fellow, I never met him before, and he had a Bren gun in his hand, and I told him, "Son, get that damn thing firing onto the causeway." He says, "Corporal, I don't know how to reload it." He was a young reinforcement. From what I gathered most of the reinforcements were

A convoy of vehicles carrying the 2nd Division on the Beveland Causeway.

A Canadian convoy passes a typical Dutch windmill en route to the Beveland Canal.

either non-combatants or artillerymen. They had no infantry training. This was the problem. Originally in Normandy on that infamous day of July 25, we lost pretty near 450 men. We had five years of training as infantrymen, and these young fellows had to learn on the job.

Russell Sanderson, Black Watch

While we were trying to get onto the causeway we took a lot of casualties, we got pinned down, and then the Maisonneuve came up and it was the Maisies that came up on the south side and they drove through and got pretty well all the way across and got stopped at the far end.

On November 1 the Canadians landed near Westkapelle on Walcheren, along with three British commando groups and the British 52nd Division. Naval support bombarded the German positions to protect the landings. The next day the Canadians managed to capture a narrow bridgehead at the causeway. Le Régiment de Maisonneuve held on as the Germans desperately attempted to dislodge them and force them back. They would not budge. The brave men held on for several hours until they were relieved by British troops.

The second wave of British commandos depart from Breskens aboard LCAs to land at Flushing (Vlissingen) to invade Walcheren Island.

The defences of Walcheren Island had been breached, and the next step was to clear the island of Germans.

Russell Sanderson, Black Watch

The British forces and our 3rd Division were coming in by sea from across the Scheldt River in landing craft. And it was through the RAF and the landing of the British troops and our 3rd Division on the south shore that we actually took the island. We got people across from the Scheldt, but we had them boxed in so that they couldn't get off of the island when they were attacked from the sea. It was like a pincer movement, and that's how it finally collapsed, their positions being flooded and most of their artillery was nullified by ours, and when they went in with the aircraft that settled it right there.

ABOVE LEFT: *Universal carriers of the 8th Reconnaissance Regiment aboard a barge move towards North Beveland Island.*
ABOVE RIGHT: *Flooded area in the vicinity of St. Phillipsland and Tholein Island.*

As the battle for Walcheren Island raged, the Canadian 4th Division in the north advanced east past Bergen op Zoom and moved on to St. Philipsland. Their tanks had engaged several German vessels in Zijpe harbour and had sunk them from the land. The liberation in the south of the Netherlands continued. The historic town of Sluis was freed on November 1.

The next day North Beveland was liberated as well. On November 3 heavy fighting around Vlissingen finally resulted in freedom for the city and its people. For the Canadians fighting along the south shore of the Scheldt estuary, November 3 was an important day. After three weeks of bitter warfare, the German opposition in the Breskens pocket collapsed, and the south shore of the Scheldt was free. Step two of the plan for the Battle of the Scheldt had been accomplished.

Charles Barrett, Highland Light Infantry

Another thing I remember quite well, I think we were on our way to clean up Breskens, and we were crossing an open field, and suddenly a machine gun opened up and started to spray the area. It seemed like a scythe working over the land, and we fell flat on our faces and I dug myself in as flat as I could to the ground. I always had that memory of the smell of mother earth, and it was the most comforting smell I could think of at the time.

TOP LEFT: *Two Canadian soldiers view the North Sea from Bergen op Zoom.* LEFT: *Bergen op Zoom, 2004.* ABOVE: *The Toronto Scottish (heavy machine gun platoon) and the 8th Recce board small metal motor boats.*

Jack Martin, Queen's Own Rifles

My friend Charlie Martin, he had gone all the way through the Scheldt, and he was so wet that he thought he could get away with walking on the dike while his men were down below. And that's when a Jerry up and let him have it with a schmeisser and tore his map case and binoculars off, but Charlie was able to pull his pistol and fire on the way down and kill the guy.

The port of Breskens, 2004.

German gun emplacement at Breskens. Similar in structure to the emplacements along the Atlantic Wall, these structures were made of concrete several feet thick, which was reinforced with metal rods, making them virtually indestructible.

Charles Barrett, Highland Light Infantry

By that time we were starting to get some of our vehicles in, and I had a jeep and a driver, and we were driving up towards Breskens and there was one town with a crossroad where we were passing through, and we were told to watch out for the heavies that they were dropping in on the main intersection. So we stopped a short distance out of the town and we'd wait until a couple of heavy shells landed on the intersection, and then you had maybe a minute to get through before the next ones arrived. So we raced through, and we're racing up to a country road and came around a corner and here's an 88 pointing straight at us. Just by instinct I grabbed the wheel of the jeep and pulled it as hard as I could and we rolled over into the ditch. We lay there for a few minutes and then I didn't hear anything, so gradually I came up and stuck my head over the edge of the ditch and I looked at this gun position. I could see the helmets of two Germans sitting there, but they didn't move. So I watched very carefully and took out a pistol, and I moved up, and these two fellows are dead.

Breskens, the key German position on the south shore of the Sheldt.

Doug Barrie, Highland Light Infantry

We were closing in on Breskens, and our role there was to hold the area around Breskens, not to attack the town itself but to let the SDGs and North Novas do the attack. That's what happened, the regiment kept a tight circle around Breskens so none of them could get out. Then we were turned south to go down to Schoondjike, and the regiment had quite a battle there. From there back to Cadzand and along the coast, clearing the way to Knocke, and that's just across the border into Belgium. The 9th Brigade liberated Knocke. There was still a little bit of fighting going on, and we had to take out some guns down on the waterfront. Other than that, the main fighting was over.

Large areas of the Scheldt were inundated throughout the fall. Recovery from the damage would take years.

Charles Barrett, Highland Light Infantry

At the end of the Scheldt operation we were up to Knocke, which is on the coast. It was a fortress on the coast with all the main armament facing out to sea, and the remains of the 6th and 4th German Divisions — they had been shrunk back into this area. We were attacking that, and I used artillery. I kept a lot of metal coming down on the position while the company moved forward, and I don't think we had any casualties because the Germans kept their heads down and it worked very well. Our men got right in, and as soon as they saw they were surrounded, they just gave up. The white flags came up, and I think there was something like eleven hundred came out of that position. Of course, there were so many of them we couldn't escort them, we just told them to go to the rear, and they all just walked down the road. I know when I was going through the position after we had taken it, one of my men came up to me and said, "You better come down here and see what's going on." So he took me down into a bunker and there was a huge trunk, and it was filled with bills, brand new bills, I think they were guilders mostly. I called up the other units in the battalion and the brigade, including the artillery, to send vehicles over, and we unloaded all this material that we relieved from the enemy, mostly liquor and also money. At the spur of the moment we were just handing out bundles of money to all these different units. The funny thing about that was at the time we found the trunk, two of my men were standing there looking very circumspect and standing at attention — but I noticed at the time that their jackets seemed very bulgy, and a day or so later I realized they had gone AWOL (absent without leave). We never heard from them again. I remember getting messages from A and Q — the administrative and quartermasters' division — asking if we knew anything about their location. The only thing I ever did hear was one of my men one day several weeks or a month later said that he had heard from one of them, got a note, and it said, "Don't worry about us, I'm married, and I've bought a hotel in the south of France." These are some of the unusual things that happen.

L.A. Hamilton of the 8th Reconnaissance Group (2nd Division) sits in a jeep surrounded by Dutch children.

Rubble from a bombed building in Steenbergen being used to fill in a hole in the road. The Engineers worked hard to maintain the roads to ensure a steady supply route from the rear.

The last holdout was the German unit on Walcheren Island. On November 6 the siege of Middelburg, the capital of Walcheren Island, provided a major victory, liberating the city and paving the way for the collapse of German resistance on the island. Two days later the Germans at Vrouwenpolder surrendered, clearing Walcheren completely. The fourth and final step of the Battle of the Scheldt was complete, and the Canadians had secured the major supply route to northwestern Europe for the Allies.

Charles Barrett, Highland Light Infantry

I think the heaviest fighting the Highland Light Infantry experienced was in the Scheldt because it was a gruelling experience. I think we lost up to 40 percent of our strength during that period. Killed and wounded.

Mervin Durham, Royal Canadian Engineers

November the eighth or ninth, we were in Bergen op Zoom. I was in the engineers — we cleared mines, built bridges, and all that went with it. When we got about a mile and a half out of the city, we got word to check the road by observation. I took off for Bergen op Zoom, and I didn't look back as often as I should have. The damn telephone wires were

TOP LEFT: *The old city centre of Bergen op Zoom, with many buildings dating back to the Middle Ages.* TOP RIGHT: *Heavily damaged house in Bergen op Zoom.* MIDDLE RIGHT: *A Dutch child poses for a picture in Bergen op Zoom.* BOTTOM LEFT: *Canadian soldiers examine items left at the German headquarters at Bergen op Zoom.* BOTTOM RIGHT: *Obstacles and damage left behind by the Germany Army at Bergen op Zoom.*

crossed over and tied me up. So they had to stop and cut that wire out. So I got into Bergen op Zoom about ten minutes before they arrive and *wham!* I got shot through the headlight of the motorcycle, and I threw off my motorcycle and crawled up to this house that I thought looked friendly enough. I waited there ten or fifteen minutes and the men came along and I was okay, and the head man of the house, Mr. Calpaert, he introduced himself and told us how happy he was to see us there. I took the troops into the town square and got ready for the night. This Mr. Calpaert came up and he said, "You come to my place for coffee." That was a nice gesture, so I went with him; it wasn't coffee he had, it was cognac! He had a nine-year-old son and a twelve-year-old daughter, and they've been friends of mine to this day. They were hungry. Later I happened to be going past this little settlement and there's a rabbit out in the yard. I thought maybe I could make a deal with that farmer for his rabbit. I went in and talked with him, and no, he wouldn't part with that rabbit for anything. So I said maybe a little petrol? Well, that hit his soft spot, and I gave him half the petrol I had in my motorcycle. I took it to the Calpaerts in Bergen op Zoom. I couldn't have made them happier with a million dollars. They were hungry. And they got the rabbit.

Roy Kelley, Lorne Scots

I guess when we got out of Walcheren Island we got left out of battle for about a week. My platoon stayed at a monastery, and I had probably the royal suite for the church there. I had a room, it wasn't fancy or anything, but I never had woollen blankets like that — anything from a half-inch thick right down to the finest wool you could get next to you. We got well taken care of. My men slept up on the fourth floor, they had electric lights, and they were in heaven. They had been outside for a long time.

We went down to the MO, and he said, "You'll have to take your shirts off," so we took our shirts off, and he said, "Let me check your chests." He did that and said, "You better go pack a haversack and go back to the hospital." I said, "Hell, I don't want to go to the hospital." He said, "You both have viral pneumonia."

J. Wanamaker and the flooded region around Bergen op Zoom.

Spillebeek church that was destroyed in reprisal by the Germans.

A downed Fortress that crashed into the woods near Bergen op Zoom.

The Canadian ship Fort Cataraqui enters Antwerp harbour, becoming the first supply ship to use the port after the clearing of the Scheldt estuary by Canadian forces.

Ted Brabers

The Germans tried to steal anything — whatever they could get a hold of. All of a sudden in our hometown [Breda] the Germans were gone. An Allied forces man was noticed, there were no Germans to be seen. Then we got the invasion, and the Polish were very fast, they were there a very short time and the Germans were gone. Everyone was stealing out of the German barracks. And then we had the liberation by the Polish, in our particular case it was the Polish.

Globe & Mail, November 30, 1944

Prime Minister Churchill announced the opening of the great Belgian port of Antwerp to ocean traffic and told of British and Canadian losses in the drive into Holland and Germany.

"In these operations, including the storming of the Island of Walcheren, which contained episodes of marvelous gallantry and great feats of arms, the British and Canadian forces suffered about 40,000 casualties," the Prime Minister said.

The operations he referred to included the month-long nightmarish struggle by the 1st Canadian Army to clear the Scheldt estuary.

Mr. Churchill was far from pessimistic during his speech, but he warned against "any indulgence in the feeling that the war will be over soon."

BATTLE OF THE SCHELDT
October 1–November 8, 1944

Minesweepers moved in and cleared the shipping lanes in the Scheldt, and by November 28 the first convoy of supply ships arrived at Antwerp. The first ship to arrive was the Canadian freighter *Fort Cataraqui*. It was a great moment for Canadians. Unfortunately, no Canadian representatives were invited to the celebration of the opening of the port.

The Battle of the Scheldt was characterized by bitter fighting, difficult obstacles, and horrible conditions. The Canadians had opened up the port of Antwerp and cleared the Netherlands up to the Maas River. It was a proud achievement, but one with a steep cost. The 1st Canadian Army suffered 12,000 casualties, of whom 6,367 were Canadians.

TOP: *Antwerp, Belgium, the major port in Northwestern Europe and the cause of the Battle of the Scheldt.* BOTTOM: *A battered Steenbergen on liberation day. The church steeple is conspicuously absent; as many were shot down to eliminate their use as observation posts by the Germans.*

CHAPTER FOUR

WINTER ON THE MAAS
November 9, 1944–February 7, 1945

After the Battle of the Scheldt, the Canadians were involved three months of static defence. They dug in and held the line along the Maas River and the Nijmegen Salient. They held one side of the river, and the Germans held the other. Close enough to see each other, both sides remained quiet, weary after months of battle. The respite was welcome, and the Allies used the time to prepare for a spring offensive. The Canadians held the front line from Dunkirk on the North Sea to south of Nijmegen, a distance of two hundred miles.

Many of the Canadian units were undermanned as they had been fighting continually since June, and so this quiet period was necessary. Usually reinforcements would be added when a unit was rotated out of combat, but that had not been the case for most of the Canadian units, and the new men were slowly filtering up. It would take months for the units to return to strength, and fortunately the Canadians had the winter on the Maas to do just that.

On November 9 the Allies cleared the last of the German resistance in central and western Brabant. The Netherlands was a nation divided that winter, liberated in the south, occupied in the north.

LEFT: *Guard duty at 3:00 a.m. at Breda.* TOP RIGHT: *A bridge destroyed by the Germans at Tilburg.* BOTTOM RIGHT: *The Waal River at Nijmegen. Across it the Germans held the line throughout the winter and prepared for the assault that would come in the spring.*

Charles Fosseneuve, 13th Field Artillery

It rained all the time. It was cold. When I was there it rained one night and then it was snow. The weather was pretty bad.

John Honsberger, 4th Canadian Armoured Division

Montgomery and Crerar wanted to make the Germans think that we would be going north across the Maas — we had to do a lot of fetes, and we would shoot once in a while, and then at one stage they brought in all of these tactical signs posted here and there for a whole new division that we'd never heard of. These were all fake signs and again were part of trying to fool the Germans to think that this whole area was being reinforced and that in the

spring we would move across there. Afterwards I read it worked because the Germans took the bait and brought in some of their good troops, which were there when the army went across the Rhine.

Jim Parks, Royal Winnipeg Rifles

When I came back [from NCO training], I went up to Groesbeek, where we were dug in. You'd try to find a place where there's an old house nearby and it had a cellar in it — you'd use that to do your resting, and the rest of the time you'd be in your trenches.

With the mortars we were firing at pre-arranged targets and getting out of the way because there's always counter-battery work. The plains beyond Nijmegen were all flooded, and the various roads were all covered by smokescreen, but you had people out there on watch all the time, what they call live watch.

Russell Sanderson, Black Watch

It was basically a holding position. You can't do a devil of a lot because there was a lot of wetlands near the area. It was a matter of going in and probing and trying to see what their strength was, or if their positions were

TOP: *Repairing the bridge at s'Hertogenbosch right under the Germans' noses.* CENTRE: *Canadian troops were rotated out from the front for rest and relaxation in Belgium.* BOTTOM: *November 1944: Jim Parks, Bill Shadlock, and Dave Skidmore attend 3rd Division NCO training school at Woarschoot, Belgium, shortly after being involved in the action at the Leopold Canal.*

ABOVE: *Many Canadians were stationed at Nijmegen and the surrounding area during the winter of 1944-1945.*
TOP CENTRE: *The bridge at Nijmegen.*
TOP RIGHT: T*he bridge at Nijmegen, captured during Operation Market Garden and kept intact throughout the winter by the Canadian Army.* CENTRE: *A damaged bridge at Nijmegen. Note the temporary bridge in the foreground.*
CENTRE RIGHT: *The bridge at Nijmegen in the dead of winter 1944.*
BOTTOM: *F.L. Russell, J. Sneddon, R.S. Marshall, and unknown member of the Lincoln and Welland Regiment in snow camouflaged battle dress.*

being manoeuvred in any way. They divided up their area: their platoon areas and the scout platoon got the forward position at a farmhouse in an orchard and a chicken coop. Way out the back and across the road behind us our carrier of the platoon moved in. They covered our flank, and with their firepower they had two German MG42s and boxes and boxes of ammunition. They had them all with it. It got to a point where I had gone through that company on patrols and it's pitch dark and you'd go in, "Hi guys! Whatcha doing?"

"Shhh! Jesus, Sandy, be quiet!"

"What? What's the matter?"

"The Jerries will hear you!"

"Well, don't they know you're here, for God's sake?"

It got to a point where they got a little tense. They listened for every little sound. The scout platoon didn't own any machine guns, we had to borrow them from the rifle companies — their Bren guns. The only one we had was an MP43, and one of the fellows cut a ring and a half off the spring just to change the sound of the rate of fire so you're not going to get fired on by your own guys. We manned this position, we did some of our cooking, we took turns — usually I didn't get too many turns because they didn't like my cooking. There was a young fellow by the name of Swanson — that man was a genius with food! At night there would be a jeep come up and bring you a hot meal. It comes up and into our position, and it was these big canisters of food, and the Germans never fired on it. And their food would come up on a three-wheeled cart with a horse and a man sitting up on it, and we never fired on him. It was an unwritten rule — you don't touch the man with the food!

Ack-ack fire at night.

While that winter was relatively quiet, the Canadian troops did have to keep the Germans alert and concerned. The goal was to make the Germans think that the Canadians were preparing for an attack, so that they would keep their defences spread out all along the line. This also reduced the effectiveness of the Germans in other areas where the Americans and British continued to run operations, aiding in their success. On the flip side, the Canadians had to be prepared in case of a German offensive — they did not want to be caught unprepared. But overall, the winter in the Netherlands was a quiet one for most Canadians.

Jack Martin, Queen's Own Rifles

Every night we would have to go down by the brickworks in case the Jerries came across the river. We would set up and wait for any attack, and then early in the morning if nothing happened we returned to our billets and we'd sleep all day. When we got home, the mother would make us a cup of tea of rose petals because the Germans had taken all their tea and everything else away from them. When we got into Germany my other driver, Tex Scott, went into one of the houses and took a whole lot of the furniture out and loaded it up onto a carrier. It was loaded about fifteen feet high with all kinds of furniture, we drove back to Berg En Dal to the house that we had been billeted in and dropped all the furniture off on the front lawn and gave them back some of their furniture that the Germans had stolen.

Charles Fosseneuve, 13th Field Artillery

In the middle of the night we were told to check where the enemy was, and that's the reason we went out on patrol. We weren't fighting, but we were just checking and sneaking around. [Charles, a Metis soldier, brought his moccasins with him from Canada and found them useful on patrols.] The boots are too heavy and you can make lots of noise. With those moccasins you can sneak around without making noise — just like a cat.

Al Armstrong, 14th Canadian Hussars

We did foot patrols. They were coming through our lines at night, and we were going into their lines at night. Out in front of the village where we were staying there was a dike, and we'd send out a reconnaissance

A four-span railway bridge at Tilburg that was destroyed by the Germans.

LEFT: *Rest time at s'Hertogenbosch.* CENTRE: *Canadians posing by a street sign near Breda.* RIGHT: *Breda 1944-1945.*

patrol, which would be three or four men, all we were after was information. We'd leave where we were at night, go over the dike, cross the marshy land, and we'd get in behind their line. If we could, we'd pick up a prisoner or two and bring them back. And on the other end there was another type of patrol, it's called a fighting patrol. Ten to twelve men would get into their lines, raise hell, shoot up everything, grab a couple of prisoners, and get back if you're lucky. And that was the extent of the winter war.

Russell Sanderson, Black Watch

I was a sniper in the scout platoon, and our job was to do sniping, and we also did patrols. You were sent out to work with the rifle company or certain locations for sniping. You went out and you lay down with your rifle with a telescopic sight on it — you could take out your objective, whatever you were aiming at from an awful long ways away. But you lay there and your scout lay beside you with binoculars. It was a job. No sadness or no worries. I'd like to think that I was good at it. There was no scorekeeping about how many you killed. It was a good assignment and I enjoyed it all the way through, and I worked with some fantastic men.

George Mummery, Highland Light Infantry

The second night we were down there the Jerries tried to bomb the bridge, and they couldn't do much with their shells. They sent down logs with explosives on it hoping to hit something, that didn't work. Then they started to send frogmen. Well, when they figured out what the Germans were up to, they got ropes on both sides of the bridge, and Harry and myself, they put us on this raft, they pulled us out in the middle of the river and tied it off both sides. We just sat there all night. Everything that was coming down the river, didn't matter if it was a duck or a cigarette package, we just sat there popping all night. We don't know what we ever hit, but they never did blow that bridge.

Jim Parks, Royal Winnipeg Rifles

Over the winter we had our share of casualties. It was shelling mainly that did it. If you kept down, fine. Our company sent out a lot of patrols, we were patrolling quite a bit. The odd time we'd have to take prisoners back to the RAP. Our purpose was to give good artillery support and to keep the hell out of the way of the rifle companies because we'd draw fire on them if we fired too close to them.

The members of the RCAF were playing a pivotal role during this period. While the action on the ground slowed down, the action in the air never let up.

Richard Rohmer, RCAF

By mid-November the British Army was pressing the enemy hard in the area lying to the east of Nijmegen and Arnhem south of the Maas, also on its west bank as the path of the river hooked south toward the large Dutch city and rail centre of Venlo. As the British mounted and maintained their attacks, the enemy retreated. Troops with their vehicles, tanks, artillery, and other equipment were trying desperately to cross the Maas. But there was only

Canadian soldiers pose by the remains of a German 88 at Best (north of Eindhoven).

one escape route. It was across the twinned railway and motor vehicle bridges that stood cheek by jowl at Venlo. A decision was made by Field Marshal Montgomery that the bridges at Venlo had to come down. How to accomplish the task?

The first choice was by air force bombers. But they would have to attack in daylight because the target was so difficult to hit. Precision bombing was required, and it would have to be done from a great height because the Germans had placed hundreds of their accurate, deadly 88 mm anti-aircraft guns in and around Venlo.

There was an alternative available to Montgomery. It was to utilize, for the first time, a Super Heavy Gun, an eight-inch artillery piece with a super long range. The massive shell had enormous destructive power. Fortuitously, such a Super Heavy Gun was within striking range of the bridges at Venlo. The 4th Battery of the No.3 Super Heavy Regiment had one deployed at Loon, some twenty-five thousand yards from and almost due west of the twin bridges at Venlo. That was a distance of 14.2 miles, yet within shooting range of the Super Heavy Guns of the 4th Battery.

A Super Heavy Gun had not yet been fired in the northwest Europe campaign. If it was to be used, it would have to be ranged, its fire directed, by an air force pilot, one experienced in artillery direction.

Montgomery made the decision. Priority would go to the Super Heavy Gun and the fighter recce pilot who would do the ranging. There were only two fighter recce squadrons available. They were 414 and 411 squadrons, both RCAF, of 39 Recce Wing, then based at Eindhoven. Both squadrons were equipped with the low-flying U.S.-built Mustang I aircraft.

The choice was left up to the wing commander operations of 39 Recce Wing, Wing Commander "Bunt" Waddell. From his nearly 50 available pilots he chose an almost tour-expired (133 sorties) 20-year-old to do this shoot. His name was Flying Officer Richard Rohmer; the number two was to be Flight Lieutenant E.F.J. Clark, known to the world as "Knobby."

Bunt Waddell and a Canadian Army liaison officer briefed me thoroughly with Clark. The targets were the twin bridges at Venlo. They were about five hundred feet long, stretching across the Maas River. I would be ranging a Super Heavy Gun fourteen miles back from the target. Time of flight of the shell would be incredibly long, about fifty-five seconds. I couldn't believe it! The line of flight of the shell would be almost due east, and the bridges' path across the Maas was east-west. So I would be ranging on a hair. We had to hit the hair using a gun fourteen miles away! Unbelievable! Waddell cautioned me about the flak at Venlo. I had been there several times. You could walk on the exploding 88 mm shells. With luck I could see the fall of the Super Heavy shells from a distance outside the Venlo 88 mm range. I was given the radio frequency of the Super Heavy battery. When the briefing was over, Bunt Waddell underscored the importance of the operation by promising me a bottle of champagne if I hit the "goddamn" bridges. That was the best incentive I'd had since I had started my tour of operations with 430 Squadron in September 1943.

It was a bleak, chilly, sunless day. There was a cover of high, impenetrable cloud at about eight or ten thousand feet. It was Sunday, November 19, 1944. Clark and I were airborne in our Mustangs over Eindhoven at 1350 hours and headed east toward Venlo, climbing to the working altitude I had selected of four thousand feet. That height would give me a good opportunity to see where the shells were landing while we stayed out of range of the 88s. We circled, and I switched to the designated radio frequency and transmitted, "Queen Baker this is Peco Blue Leader. Do you read me? Over." The response from QB was instant. It was a crisp, clear British voice coming in at strength five by five. Perfect.

I explained to the voice the procedure I wanted. Given the time of flight of the shell to the target, I would give the order to fire when I was within easy sight of the target so I could see the shell land. But at the same time I would be far enough out of range of those deadly 88s when the shell hit the ground. The timing for fire was therefore my call. I would give QB a ten-second warning before calling for fire. That settled, I then headed again toward the bridges. If I called for fire in about ten seconds I would be in the perfect position to see the first shell land. I gave the warning to QB. Would the first shot land on the bridges, on the east bank of the Maas, or the west? Would I see it land at all?

"Fire!" I shouted into my face mask microphone. "Fire!" was the immediate response from QB as he repeated my order. His transmitter open, I could hear the blast in my earphones of the shell being fired. The radio operator then said, "Shot," which meant that the shell had been launched at the target. I then had some fifty seconds to get myself into position to pinpoint the spot where that first shot fell. At ten seconds before the shell hit QB warned me, "Splash!"

There it was! The explosion was massive. Smoke and debris and flame billowed up in a huge cloud. The shell had hit the east bank of the Maas. The devastation was … well, I'd never seen anything like it. I turned and headed west again in order to stay away from the 88s. My correction decision was made after I plotted the shot on my special scale map. "QB drop 400," I ordered. That was four hundred yards to be taken off the elevation of the gun so the next shot would land on the west bank of the Maas within a few yards of the entrance to the bridges. My objective was to bracket the target as to distance. Drop four hundred. Up two hundred. Drop one hundred. Up fifty. Bracket until I had the shells dropping exactly as to distance. Then it was to be the same bracketing as to the line from the gun. When the distance bracketing was finished the shells were falling to the left of the fifty-foot wide twinned bridges, the hair, by about forty yards. Right eighty. Fire — splash. Then left forty should put it right on line.

When I finished ranging at 1525 hours after firing thirty-six rounds in an hour and fifteen minutes, I had the shells landing within a few yards of the centre span of the bridges. They were missing the hair by a hair's breadth. We couldn't stay any longer. We were running out of fuel, and I could see a gaggle of medium bombers heading north toward the Venlo bridges, their obvious target. We left and landed back at Eindhoven at 1545. It had taken one hour and fifty-five airborne minutes to do the bridges at Venlo. All I had to show for it was a hit on the approaches and some near misses.

But wait! Word filtered down from high headquarters the next morning that the battery had used my ranging to keep firing at the bridge all night — and the bridge was down!

Two days later, on November 21, 1944, Knobby Clark and I climbed into our Mustangs again to go and take a confirming look at what we and the Brit Super Heavy gunners had wrought. It was late in the day, 1620 when we were airborne. As the ops book says I reported, "Railway bridge appears to have one span down." No question. The

Canada's game made its way to the Netherlands as the men looked for a little recreation during the winter.

Super Heavy gunners and I, with the intelligent assistance of their radio operator, had knocked down the bridges at Venlo. The enemy's only escape route had been destroyed.

The winter months spent on the Maas provided a range of experiences for the Canadian servicemen. While the war was still in evidence, the extended periods of time in the same area led to lasting friendships with the Dutch. It was a winter they would never forget.

John Honsberger, 4th Canadian Armoured Division

It was a very, very cold winter — I think the records show that it was the coldest in several years — it gave us a problem, and I'm talking only about our little part of the Armoured Division. We were issued no antifreeze. During that cold part of the winter we had to get up, start the tanks and self-propelled vehicles every hour, and run them for five or ten minutes to keep them from freezing. We had reoccurring problems with the vehicles, the guns, and tanks — they would slide off the dikes because of all the snow, and we were always having to rescue these vehicles.

Jim Parks, Royal Winnipeg Rifles

The rifle companies were dug in, and they had listening posts down in the valley — they went in at nighttime to listen for where the Germans were. If you had good binoculars you could see across the valley about five hundred yards, you could see some of the faces, the odd time you'd see them moving and heading into the bush — they might have had a latrine. So we had a couple of mean guys, and they'd wait until they headed into the bush and they'd fire a volley of mortar bombs at them. Didn't know what they were doing in there, but that's war I guess. You take the humour with the bad.

Russell Sanderson, Black Watch

There was a chicken coop in the back end of our place. The door was on their side. Now there was a slit trench on our side and a slit trench on their side, and we would have to occupy that at night to make sure that they didn't move in and try to get past us. If you got out there first in the evening and get into the slit trench we'd hear them coming to occupy the slit trench on their side, and then you'd hear the door on the chicken coop open up and there's great commotion, and we'd be, "Leave those eggs alone!" All kinds of silly stuff. And they'd just laugh. It's a situation that comes from men who have been under pressure like that — they can laugh at things. We could have killed each other without any trouble at all. That chicken coop couldn't have been any more than twelve feet high. All you had to do was pull a pin and throw a grenade over the roof and it would land into their trench. They could have done the same thing to us. It was never done.

John Honsberger, 4th Canadian Armoured Division

At one stage that they thought that we might be overrun, and we had to phone back every hour, on the hour, every night to say that we were still there. Somehow or other I got the duty. They wanted the same person to phone back each hour to make sure that some English-speaking German hadn't taken over our position. For six or seven weeks I never slept more than about forty minutes at a time because every hour I was shaken to say what I had to say and I would take five minutes to go back to sleep. I think it had quite the effect on our collective nerves.

Jim Parks, Royal Winnipeg Rifles

The roads were always getting smashed up and shelled out, and so on one particular time they sent out a crew of the pioneer platoon to repair it. On the way out there they were shelled, and the fellow lost control of his carrier and it went into the side where all the water was and it tipped over. They lost seven people. I was part of the group that helped to retrieve them. We buried them the next day. There were two padres — a United Church padre and a priest from our brigade for the seven people. It didn't really matter who you were, denomination didn't mean a thing, the fact was there was some respect given.

Bridge over the Maas at Grave.

Roy Kelley, Lorne Scots

The Dutch enjoyed having the Canadians come in, and they took good care of us, and they were only too good to try to do the laundry, and the Canadians paid in kind with soap and cigarettes. They always had them, and the poor Dutch hadn't seen them in so many years.

The canal at s'Hertogenbosch. Note the steep embankments that made crossings of such canals in combat a deadly affair.

The city centre of s'Hertogenbosch, 2004.

John Honsberger, 4th Canadian Armoured Division

The level of starvation was so bad that at one time we'd have Dutch children that would come to the cook and take away the old coffee grounds. The cook would be throwing them out, but they would take these old coffee grounds — they were really treasured — and they'd take them back to their families and the families would use it.

Ed Newman, Royal Hamilton Light Infantry

We were really made well aware of that [starvation] during our winter stay at Nijmegen. They had bugger all to eat, and we passed out anything that we could pass out to the public. We were living on what they called compo rations, which was a box of food, and now these boxes had letters on them from A to H, and there was enough food in there to feed twelve or thirteen men for three meals. It didn't take long before the guys got to know which were the good boxes and which were the bad boxes, and if we were unlucky enough to draw some bad boxes we had a lot of stuff left over because the guys wouldn't use it. The Dutch people were only too glad to get a hold of anything we would give them.

To the south, the Dutch were ecstatic about the return of their freedom, but to the north, the people suffered more than ever before. The Nazis were desperate and vengeful. On November 10 the Germans rounded up fifty thousand men for forced labour in Rotterdam and Schiedam. The Germans were preparing, since the Allies had reached their final line of defence for Rotterdam. The mass roundups for forced labour would be repeated in the following months.

ABOVE LEFT: *Breda on New Year's Day 1945*. ABOVE RIGHT: *Life in the city back to normal after liberation in the south*. LEFT: *Relaxing at Breda*.

Martin van Denzen

In the last year of the war the occupiers were getting kind of desperate, and they were picking up men off the street. I can remember coming back from school, and we saw this German truck and they were picking up any able-bodied men off the street. So we ran home and told my dad, and he had a little shack at the back — they built a little loft in there, and him and his neighbour hid up there for almost three weeks. We had a little field at the back of our house, and we saw our schoolteacher running. So we ran to him, and he hid up there as well. They were never found. After that, when the pressure was off my dad was picked up, and he had to work for the Germans and dig trenches in and around our neighbourhood. He would be picked up every morning by a horse and wagon by an old German soldier, they would have to labour for the Germans, and they would then be brought back. This old soldier would bring a little loaf of bread to our family once in a while. He was forced to do things as well. Years later after it was over his kids came to Holland for a vacation, and they stayed with my parents. It's amazing some of these relationships — because not all Germans were bad. It was the Nazis that were really bad, and there were a lot of German soldiers that if they didn't fight, well, it would be the end of them as well.

The steeple in the distance at s'Hertogenbosch was used as an observation post across the Maas by the Germans.

Another disaster was shaping up at that time. The flooding of the polders as a defence had reduced the local crops and ruined the land with the inflow of salt water. Some communities were isolated, surrounded by flooded areas, and the people were going hungry. On December 1 Reichskommissioner Seyss-Inquart permitted the distribution of food by river barges to the starving towns. On December 4 the Germans opened the Rhine dikes as a defensive measure, aggravating the problem even further. There was another reduction in food allotments, as every commodity was scarce. By December 10 the situation was so desperate that Seyss-Inquart allowed the Dutch churches to help in the food distribution. On December 14 the Germans forbade the use of electricity in North and South Holland provinces. The Dutch were facing a brutal winter.

Henry Schogt

One of the things that I remember more vividly than the hunger is the darkness. It was always dark, it was cold because there was no electricity, there was no gas.

Corrie Schogt

A lot of houses had one stove. But even with that stove you didn't have enough coal, so on top of the stove you'd have a can, like a little coffee can, that would be your only source of cooking and heating.

Elly Dull

The stove was too big, it consumed too much fuel, really it was no more than a cookie tin, and we had the tiniest pieces of wood, and it was us children who kept that fire going, feeding all these little splinters of wood. We stripped down the frames along the doorways, the windowsills, any little wooden furniture that we didn't need — we would hack it into pieces to feed that little tin that was our only source of heat.

Desperate Dutch civilian sorting through garbage and old tins for something of possible use. Food and heating supplies were almost non-existent.

Scavenging for supplies was everybody's responsibility during the hongerwinter. It was a matter of life and death.

We had to darken all the windows by eight o'clock, and that was my job, I was about seven or eight at the time, to fit these drapes inside the windows, and if it showed any light at all the Germans would come and knock on your door and shout. All the lights needed to be out so that the Allies would have no orientation as they were flying over-head to see that this was actually the city. It was all dark. We were not allowed out after eight o'clock. The neighbours tried very carefully to saw down a tree after eight o'clock, a little bit every night until the point that the tree actually had to come down, and there was a great commotion. Little bit by little bit they hacked the tree to pieces and they divided the wood among us.

Henry Schogt

In our case there were close calls. Three actually. The first was on the fifth of December, and I remember that because it was St. Nicholas Eve and there was banging on the door. Well, we first thought, *It can't be.* Part of the celebration is bang on the door, leave a present, and race away so that you can't see who gave the present. But this time it was no present. The Germans had come, and they wanted cigars my father had taken from a colleague to hide. The Germans came,

Near Bastogne, where the American 101st were surrounded by the Germans. The 1st Canadian Parachute Battalion held the line nearby.

An American soldier takes shelter from the cold at Berg.

Interior of a bombed church during the Battle of the Bulge.

Patrols in the snow were gruelling tasks due to immense snowdrifts and frigid temperatures.

The devastation from the Battle of the Bulge was widespread, and the Germans couldn't afford to sustain such losses of both men and matériel.

and they said, "We want your cigars, and if you don't give them to us we'll take the Jewish child that you have in hiding." And we figured out that the only one who knew about those cigars was a cleaning lady who left soon after the cigars came, and she knew about the little girl, but apparently she didn't know about the family [the Schogts were hiding as well at that time].

For months the Germans had been beating a fighting retreat, and during the winter lull the unexpected happened: the Germans launched a massive counterattack. The date was December 16, 1944. Gerd von Rundstedt masterminded Operation Herbstnebel, a bold move through the Ardennes forest that planned to push the Allied advance back, allowing the Germans to retake the strategic port of Antwerp. The Germans felt that if they could cut off that supply route, they could defeat the Allies and eventually push them back into the Channel. The Allies never

considered a German attack through the Ardennes — it was heavily wooded and contained treacherous terrain that would be difficult for an armoured advance.

The Germans advanced swiftly, bursting through the front line and penetrating as far as North Brabant at Hedel. The Allies countered quickly, battling the German breakthrough in what is known as the Battle of the Bulge. It was the coldest winter in memory, with deep snow and frigid temperatures. Low clouds eliminated support from the air force. It was left to the men on the ground to repel the German army. In the desperate race to get men to the front, the Allies did not have adequate winter clothing for them. It was a horrible experience for all involved — dreadfully cold and short on supplies of every kind. The men lived in constant tension, waiting for an attack at any time, fearful of being overrun.

The Battle of the Bulge involved the Americans and the British. Only one Canadian unit participated in the Ardennes — the men of the 1st Canadian Parachute Battalion. Only a short distance away from Bastogne (where the American 101st Airborne, a unit that had trained with the Canadians in Fort Benning, Georgia, was surrounded), the Canadian paratroopers suffered the freezing cold and held the line.

ABOVE: *Tanks at Manhay during the Battle of the Bulge. Primarily an American and British engagement, one Canadian unit (the 1st Canadian Parachute Battalion) participated and many other Canadian units were brought south in case the Germans succeeded in breaking through the line. The German advance stalled, and their last attempt to turn back the Allies failed.*
LEFT: *Canadian paratrooper in a bombed church in the Ardennes.*

Jan de Vries, 1st Canadian Parachute Battalion

We were called into the Ardennes to fight in the Battle of the Bulge. The freezing temperatures were extreme, it was an unusual winter, and the hobnail boots brought the frost into the feet, since we had the same uniforms that we did in Normandy; the result is that we had more casualties from frost than we did from fighting.

TOP LEFT: A member of the 1st Canadian Parachute Battalion prepared for action in the Ardennes. TOP CENTRE: Group shot of Canadian paratroopers in the Ardennes. TOP RIGHT: The winter weather was the coldest in memory that year, made worse by the fact that the Canadian paratroopers did not have winter clothing (they held the line for several weeks in the same uniforms that they landed in on D-Day). BOTTOM LEFT: A pair of Canadian paratroopers trying to stay warm in the Ardennes. BOTTOM RIGHT: The 1st Canadian Parachute Battalion was attached to the British 6th Airborne, and as such they were involved in various actions that no other Canadian units participated in, including the Battle of the Bulge.

When we met the Germans, they were at the maximum extension of their attack. They started retreating, so we just stayed right on their tails. They'd go to ground and fire at us, we'd go to ground and put in an attack, and they'd pull back and disappear. So we'd have to find them again. This went on for a while. At the same time Bastogne was on, and the colonel sent a message over to the Americans that we could easily run over and give them some help, they were less than ten miles away. He got a message back: they didn't need any help, the Americans were on their way. So we didn't have to go to Bastogne.

T. Garry Gould, Sherbrooke Fusiliers

Some time around the twentieth of December the good ladies of Nijmegen decided that we had gone without female company for six or seven months and there was a great big dance. The ladies turned up, they were on the far side of the room at this tremendous town hall dance floor, and we could hear the rustle of their skirts, and some of us got up enough nerve to cross the floor and were introduced to their mothers who had come with them. But just as we were trying to get the first sentence out the adjutant comes through the gall darn door and blows the whistle and we head south all night long for the Battle of the Bulge. We bid a fast adieu to the ladies and their mothers without having hardly said hello. That was our introduction to the kindness of the Dutch ladies who turned out for us, but unfortunately we stood them up. A tragic story.

Patrolling in the frigid conditions of the Ardennes in 1944.

We were a counter threat. The Americans didn't take kindly to other people trying to interfere with what they were trying to do. They let their own people tough it out. We were down there as an insurance policy for the Canadian shipping line. Maple Leaf Up was the name of the shipping route up, and Maple Leaf Down for empty trucks going back. We went down in one night's drive. Fifty minutes in the hour, and we must have driven a good eight or nine hours. I'm amazed at how far we could have gone, it would be a long way down. We were prepared in case they broke through the Americans, because that was Hitler's plan. We weren't down there very long.

Mervin Durham, Royal Canadian Engineers

We went to the Ardennes. Christmas night we had good cooks, really anxious to please the guys. So they did a little Christmas cooking. They scavenged things around the country. They were getting the berries for Christmas tomorrow, and then we got the word that we had to hit the road, to head towards the Americans. We had our Christmas cancelled.

Along the Maas River the Germans had planned an attack to coincide with the von Rundstedt offensive, but those plans were foiled by the Dutch Resistance. Quick to observe troop movement and concentrations, the Resistance got word to the Canadians stationed at Kapelsche Veer that an attack was imminent. The German offensive over the Maas resulted in a small bridgehead south of the Maas. It then turned into a month-long engagement over that thin strip of land.

Training by the Lincoln and Welland Regiment in canoes, preparing for the assault on the German stronghold at Kapelsche Veer.

Mervin Durham, Royal Canadian Engineers

Things were going good in Holland for a while until this snow came down and ice — it was a real Canadian winter so to speak. That was when the battle of Kapelsche Veer took place. I was in charge of building that bridge — partly Bailey bridge and partly improvised — on the Maas River. We were about four days getting that bridge together. We got strafed, and then the battle did go in with the Lincoln and Welland Regiment. They lost a lot of people in battle on that island.

Bailey bridge erected across a canal.

Bailey bridges were constructed in ten-foot lengths and connected together to bridge gaps of up to two hundred feet.

Damaged Dutch trains at s'Hertogenbosch.

Not far from the Maas River, Waalwijk provided a safe resting place for the Canadian soldiers while keeping them in close proximity to the front in case they needed to be mobilized at a moment's notice.

Kayaks were used, but that's misleading. They were nothing but two and a half feet by five feet of kapok. If you didn't move fast it would sink under your feet.

The bridge was called the Mad Whore's Dream, makes you think of what that description brings to mind. When my officer called me one day from Waalwijk on a telephone system set up, he said, "How's it going?" And I said, "Sir, it's a mad whore's dream." It was that bad, there was quite a bit of small arms fire. They were not too far from us, the Germans were dug in, and they were using machine guns a lot to try and keep us off this bridge that we were building. So then they finally started to use mortars, which is a nasty thing to do. That was one of the nastiest deals in the whole campaign. Kapelsche Veer. The Lincoln and Welland Regiment was the one that got the fame, it's well deserved.

On December 22 General George Patton launched a counteroffensive to relieve the men who were surrounded at Bastogne. While some heralded it as a rescue, the men of the 101st made it clear that they were never in need of rescue and that they had been holding up fine by themselves.

Bill Clifford, RCAF

We had to be ready for diversions, for example the Battle of the Bulge. Early on in that attack, General George "Blood and Guts" Patton called for help from the Typhoons. This intrusion took up approximately 75 percent of our operations in December. The fighting there was vicious and our casualty rate soared. For the American and German fighters on the ground the casualties numbered in the tens of thousands. For us it was doubly hazardous, not only in fight-

The Maas River and the damaged bridge over it.

Canadian R. Goddard enjoying a ride around Schijndel on a motorcycle.

Major General Vokes celebrates Christmas with local Dutch children at a party thrown for them at the 4th Division Main Headquarters.

ing the Germans, but also being attacked by American Thunderbirds and Mustangs who thought the Typhoons were Focke Wolf 190s.

South Saskatchewan Regiment War Diary, December 25, 1944

This is the fifth Christmas that the Battalion has spent overseas. There were two sittings for dinner … 1230 and 1400 hrs. The menu for the dinner was put at each man's place on the table. 25% alertness was laid on in the Battalion for the night.

Russell Sanderson, Black Watch

It was a strange situation before Christmas — there was a dike over in the German area, and they came out and sang Christmas carols in German and in English, and it was fantastic! I think it was the Calgary Highlanders — they put a piper out way off to our left and we heard the piper out there. Those Germans came right out of position and sat right up there on the dike and sang.

T. Garry Gould, Sherbrooke Fusiliers

Starting around D-Day I began to write home explaining that I was under the palm trees in southern England and life was boring, and I kept that up for about six months, and my address to back up my claim was general list at some innocuous general address, and never the regimental address. The thorough people in the post office in the army caught up with this idiot's statement that his general list wasn't the correct address, and just before Christmas in Holland, in Nijmegen, three bags of mail arrived at the idiot's address, which made the squadron officers very happy because they all pitched in and ate up six or seven months of chocolate, cookies, and all this stuff that could be sent over that wasn't available normally in the mess menu. And that was yours truly who was such an idiot to have pulled that trick on his own family, not wanting them to worry, but on the other side of the coin, I was one of seven of the regiment wounded twice. One of the boys came home early from the repat depot, and he went around to my parents' home in West Hill because I asked him to and suggested to them that I was in fine shape and I'd be home in a few weeks on a July sailing. He tells me to this day that they would not believe him.

Russell Sanderson, Black Watch

I had a Christmas that I'll never forget. Just before Christmas we were in this place called Mook, and we hadn't had a bath for several weeks. They took us up by truck to Nijmegen. I think there was about ten of us who went up in the first bunch.

My brother was a dispatch writer for the Cameron Highlanders of Ottawa, and there was an officer there from his unit. I went to him and asked him where his regiment was stationed, and he said he'd been detached since he'd been wounded. He'd been detached for about a month and a half and he wasn't sure but he thought they were south of the city.

So we went back to the platoon and I went in to see the sergeant, and I said to him, "Tommy, my brother, is up near Nijmegen and I wonder if I could go and see him. I'll be back tonight." He said, "Okay, as long as you're back for your patrol." So I hiked it out of the place and I got rides from trucks until I got up to Nijmegen, and just go by signs — some were rather vague, but I got picked up by a sergeant from my brother's regiment. He took me right down to the platoon headquarters, and as I walked in the room where the platoon officer was, he looked up and he said, "Sandy, I've got a job for you."

And I said, "I think you're looking for my other half, sir." I took my balmoral off.

"Oh by god," he said, "and who might you be?"

"I'm your Sandy's brother."

So it was quite a thing, so he sent one of the fellows upstairs to get my brother. So instead of my brother coming down, another fellow comes down.

"Where's Sanderson?"

"He's sleeping, sir."

"Get up there and tell him to get down here!" So when my brother came down I was standing behind the door. The officer said to him, "Close the door there." So he closed the door and I'm standing behind it. So we had quite a little celebration there for a while. The officer said, "What are you doing tomorrow?" I said, "Nothing that I know of, sir." So he said, "Well, we're having a turkey dinner tomorrow. We have one turkey to the whole company, and I won the raffle, and we're having a turkey dinner, and we'd like you to stay and have dinner with us." Now I hadn't seen my brother in three years, and so it was quite a momentous occasion.

Jack Read, Regina Rifle Regiment

Then getting on towards Christmas our 2 IC arranged for dances in Nijmegen for all the companies. There were nine different dances that were set up with the local girls for the Regina Rifle people. As we got closer to Christmastime we were granted Christmas dinner, and at that time we the officers and the NCOs served the men Christmas dinner. However, it was set forward a day because we had to get ready to move out, therefore Christmas was cut rather short. The next day we had to move back into the line, in Groesbeek.

Allied soldiers celebrate the Jewish feast with a group of Jewish children at Tilburg: Shown: A. Lobsenzer (Coney Island, N.Y.) U.S. Army, Eve Keller (Regina, Saskatchewan) C.W.A.C., H. Fishman (Montreal, Quebec) Canadian Army, and E. Sassoon (Manchester, England) British Army.

Bill Clifford, RCAF

On the first of December I flew through the premature detonation of two thousand-pound bombs while doing a low-level attack. The concussion left me with a persistent bloody nose. I kept flying for a couple of days and finally had to seek medical aid. A specialist in Brussels grounded me for three weeks. During the confinement I helped arrange a Christmas party for the local Dutch kids. The custom is that St. Nicholas [a bishop] comes accompanied by two Black Peters. We had them dressed and made up to look quite authentic, and I packed them into an Auster [observation aircraft] and taxied them to where the airman's mess was located, the site of the party. The children were overwhelmed and extremely excited. This all had never happened before in their young lives. They all got presents and lots of goodies along with doggy bags to take food home to their hungry families as well.

By this time I was in contact with a local family, and they welcomed me into their home many times, and I was able to bring with me food items like canned Spam, cheese, bread, just whatever I could scrounge from the mess sergeant. They were a family of six, mom and dad, two boys twelve and fourteen, a daughter eighteen, and a little two-year-old girl. The father was city treasurer of the city of 110,000, and he spent a lot of his time on a bicycle searching for food and milk for the baby in the country. The boys went with him along the railway tracks hoping to find pieces of coal for heat in the home. They had a rabbit that got lots of greens to eat, and it was going to be Christmas dinner, but when the time came they loved it too much, it had become part of their family.

Doug Shaughnessy, Royal Hamilton Light Infantry

I can remember Christmas Day in 1944, we were staying with a Dutch family. When we were going out to get our Christmas dinner, they were sitting down for theirs, and there were two pieces of bread on the table and a little bit of butter or cheese or something, and there were three or four people to eat it. So when we went down to have our dinner, they had a special Christmas dinner for us — two bottles of beer and turkey and all that sort of stuff that they sent over from Canada. So after we finished ours we washed our mess tins and went back in the line again and filled them up with turkey and potatoes and gravy and stuff like that and then we took it back to that family. That was the best Christmas I ever had.

John Honsberger, 4th Canadian Armoured Division

It was decided that we would put on a party for these Dutch children. These children would come and we'd put on a little concert — those who had some musical instruments — with a play, and I remember one fellow getting up and doing a kind of a tap dance, which was quite a thing with big heavy army boots. It was amazing with these children laughing and so on, and then we gave them a feast. It was impressive — we had our rations, but that didn't go very far, but what was interesting is that almost everybody seemed to have something in their packs from home and we'd donate all of these things to the party and to see the eyes of these children, this was not very exciting type of food, but to them it was something unbelievable. For many they were of an age that they could not remember that kind of food. It was unbelievable how happy we made these little children. I know that I have never made anybody happier than those children.

Al Armstrong, 14th Canadian Hussars

Christmas '44 was something else. Being an armoured regiment our mail was always slow in catching up to us because we're always on the move. But just before Christmas our mail caught up to us, and we were getting food parcels, Christmas cakes, and so on. We took a sergeant-major, we got a Santa Claus outfit, put him into a jeep with all our mail

Christmas Day 1944 in Schijndel.

General H.D.G. Crerar celebrates Christmas with the Dutch children of Tilburg. St. Nicholas (Lieutenant H. J. Tingle) delights the youngsters at the party held for them at the First Canadian Army's Main Men's Mess.

parcels. They had all the local children in the town hall, and he comes in and distributed it, whatever we had. A lot of the gifts were put in their wooden shoes, and they couldn't understand how they were getting shaving cream and razor blades in their shoes because the guys didn't go through the parcels too thoroughly before they turned them over. That was Christmas in Holland.

Jim Wilkinson, Black Watch

We were assigned a job, Dale Sharp and myself, to go out and see what we could find in that particular location, and we thought we were smart, we came across two Germans and we were chasing them. They were smarter than us, they had two friends behind us, and I was just about to shoot one of these Germans when I picked up a bullet, I picked up two actually, in my right leg, and then his pal hit me with a hand grenade. Dale Sharp, who was a big strong man, he was able to fight them off and he helped me back to our lines. That was December 27.

LEFT: *Schijndel 1944-45.* TOP CENTRE: *Celebrating Christmas in Schijndel with Dutch friends.* TOP RIGHT: *View across the bridge at Grave.* BOTTOM CENTRE: *January 1, 1945: the aftermath of the Luftwaffe's New Year's Day attack on Allied airfields. Shown here on the left is a Spitfire (P.R.Xi of No. 400 Squadron [City of Toronto]) at the RCAF base at Eindhoven.*

One of the bullets went right into and fractured my right leg and the other one just missed my patella on the right leg and shattered a little bit — it wasn't bad — but it made me lame for the rest of my life. The guy who hit me with the hand grenade, I still got nine pieces of shrapnel in my body.

On December 30 the Allies launched counterattacks throughout the Ardennes and began driving the Germans back. A few days into the counterattack, the Germans launched Operation Bodenplatte. The Luftwaffe had mustered eight hundred diverse aircraft to use in a desperate and daring attack on Allied airfields in the Netherlands, Belgium, and northern France. The skies had cleared over the Ardennes, and the Allies were using their air force to aid in the campaign there. The Luftwaffe's attempt to neutralize these airfields failed, due in part to the lack of experienced pilots that they had left. They managed to destroy three hundred Allied aircraft in the raids, but they lost two hundred of their own in the process. While the Allies were quick to replace their losses, the Germans could not. The operation was devastating, leaving the Luftwaffe virtually powerless in Western Europe.

Bill Clifford, RCAF

New Year's Day our airfield was attacked. Most of the aircraft were destroyed. Buildings were destroyed and runways bombed. It was a major setback, and we had casualties. As soon as the runways were patched up, my flight group went to the U.K. for new aircraft. We were back in business at Eindhoven in a couple of days with new aircraft.

In January and February we continued our drive into Germany, hitting railway marshalling yards, cutting mainline supply routes, enemy airfields, and V1 rocket launching sites (some near Rotterdam). The targets were unlimited, and the anti-aircraft fire intensified.

Pierre Faribault, Fusiliers Mont-Royal

I joined my regiment in early January because I was a reserve officer, and the first battle I had in Holland was in Groeningen — a small village near the border down south. We fought for two and a half days, street fighting from house to house. I was awarded the military cross for an action in that village because the first platoon commander was killed and the Germans were firing mortars and machine guns, and I took over the two platoons and took the village and seventy-five prisoners.

Canadian soldiers at Waalwijk.

Al Armstrong, 14th Canadian Hussars

There was one Dutch family — we had to use their barn. It was too cold to sleep outside. We took over part of the family's house — the ground floor and the barn. We used the barn to put our vehicles in so they couldn't be spotted from the air. The mobile baths started catching up to us, and our mail, they brought in a mobile

A two-inch mortar crew of le Régiment de Maisonneuve in action. (Left to right: Private Raoul Archambault and Private Albert Harvey).

Some members of the Fusiliers Mont-Royal chat with a Dutch woman by their carrier in Cuijk (south of Groesbeek). (Left to right: Sergeant Rene Laberge, Dutch woman, and Private Gerrard Provencal).

bakery. I had to go back with the jeep and pick up rations so I got to know the guy in the bakery. Cigarettes and whatnot changed hands, and I came away with three loaves of fresh baked bread. They were still warm. This Dutch family, they had three children — very young ones. I walked into the kitchen and I handed the lady of the house a hot loaf of bread. She broke down and cried. The kids gathered around her, they didn't know what it was. White bread.

T. Garry Gould, Sherbrooke Fusiliers

We were straddling a road and it's a little bit quiet, and we're settling down, and all of a sudden I hear a jeep pulling out. Oh, it's okay, it's a couple of sergeants going to make their way back checking on and making sure the pubs are closed, or they'll be closed as soon as they leave them. So sure enough around one or two o'clock in the morning *putt-putt-putt-putt* we hear the jeep coming roaring back up — my God he's not stopping! Look out! Nobody put a barrier up, nobody put a tape up, and they're gone. Right into enemy hands. They checked out the bar that they wanted to close and they went too far.

Few Canadians experienced such cold as the members of the 1st Canadian Parachute Battalion that winter. They shivered in their slit trenches with only their summer battledress for weeks on end.

The icy roads and treacherous conditions led to numerous accidents as equipment was moved into action. Here a tank slid off the road leading to Zetten while going into action.

The Ardennes campaign ended on January 16, 1945, when the British and American troops met at Houffalize. It would be the last major offensive of the war for the Germans. In the end, the Ardennes campaign would cost the lives of 32,000 soldiers (24,000 German and 8,000 Allied), 2,500 civilians, 1,300 tanks, 1,280 airplanes, and 6,000 vehicles. The losses were greater for the Germans, and they could ill afford them. The Allies could replace the war *matériel* quickly from factories in North America (far from the reach of the Luftwaffe bombers), whereas the Germans were losing their factories to Allied bomb runs daily. Even greater was the loss of life — the Germans did not have as large a population base to draw on as the Allies did. For several years the Germans had been employing soldiers from their occupied territories, throwing out their notion of racial superiority when necessity dictated. They were in retreat with dwindling resources.

In the north, the Dutch plight became more difficult every day as the desperation of the Nazis led to greater oppression.

Henry Schogt

They confiscated everything. I remember that I was on the bicycle in the last winter of the war, and it was a very good bicycle because it was the bicycle of a medical doctor, and he said, "You can have my bicycle," and I had distributed some bulletins — illegal bulletins. The bicycle was fantastic, and then a German came and said, "Your light is too bright, get off!" He got on the bicycle and off he went. So I had to tell this nice doctor that his bicycle was stolen — confiscated.

The Germans stripped the Netherlands of everything of value. Streetcars were loaded up and taken to Germany to use the metal in their war effort.

Helena van Doren

We were a small town, so they didn't bomb much, but there were Germans on our street living in some of the houses. We had a store and we sold postcards, and they came in the store and I had to help them, I had to give them the postcards that they wanted, and I said, "I hate to help them," and they said, "But, Mom, what can you do? They might kill you, you're standing behind the counter with a baby." It was five horrible years — with the shooting, you could hear it, we could hear when they were shooting people. They put seven young people out hand in hand and they shot them all in the neck right in the street.

In the Netherlands the resource in the greatest demand and the shortest supply was food. In December starving Dutch women, children, and elderly people went in search of food. People from cities wandered through rural areas hoping to find something to eat. Many were reduced to eating grass or whatever else would ease the hunger pains. Starving children were evacuated to the east, where food was not as scarce. It was a disaster of national proportions. Hunger was a daily way of life for the Dutch, and the suffering seemed to have no end. It would be called the *hongerwinter* ("hunger winter").

Douglas Lavoie, Fort Garry Horse

Holland thought that the war was going to be finished before Christmas. They had to live through that winter, it was probably the toughest winter that they had. The Germans were retreating, taking everything that they possibly could, and left the Dutch with very, very little.

Ada Wynston

I was lucky that when the hunger started to become very rampant, I was in this place where they had a farm, so I had no hunger. None at all. You ate what you got, and we ate potato peels — now it is fashionable, then you had no choice.

Liedewij Hawke

I especially remember the hardship. I don't really remember being hungry. We were always hungry, but I don't remember it. My parents had to scramble, and it was very hard to get food. I do remember Sinterklaas, which was the fifth of December, and it's comparable to Christmas over here. In the morning you would always find gifts and a letter from Sinterklaas in your shoe and candy. This time all there was a spoonful of some sugar substitute, it wasn't even real sugar, and I remember that we were ecstatic, we were just so excited, and we thought that this was just the most wonderful gift. So I guess that shows that we must have been very hungry, otherwise I wouldn't remember that.

Corrie Schogt

We have different experiences. I was with a family in Rotterdam who had an estate in Brabant. She was from a noble Huguenot family, and they held on to this estate, and we went there every holiday, even during the war. They always had their provisions from the farmers around that estate because they rented it, it was a feudal system. So every time we went we took back beans and grain and whatever — so the last time we were there was in August 1944.

TOP LEFT: *A soup line to help the starving Dutch population. Often the soup would be made from tulip bulbs or other improvised staples.* TOP RIGHT: *Despair enveloped the Dutch people as the hardships grew.* RIGHT: *Children suffered greatly through the hongerwinter. Between the starvation and the cold, tens of thousands would die that winter.*

At the very end of August we were all listening to the radio, the underground radio, and we heard that the Canadians were close. So it was a debate in the family whether we should go back to Rotterdam or not, and they decided to go back because he was a lawyer, like my father, and he said, "I can't leave my work and the house in Rotterdam." We went back and the house was unfortunately quite badly damaged. So we were in Rotterdam without any provisions. It was very bad, and you didn't get anything. So the father and the daughter of the family went on their bicycles to the east of the country to get some food, but it was very, very little.

Jan de Vries, 1st Canadian Parachute Battalion

When we got to Holland, we relieved a division in the large town of Roermond. The Germans had cleared out all the inhabitants — just pushed them out and told them to go somewhere else, they didn't care where. Cleaned out most of the houses and took the stuff with them and didn't leave a lot. We

TOP LEFT: *A starving couple with their child on Kalver Street suffering through the honger-winter.* BOTTOM LEFT: *Barges filled with sugar beets. Food was taken to Germany instead of being distributed amongst the starving Dutch population.* ABOVE: *Special meal programs were arranged for the children.*

did discover some preserves in jars, but we hated to touch that because we knew the families would have nothing to eat if we didn't leave that alone. The Dutch were very good at preserves. If you knew where to look in the hideaways, under the floor … there was even one big cache under the community hall — found the trap door in the floor and lo and behold there was all kinds of stuff there in jars, but we left that alone.

Martin van Denzen

I lived in a small village called Noordwijkerhout, which is right along the coast of the North Sea between Haarlem and Leiden. The thing that I can remember of the occupation was when I was five or six was how hungry we were. We had five kids at the time and there was no food. I can remember that we were hungry saying things to my mom like, "Oh, you have something, it's just you won't give it to us." How we hurt our parents, but there was just no food to be had.

Helena van Doren

Everybody was hungry. We had no water, we had no light, we had no heat, and I said to Peter, "I want a baby, I am twenty-seven years old, I cannot

Essentials such as clothing and footwear were rationed, but not always available.

wait." He said, "Mum, the war can take ten years and you cannot live through that." I said, "I'm getting too old for a baby." I had it in '44 and I had six diapers from the matron, they were bedsheets because you couldn't get anything in the stores. We couldn't get anything, so I had to make something. That was five lost years of your life. We had a store where we rented books, we called it a library, but they paid ten cents a book per week. They went home with eight or ten books a week. They were reading by candlelight, they had nothing else — no radio, the movies were all German.

Martin van Denzen

I can remember we had a little canal at our place, and one day there was a German that was throwing grenades in the water to render unconscious the fish, and they would come floating up. And I remember we saw this fish floating in the water and we kept throwing stones so that it would come closer to the side, and we quickly picked up that fish and we ran like mad, we ran home and my mom cooked it. These are the things that stand out in your memory, you'll never forget those.

Jack Heidema

I remember some people pay as much as five guilders for one little potato. It was worth two cents. The black market was very much in evidence. I don't know where they got this stuff from, they went out to the farms, bought stuff, and then sold it at high profits, so they had more money to buy more stuff off the farms to sell it again. A lot of black marketing was going on in those days.

Elly Dull

I remember that a potato was a guilder, a potato with salt was a guilder-ten, butter … you can't even buy it, bread was so stale and full of mould that if

LEFT: *Hunger written all over the faces of desperate people in a very dark time.* RIGHT: *Food was a precious commodity. It was the key to life itself at a time when nothing else mattered.* BELOW: *A boy waits outside a black market restaurant hoping for a handout of a morsel of food. Many children would carried a spoon with them everywhere – just in case.*

you gave it to the goldfish at the museum they wouldn't eat it. We ended up eating sugar beet pulp, which was so nauseating and so sweet I can still taste it. And we ate tulip bulbs. There was no food. There was no school at that time, everything was closed, there was no transportation. Our school became a central kitchen, and every member of the family would get a card and every day we would go to the central kitchen and every stamp would be one scoop of whatever they were serving, and it was usually sugar beet pulp. People were very ill, with skin diseases, and I think what's left over with me is that I fear cold more than hunger. It was incredibly cold that winter, the moisture just dripped off the inside of the walls. We all went to bed at seven o'clock with everything that we had that we could wear, and the only thing that really supported us is the fact that in '44 there was the Underground news of D-Day and there were the wildest rumours about they're there, they've got blankets for us, they've got food for us, and all this.

We didn't have anything — the streetcar rails were all broken up. We used that to make wood for the fire. Anything that had a bit of rubber on it we used it to put underneath your shoes. Our shoes were cut open at the top, the front, and the back

TOP: *Lining up for food.* LEFT: *Group of children heading out for food with their pots in hand.* CENTRE: *So desperate for wood for heat, the rail ties were stripped from all of the streetcar tracks, leaving them unusable.* RIGHT: *With no supplies of any kind, shoes were worn out but never disposed of.*

to allow for growth in the shoes, because we couldn't get new shoes. It was very inventive, but it was very marginal, and I don't know if we could have lasted another month even.

Liedewij Hawke

My father went on hunger trips. I remember one day very clearly, my mother had said, "When Father comes home, we will have pancakes," because if he made it back safely, he would have flour, he would have eggs he would've

LEFT: *A contrast in conditions: Dutch police enjoy a meal while a group of starving civilians wait for leftovers.* RIGHT: *With rations of bread down to four hundred grams per week, desperation necessitated police presence at breadlines.*

bartered against supplies that we had, like soap or whatever. He finally did come back, and I remember running along the narrow corridor of the house to the front door and I said, "Father, we're going to have pancakes!" and he never even said anything to me, he didn't even look at me. He walked past me and then into the kitchen where he just dropped down into a chair, he was so exhausted. I was extremely puzzled because he was always a very warm father, and so my mother said, "Well, he's very tired, he's exhausted …" He was very thin then, and he just sort of sat there. He would've had to sleep in ditches, for several nights, maybe not even sleep. To hide, and hide the bicycle, so that he wouldn't be arrested, or so his food wouldn't be taken away by the Germans, which often happened.

Martin van Denzen

There was distribution at different farms, and we would walk for miles to get a little sack of grain that mother would be able to bake a loaf of bread from. As young children, we were also sent to more well-to-do families for a meal. We would take turns, and one day you'd go to this family and another day you'd go to another family.

I can remember eating tulip bulbs. All I can remember is that it tasted very sweet. We'd get them from the communal kitchens that the Germans had set up, and you'd go over with a pot and you had a number, and they ask how many kids and that's how many spoonfuls you got.

Liedewij Hawke

I remember clearly that we went to a special soup kitchen, where the children would go. It was kind of a gruel, I remember the taste. It seemed delicious to us, and occasionally I get a whiff of it or a taste in some other soup, and it brings back that soup kitchen. Maybe it was made with potato peels. During that last winter, the

Soup being served to Dutch children.

When the Dutch expected liberation in the fall as the Allies advanced north in the Netherlands, some began to document Dutch life through photography. They hoped to capture the liberation on film. Instead they documented the horrible events of the hongerwinter.

Desperately searching for scraps of food in empty tins.

worst winter, there was no power, there was no light, there was no gas or electricity, so everybody was frozen and there was no food either. There would be a constant stream of people who had nothing to eat. They would ring our doorbell, because we lived in a village closer to the country and there were some farmers in our area that we sometimes managed to barter with. But the people from Utrecht, they had even less food, so they would come and ring our doorbell, and my mother would usually have to say, "No, I'm sorry, I haven't got anything." There was one man who my sister and I were very scared of, because he looked kind of wild, he had long hair, he looked unkempt, and he was in rags. He would ring the doorbell occasionally, and my sister and I would call out, "Ooh, the boogie man, the boogie man." We would hide under the chairs, and yet my mother said he was really a nice man. He would come once a week, and then one day he didn't come. We found out that he had starved to death.

Corrie Schogt

How many calories were we allowed by the Germans?

Henry Schogt

The official ration at the worst was five hundred calories per day. But you couldn't get that because you had to stand in line, and the bread was awful.

Martin van Denzen

I can remember one time when there was a German food convoy going by, and it was slippery and a truck had overturned, and after they had scraped up most of the stuff we sat in the gravel with a sieve and sifted out the sand and the stones for the little peas so we would have a little bowl of peas to eat.

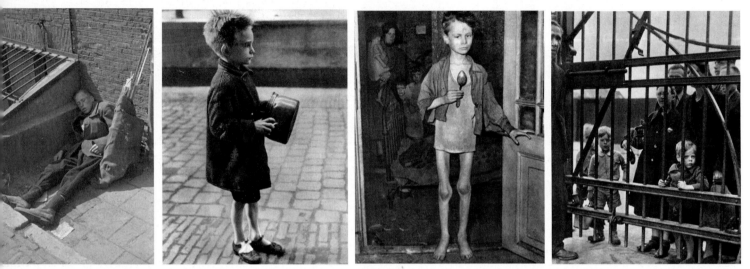

LEFT: *A starving youth collapsed while gathering wood. A few days later he died.* CENTRE LEFT: *Pathetic figures moved through the streets of the larger cities in search of sustenance.* CENTRE RIGHT: *Malnutrition ravaged the population in the north and the west regions of occupied Netherlands.* RIGHT: *Desperation etched on the faces of the hungry.*

LEFT: *The elderly, like the young, suffered the greatest during the hongerwinter.* CENTRE: *Food lines were a way of life during the last winter of the war.* RIGHT: *The Netherlands suffered one of the worst man-made catastrophes in its history during the winter of 1944-45.*

Jack Heidema

Hunger is a terrible weapon, and the Germans deliberately did this to the Dutch, there was no mistake. They deliberately starved the people, thousands died from hunger. I saw people collapse right in the street, buckle to their knees and die on the sidewalk. Smaller towns were spared because there were farms around, and there was always something to be had on the farm. It was the city people who suffered badly.

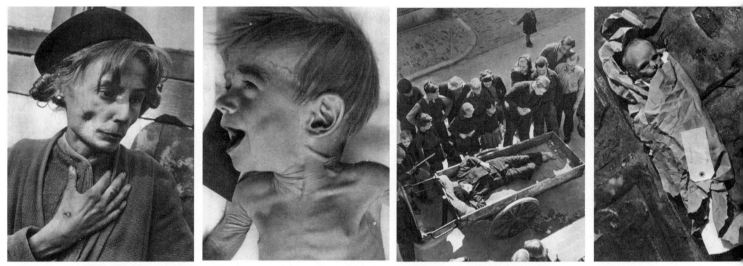

LEFT: *Many would go days without food, only to enjoy a morsel that was not nearly enough to sustain life for any length of time.* CENTRE LEFT: *Grim results of lack of food.* CENTRE RIGHT: *The result of the hongerwinter was a weakened population, sick and on the verge of death.* RIGHT: *Some never had a chance in life. The Canadian soldiers would soon find out what they were fighting for.*

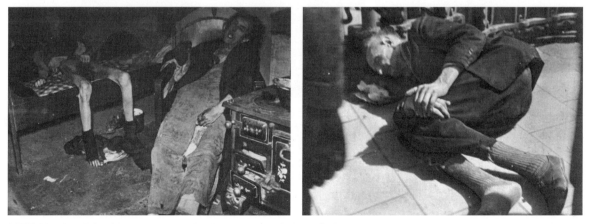

LEFT: *Two found dead in an apartment, having starved to death.* RIGHT: *People reached such a weakened state that they collapsed and died on the street. It became so commonplace that no one paid attention.*

The lack of food proved deadly for the Dutch in the early months of 1945. While liberation was close, there was no relief from the hunger. Thousands died from hunger in January and February. Meanwhile, members of the Dutch Resistance were being hunted down and executed, and tens of thousands of men were forced into labour. In the depths of such despair, thirty thousand Dutch civilians perished from starvation during the dreaded hongerwinter.

Food reserves were so low that on January 25 there was no other choice than to reduce the food rationing at the central soup kitchens throughout occupied Netherlands. Two days later the Germans stopped food transportation to the west, which was the hardest-hit area. On January 28 Swedish ships arrived filled with food and supplies, but the Germans prevented the distribution of these desperately needed items. It was one deadly month later that the German authorities finally allowed the Swedish humanitarian aid to be delivered.

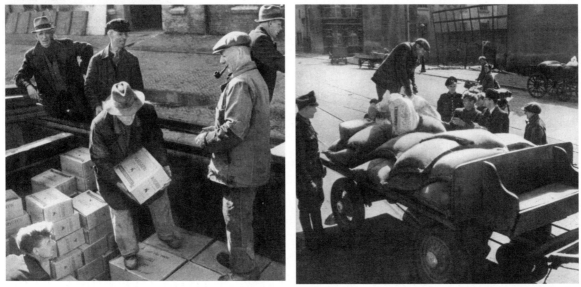

TOP: *Swedish Red Cross supply ships arrived in occupied Netherlands to try to help the starving Dutch population. Seyss-Inquart held up the distribution of the food for a month, costing countless thousands their lives.* LEFT: *Unloading the Swedish Red Cross boxes.* RIGHT: *Preparing to distribute the Swedish Red Cross supplies. It would be a month before they were allowed to be delivered.*

Jack Heidema

In February 1945 it was doomsday for our Resistance group. I went to a printing shop where they made falsified documentation. So I called at the door, the printer lived above his store. There was a staircase going up, and there was a strange man at the top of the staircase. I had never seen him before. I said, "Is Mr. Van Dreel in?" And he said, "Well, come on up." And I said, "No, I think I'll come back." At that very moment he pulled a gun on me. I had a gun in my back because someone had come into the door behind me, so I was in between two armed Dutchmen. So I was taken upstairs, and what was I doing there? I said, "Mr. Van Dreel is a member of my church, and I just wondered how they were doing, I heard they weren't all that well." So they brought the printer into the room. "Do you know this young man?" and he said, "No, I do not." They brought in his wife, and the same story repeated itself, she also denied knowing me. I got belted around pretty good after that. All these guys were Dutchmen, Dutch traitors working for a branch of the Gestapo. They eventually took me to the centre of The Hague to Gestapo headquarters. From there I was again interrogated, and I kept on repeating that I was inquiring about these people's health. I was transported to the prison in s'Gravenhage, called the Orange Hotel, named after the House of Orange because that place was full of Resistance people. I spent two weeks in solitary. Many mornings we could hear rifle shots outside. Later on we found out that Resistance people had been taken out into the dunes and shot. So one morning they came with a little suitcase, and in the suitcase was a jacket, and I recognized it as one of my brother's jackets, and a pair of boots. I did not know at the time that my brother was dead. I was arrested at noon on February 13, and my brother was involved in a firefight with a Gestapo unit, and during that firefight he was killed. I didn't know because I was in jail.

About two weeks later I was transported to Germany, to the city of Gronau, which is just across the Dutch border, and I was at three consecutive slave labour camps. That was pretty well the end of my Resistance period.

Henry Schogt

The second close call was when a German and we suppose Dutch Nazis raided our house, and we later heard that two suspect people were standing outside our house with burlap bags waiting for the loot. So it was not really an official German invasion, but it was the Germans who were ransacking people who they knew were vulnerable. So in this time there was one of the two Germans inside, he said, "This is disgusting what we are doing," and my mother said, "Why are you doing it then?" He said, "I don't know — let's go." And they left.

Helena van Doren

My brother was in the Underground, we had him and his wife living with us. My brother had seven people every night, and he was instructing them how to use rifles and things like that. One night after eight o'clock there was banging on the door, and I was expecting any day, and my husband said, "You open the door and see who it is." So the Germans came in and they shoved me aside, and I was so mad I said, "If I lose my baby, it is your fault!" As if they would care. So three of them came in and they had rifles. The Germans were so stupid, they threw a grenade up the steps so they couldn't go upstairs, and my brother and his wife went out the window in the back and over the rooftops, and they got away. But they finally got my brother when I was in hospital having my baby, and I got a letter smuggled in from him, and he said, "Helena, they shot me through my kidneys and they operated on me. If

I don't see you anymore, I wish you and your baby all the best — I hope your baby grows up in a better world with no war and no hate towards each other." They operated on him, made him better, and then they killed him. Why not let him die? Oh no, they killed him after that. I lost my brother, that was the hard part.

TOP: *Gent Belgium, a rest and relaxation destination for Canadian soldiers on leave.* BOTTOM: *Guns providing supporting fire as the Canadian infantry attack across the Maas River.*

Douglas Lavoie, Fort Garry Horse

I didn't get back into there until February. Then we were in Holland after I got out of the hospital. We trained the new guys coming over from Canada for about a month. It was a really boring time after a while for my friend and myself, Harold Little, who landed on D-Day — he got shot up pretty badly on the beach, so he was in England until I met up with him again. One day we said, "Let's go back," so we put our names up. It must have been a couple of weeks before we saw our names on the list. So we went back and we ended up at Gent for a couple of days, which was sort of the collection centre for all the guys coming in and then to be sent out to their regiments. You didn't always get sent to your regiment, but Harold and I did. A couple of trucks had about forty guys all together, and Harold and I were the last two to get dropped off. The truck stopped, and they said, "Okay, you guys, out you get!" We said, "Well, where's the regiment?" He said, "Right there across the field, don't you see those tanks over there?" They were all camouflaged and sitting there quietly. So we started across the field and down came a mortar. We could hear the darn thing coming, so we hit the ground. I turned to Harold and I said, "What the heck are we doing back here?" He said, "Don't ask me, it was your idea!"

While the von Rundstedt offensive failed and ended in mid-January, the vicious Battle of Kapelsche Veer raged on until January 31. The Germans were tenacious in their hold on the bridgehead south of the Maas River, but eventually they were forced back. The Dutch Resistance members who had discovered the planned attack and communicated it to the Canadians paid for their heroics with their lives.

CHAPTER FIVE
THE RHINELAND CAMPAIGN
February 8–March 11, 1945

With the winter coming to an end, and wishing to take advantage of the momentum that they had gained in counterattacking the Germans in the Ardennes, the Allies launched Operation Veritable. Commencing on February 8, the operation was designed to move the offensive over the Rhine River and eventually lead to final victory. This was a different type of battle for both the Germans and the Allies. It was the first time that the Germans had to defend the Fatherland on German soil.

Led by Field Marshal Montgomery, Operation Veritable included the combined forces of the British, the Canadians, and the 9th U.S. Army. The plan called for two separate thrusts across the Netherlands and into Germany. The first thrust would see the Canadians attack to the southeast from the easternmost reaches of their front (the Nijmegen Salient) and then proceed to clear the region between the Rhine and the Maas rivers. Due to the formation for the operation, the 1st Canadian Army included II Canadian Corps, nine British divisions, and some Belgian, Dutch, Polish, and American units. General Crerar took charge of the largest formation ever commanded by a Canadian officer. The second thrust would see the 9th U.S. Army advance to the northeast. The two forces would meet on the Rhine opposite the town of Wesel.

The Canadians faced several tasks en route to Wesel. They had to clear the densely wooded Reichwald Forest and break the Siegfried Line. Next they needed to clear the

Hochwald Forest and the German defences in that area. Finally they had to clear the territory all the way up to the Rhine. The defences were daunting.

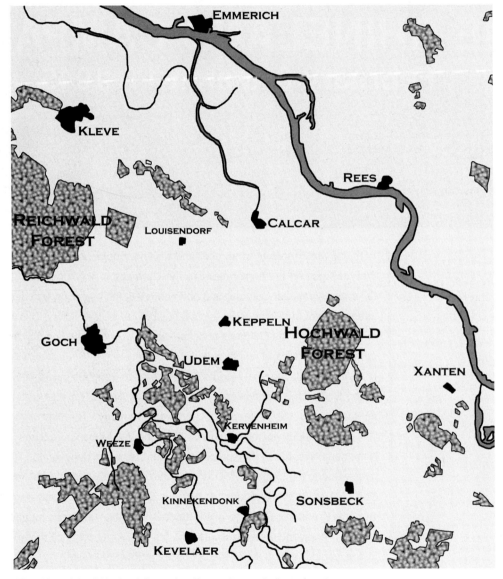

The cities of the Rhineland Campaign. Textured areas indicate forests.

Construction of a road by the 1st Canadian Army Engineers.

Lieutenant Louis Woods observing the German line before the attack.

Doug Shaughnessy, Royal Hamilton Light Infantry

The eighth of February, 1945, we went into the Siegfried Line at Kleve, and if we could have made it a little bit earlier it would have been great. The spring thaw came, and our tanks got bogged down, but we got through it all right.

Douglas Lavoie, Fort Garry Horse

We were in Germany. We crossed at a place called Kleve, and the history says that we were the first Canadian tanks into Germany, but we didn't stay there. We just went in,

The Rhineland Campaign took the war onto German soil, where the defenders became more motivated to stand and fight.

and in a couple of days we turned around and went back into Holland again. From there on it was a whole different type of war then. It was just getting it over with, and yet guys were still getting killed. Every day there'd be somebody getting knocked off, and you'd say that's too bad because they knew that the war was over really, all we were doing was driving up the roads.

Kleve is a medieval town that is situated on high ground between the Rhine and the Reichwald Forest. "Kleve" translates to "cliff."

The castle at Kleve.

Kleve.

Jim Parks, Royal Winnipeg Rifles

The thing that I remember about the Rhineland is the muck — you couldn't even drive some of these tanks. Our mortar carrier had a helluva time getting in there. Sometimes we'd have two mortar carriers, one pulling another just to get them out. We'd dump off all the bombs and lower the weight, pull it out of the mud, and then we'd put them back on again All I remember is being wet and cold most of the time. They'd bring blankets up to the front for the night and a greatcoat.

Roy Kelley, Lorne Scots

I just got back out of the hospital when they made the push. They brought me back, and I was still weak as kitten. I was up twenty hours a day, and I guess I just got too bloody weak. When we moved from Nijmegen there was a thaw and everything was muddy as hell. The nice part about it was, I don't know how many miles of electric wiring that 3rd Division headquarters left, it was frozen in and they couldn't take it. So after the thaw I had electric lights all over the place. That was great!

Support company of le Régiment de Maisonneuve with Bren gun carriers moving up.

The advance was slow. The weather was milder than usual, and that, in combination with the extreme winter they had just experienced, made the ground muddy and slick. While it was difficult for troops, it was dangerous for the larger vehicles. When it came to launching an attack, it severely hampered the ability of the mobile units to progress with any speed. In some areas there was flooding, forcing the men to advance through three feet of water. This was most uncomfortable with the chill of the February air. Whenever the Canadians did launch an assault on an enemy position, they enjoyed considerable artillery and air support.

Charles Barrett, Highland Light Infantry

When Operation Veritable started, the 3rd Division was on our left flank, and the 2nd Division that I was with was on the right flank, and there were British on our right. We attacked the Reichwald Forest under one of the heaviest bombardments that the artillery ever put on during the war. I understand that there was something in the neighbourhood of over thirteen hundred guns firing, aside from other assorted firepower such as rockets and so on. It was a tremendous barrage, and we did have some advantage because prior to this we had been locating German positions and artillery knew where to zero in. That helped the advance to a certain extent, but it was a difficult operation.

Norman Edwards, 14th Canadian Hussars

We had artillery on our side, and they were very effective. The infantry did most of the clearing out, and our job was to locate the spots where they were still strong. The Germans were very well fortified. They were very radical some of them, and they didn't want to give up — we were right on the border of Holland and Germany.

The 3rd Super Heavy Regiment, Royal Artillery, supporting the attack by the 1st Canadian Army. The 240-mm Howitzer had a 22-foot barrel firing 360-pound shells with a range of 2,400 yards. Here it is bombing the Siegfried Line as the Canadians advance.

The Canadian Scottish Regiment firing 3-inch mortars at the Germans situated on islands in the flood waters of the Rhine.

The results of pattern bombing at Kleve.

The devastation of the town of Kleve.

A massive 240-mm gun shelling the Germans from Haps, part of the huge barrage in support of the Rhineland Campaign.

North Shore Regiment troops prepare to load up into Alligators for an amphibious assault on the Western Front.

Ed Newman, Royal Hamilton Light Infantry

It was a helluva big bombing in the early hours of the morning by the RAF, and then all hell broke loose. A little later on the artillery were put to work, and this was the grand assault on Germany proper.

Al Armstrong, 14th Canadian Hussars

The battle started on the eighth, by the twelfth I was out. During training I had my shoulder smashed and my arm, but I still managed to get back into Europe and I had a reoccurrence, I lost the use of my arm and my shoulder when I was knocked off the back of a vehicle, and I had a load of this jaundice. Now I don't know which is the worst, but the medical officer told me the jaundice is liable to kill you before the other injury. It was very unsanitary conditions, we're drinking bad water, we're living dirty, and for me it was over. I was sent back to England.

Decimated street in Kleve after Allied bombing.

The railway yard at Kleve after being captured by the Allies.

Members of le Régiment de la Chaudière march along a dike with a smokescreen in the distance. Some of the men in this unit were veterans of the D-Day landing.

The Canadians made significant gains. The area north of the Nijmegen-Calcar road was flooded, but the Water Rats of the 3rd Division used amphibious vehicles to great advantage. Using what they had learned from the Battle of the Scheldt, the Canadians were able to move forward successfully, even without tank or artillery support in the flooded areas.

The outer defences of the Siegfried Line fell. German resistance in the area varied: some positions were defended vigorously, while others were surrendered without much opposition. As they had been at the Scheldt, conditions were wet and miserable for the men; it was raining most of the time.

The Reichwald Forest presented the Canadians with a difficult assignment. The Germans had spent a lot of time preparing the defences there. They had installed trench networks, fortified positions, and anti-tank ditches. The Canadians would have to face an enemy dug into a far superior position while advancing methodically through some of the most uncomfortable conditions imaginable. The ground was waterlogged, and every inch of it was hotly contested. To make it worse, the complementary American attack had been stalled by the flooding of the Roer River, and the Germans threw their reserves into defending against the Canadians.

ABOVE: *The Reichwald Forest is a wooded region of Germany south of Kleve. The density of the trees made an armoured assault impossible. Clearing the Reichwald was the responsibility of the infantry. The Germans were excellent combatants in the woods, slowing down the Canadian advance and inflicting heavy casualties. Artillery hit the treetops and rained shrapnel and debris down onto the soldiers. The situation created unique circumstances where a typical slit trench provided little to no protection from the shrapnel hurtling down.* RIGHT: *Captain B.D. Graham (former reporter for the Toronto Telegram) tries to locate the source of some artillery fire while seeking cover behind a glider.*

Jack Martin, Queen's Own Rifles

We were in support on both the Reichwald and the Hochwald forests. Well, being mortar men we didn't get in with the infantry, hand-to-hand fighting or anything like that, we were in support. When they needed help they would say, "Lambaste this area," and we'd fire on there and get rid of some of the opposition. But the rifle companies were tremendous, they were really good at that. My former platoon officer had been elevated to a major, he was in charge of D Company. He found out that a lot of the fellas were stepping on mines in the pathways, so he ordered them to use the trees for protection by jumping in behind trees instead of using the pathway, and that seemed to work. But that was terrible when you'd get all those airbursts and shells hitting trees and it splatters everything. Not like a direct bullet hitting a guy or anything.

On February 16, 1945, the Royal Winnipeg Rifles, the Canadian Scottish, and the Regina Rifle Regiment ran into fierce opposition. The German 6th Parachute Division had recently been deployed there, and they proved to be tough opponents. Unleashing volley after volley of machine gun fire interspersed with mortar and shellfire, the fresh German troops held the Canadians at bay for a few days.

Lockhart Fulton, Royal Winnipeg Rifles

We were in reserve as far as brigade was concerned, and the Canadian Scottish and the Reginas moved ahead of us and moved out to the Siegfried Line. We were finally told to move, and we were just to clear the end of that line. That was our objective. It was flooded, so we were moved in Alligators and actually found no opposition. All the opposition we had was water. The Canadian Scottish and the Reginas had a little more difficulty, and the CO, Des Crofton, of the Reginas was hit, fairly badly, which was a very unfortunate thing because Des was a good CO and we knew each other pretty well.

One of the company commanders found a horse, and he rode around to his platoons to see how things were going. At one point I began to worry a little bit about keeping contact with the brigade because we'd have no way but swim out if they didn't come in with the Buffaloes. There was nothing to do there so they brought us back to dry land, and we moved behind the attack that had gone through Kleve.

Jack Read, Regina Rifle Regiment

In the Moyland Woods operation I led my flamethrower section into a wood in support of one of our companies, and later on two more of the companies. So we attacked into the woods and spraying the German trenches and chased most of them out, but it was pretty heavy going. After we expended our fuel we had to go back and refuel. On the way back we ran into a land mine that blew my carrier and the crew completely upside down. At that time I was pinned underneath the vehicle, and it was on fire. My driver was injured, and my gunner was killed. The crew commander of the section that was following me got out of the carrier and came over and dug me out by hand. Of course there was fire all around, and the danger of the fire was pretty high, so they had to work pretty diligently to clear the area and to clear

me. They saved my life. After that I was not able to participate in any further action for some time, and one of my section leaders took over and commanded the section. This went on for several days, and we had lost a great number of men — probably in the area of 150 to 200.

The offensive moves towards Kleve. A smoke screen is used to cover a dike near the Rhine River.

Lockhart Fulton, Royal Winnipeg Rifles

Simonds was getting pretty upset about the speed of the attack. The 15th Lowland Division had tried to take Moyland Woods and was unsuccessful, and the reason that it was important to capture it is that it overlooked the access that Simonds wanted to put the army down.

The 15th Lowland couldn't overcome the opposition, they were brought out and the 7th Brigade was moved up, and the Reginas were picked to attack the Moyland Woods and the high ground that was a part of it. We were told to capture Louisendorf, and I think we're around the fifteenth or eighteenth of February. The opposition was very strong, and we weren't given a lot of time. We were to get the old ram tanks and also in the attack we were given two divisions of the Scots Guards with the old Churchill tanks. Once we got the thing organized my battalion was loaded entirely in ram tanks. Our attack started early in the afternoon at the same time the Reginas were attacking the Moyland Woods. We were totally successful, rode right into the town of Louisendorf. But the Reginas in Moyland Woods had no success, and General Simonds was so exasperated with the part.

The next thing that happened was that the 2nd Division was brought in to take over from me and our battalion in Louisendorf, and they were to attack the next village south. While we were still in position the Essex Scottish were to move past our forward defences and put in an attack on the next village, which was a quarter of a mile ahead of us. Our scout platoon was in the village that they were going to attack, and I had telephoned and had been relayed to the sergeant, who had a couple of scouts with him, and asked him if he wanted us to lay salt and let them make their way back before the barrage and the attack started, and he said naw, he didn't want to do that. They were in a basement and the Germans were above them anyway, and he wasn't concerned. So the attack went in, and they were being supported by a squadron of the Fort Garry Horse. Instead of staying with the tanks when the return fire from the Germans began to land, the infantry went to ground. The tanks got into the town but had no infantry support, and the Germans were blowing their tracks. The squadron commander told me later that they couldn't believe their ears but there were three Winnipeg Rifles jumped up on his tank and wanted to know if he needed some help. He said from that point on they cleared that village and the next thing we saw was the scouts bringing back about fifty to sixty Germans out of the village. We were marching them back to the positions that we held in Louisendorf and the infantry from the Essex Scottish were getting to their feet and moving forward to take over the village. We were then pulled out, and I knew for sure that our next assignment was going to be Moyland Woods.

For six days the fighting continued. The Canadians systematically moved through the forest and cleared out the remnants of the German opposition. By February 21 the woods were secured, at a cost of 485 men who had been killed, wounded, or captured. The German 6th Parachute Division, which had put up a tough fight in the Moyland Woods, fell back to the Schlieffen Position. The Siegfried Line had been breached.

Ed Newman, Royal Hamilton Light Infantry

Kleve was our objective at the time — it was Kleve, Goch, and Calcar where the 2nd Canadian Division was involved. There was some pretty heavy fighting, but then the Germans really started to fall back.

Mervin Durham, Royal Canadian Engineers

Kleve, Calcar, Uedem — that's where we entered into Germany, and it was pretty darn rough going. The last battle we had was in a convent at Sonsbeck, I think it was, a Catholic convent that kept nuns. We blew the wall to get the Germans, and when we got there the men had all pulled out and left the women and children there. Some of the women were German and some of them were Polish. That's the worst mess I've ever had in my life. A young lad about twelve years old came running after the German woman with a butcher knife, he wanted to

kill her. We had a hard time holding him back. We moved the German families down where they had the Polish women and all and let them take over the officer's quarters. That was one of the best things I ever done in my life. That young man almost cut that woman's throat.

RIGHT: *Goch was a key objective during the Rhineland Campaign.* LEFT: *The church at Goch suffered severe shelling, and the steeple was rebuilt after the war.*

As the fighting in the forest wound down, the 4th Brigade found itself stuck in the mud along the Goch-Calcar road. The larger vehicles fell victim to the soggy, mud-covered roads. Then the Germans attacked — with hidden 88 mm guns. The 4th Brigade got tied up in an action that pushed back and forth on the road until finally the Canadians prevailed, gaining some ground but losing four hundred men in the process (including some taken prisoner).

The overall cost of Operation Veritable had been steep thus far. The Canadians had lost 111 officers and 1,683 other ranks, and battle fatigue was taking a huge toll. The Germans suffered greatly defending their positions: 11,778 were taken prisoner, while another estimated 12,000 were killed. The German ability to protect the front was weakening greatly.

On February 23 the U.S. 9th Army crossed the Roer River, putting the Germans west of the Rhine in a precarious position. The only obstacles between the Canadians and the Rhine were Hochwald Forest and Balberger Heights. It was believed that the Germans in the positions in front of the Canadians would weaken their defences to reinforce against the approaching Americans. Operation Blockbuster was to use a concentrated attack that would capture the Calcar ridge, break through the Schlieffen Position (the last major defence west of the Rhine), capture Xanten (thirty miles north of Dusseldorf in Germany), and clear the Hochwald Forest.

The Hochwald was not only densely wooded (once again eliminating the effective use of armoured support), but it was also on a hill, creating even greater issues for assaults on German strongholds.

Russell Sanderson, Black Watch

In the Hochwald we watched the engineers knock down houses — big houses — and bulldoze them to build a road right up to the forest. I don't know what the German civilian thought when he came back, there's his house all laid out horizontally. They just knocked it down to build a road. That way they were able to bring up some of our guns and some tanks.

T. Garry Gould, Sherbrooke Fusiliers

The ground was marginal, you couldn't use the roads, you couldn't destroy the roads with tanks or you wouldn't be able to move your supplies up. So we were trying to stay off the roads. The defenders were stoutly defending the entrance to the Rhineland, and they blunted the nose of the Canadian offensive. When one of the other armoured regiments in our brigade took a hit, and the infantry they were escorting took a hit, we got nominated to go in over the same ground. A Squadron was given the outside position of three, our position was to the left, so we had the long course over the start line. I said, "Well, fellows, we're going to do a recce," and I called for friends of mine like Charlie Williams, who was an excellent soldier, excellent marksman. I was taking them all up and we were going through piles of dead bodies — they could pile the bodies at night, but they couldn't get them out by day. We were doing our recce and we were under fire. We came back to the infantry headquarters when they were blasting away at us, trying to get us. Finally at eleven o'clock one night we were all lined up, we had overhead tracers from all four guns. We had no backup, flails, and so on. To our left was B Squadron and parallel to B was C — so we had to go in diagonally through this line because it defeated the Canadians before. We started off, and we ran into mines, and we had to negotiate over the radio to tell the boys in the lead to go around the mines, which they did successfully, then we proceeded on after that. Then there was some difficulty getting on to the target on time, but in the meantime I was diverted to have a meeting with the Queen's Own colonel. We were under fire — the Queen's Own colonel was killed, I was blown off of a tank that I was on. I was picked up and I was shot a couple of more times before I got on my feet. Finally I got heaved out of there.

Jack Martin, Queen's Own Rifles

We made a thrust into Germany at a little town called Mooshof, and that's where Sergeant Aubrey Cosens won the Victoria Cross. That was a real bunch of fanatics because they were defending their own land. They fought hard and long.

Sergeant Aubrey Cosens (Queen's Own Rifles).

In the early hours of February 26 the attack commenced, with the 6th Brigade advancing with the support of the Fort Garry Horse and the Sherbrooke Fusiliers in an icy rain. Late in the day all of the initial objectives had been secured and counterattacks were repulsed. The Queen's Own Rifles, along with the 1st Hussar (tanks), moved on Keppeln, Udem, and Mooshof. D Company advanced on Mooshof and met with harsh resistance. During that battle Sergeant Aubrey Cosens's actions won him the Victoria Cross (posthumously — Cosens is buried in Groesbeek Canadian War Cemetery in Nijmegen). The Victoria Cross is the highest honour for gallantry that can be awarded to a member of the British Commonwealth armed forces (fourteen non-Commonwealth recipients have also been awarded the VC). Instituted in 1856 (although awarded for action back to 1854), the Victoria Cross has been awarded to only 94 Canadians of a total of 1,354 awarded. During the Rhineland Campaign, three Canadians earned this ultimate honour.

Thanks to the efforts of the tank units of the 1st Hussars, the Queen's Own Rifles captured Mooshof and took more than three hundred Germans prisoner. At Keppeln the Queen's Own Rifles and le Régiment de la Chaudière cleared the flanks for the North Shore Regiment to take the village. The fighting was intense, and casualties were substantial.

Aubrey Cosens' grave at Groesbeek Canadian War Cemetery.

Operation Blockbuster continued, pressing into the Hochwald Forest at the end of February. The 1st German Army was dug in there and was prepared to put up a brutal defence. Within the forest was a narrow passage with a railway embankment just south of it. This passage was known as the Hochwald Gap, and it was the fastest route through the forest. The Canadians had plans to use the railway line for supplies once the area was cleared. On February 27, the South Alberta Regiment and the Algonquin Regiment made a drive towards the Hochwald Gap. The Germans brought them to a halt with heavy fortifications in the area. That evening the Argyll and Sutherland Highlanders of Canada arrived, and in the early hours of February 28 they led the attack on the Gap. With poor radio communications due to the woods, the Argylls battled their way along the Gap. The tanks of the South Alberta Regiment got stuck in the mud, and the Argylls pressed on. After a long, bloody day, the remnants of the Argylls were relieved by the Lake Superior Regiment and the Algonquin Regiment, who pressed on through the Gap.

On March 1 the Essex Scottish Regiment battled in the northern section of the Hochwald Forest, where Major F.A. Tilston acted so heroically that he became the second Canadian in the Rhineland Campaign to be awarded the Victoria Cross. (Tilston lived in Toronto until his death on September 23, 1992.)

LEFT AND RIGHT: *Frederick A. Tilston (Essex Scottish Regiment).*

Charles Barrett, Highland Light Infantry

We had one very bad experience near our line. We were to reach the Goch-Calcar road, which is after the Reichwald, and the Essex Scottish of our brigade was on our right flank, and during this night I remember we were not receiving any reports, we couldn't contact them. I got a liaison officer to take another radio set in a jeep down to my officer, to try and find their headquarters so as to contact them. It turned out that they were completely surrounded by the Panzer Division, which had come in on our right flank. Apparently the British hadn't moved forward in this particular attack. We contacted them, and they said that they thought they could handle it. The British never told us they weren't going to move, so our right flank was completely exposed, and the Germans were not lacking in sensing where the weak spot was and they just moved right in and they overran the Essex Scottish position, and I think we first realized that they were overrun when the artillery was being called down on their position. They were able to get through to the artillery and fire on their position, which was done more than once, because the enemy would be out in the open and you were more or less in the ground, in position — you had a better chance of surviving the artillery. It was a nasty affair, and I think there was something in the number of four hundred of the Essex that were unaccounted for the next day when finally the position was brought under control again. There was a lot of very heavy fighting at that time.

On the day of Major Tilston's heroics, the 3rd Division attacked the Hochwald Layback, the main defensive line in the forest. At the same time, the II Canadian Corps were advancing on Xanten, the anchor of the German defences in the area. The fighting continued until March 3.

Distribution of food to the Dutch by the Red Cross. It was desperately needed relief, but for many it came too late.

During the campaign in the Hochwald Forest the Dutch government urged Bedell Smith (Eisenhower's chief of staff) to start the offensive to liberate the rest of the Netherlands. Concerns were raised about preparations for civilian aid after the liberation. The conditions in occupied Netherlands were dire, and finally on February 27, after a month of stalling, the German authorities allowed the distribution of Swedish aid to the regions most in need.

Elly Dull

The Swedish Red Cross came. From my feeling I don't know how we could have lasted another month, it was just in the very, very nick of time, and for many people it came too late. I remember people in handcarts with paper bags, and they had bodies of people who died. They sort of try and bury them somewhere. There were many people who died just purely of starvation. Especially children and older people suffered.

LEFT AND RIGHT: *Horrific conditions met the Canadian and British forces that liberated Bergen-Belsen on April 15, 1945. Thousands of bodies were piled throughout the camp as the Allied forces arrived. It had been transformed into a concentration camp in December 1944. Prior to that it had been a POW camp and a "residence" camp for Jews who were to be exchanged for German nationals held by Allied nations. Inmates were evacuated from other concentration camps due to the advancing Allied forces, and many were sent to Bergen-Belsen. The camp population grew from 22,000 to over 60,000 in a matter of months. Due to the overcrowding and poor sanitary conditions, a typhus epidemic broke out that killed as many as 35,000 in the last few months prior to the liberation of the camp. Anne Frank and her sister Margot were both victims of that epidemic. It is estimated that 110,000 to 120,000 people were imprisoned at the camp. The SS destroyed their prisoner registry prior to the arrival of Canadian and British forces. Today the location of the camp has several memorials erected to the victims of Nazi brutality there.*

On March 1 Allied troops crossed the Maas to liberate the towns of Venlo and Roermond in Limburg. During this period Anne Frank died at Bergen-Belsen concentration camp within days of her sister Margot, both of typhus. (A month later the camp was liberated by members of the 1st Canadian Parachute Battalion and the British advancing through Germany.)

The Canadians pushed on through Hochwald Forest, fighting every inch of the way. Other units pressed forward towards Xanten, finding tremendous opposition.

Mervin Durham, Royal Canadian Engineers

The Hochwald was terrible. When we arrived at the Hochwald, there's a railroad track. We blew the railroad track and used the ties to make a herringbone up to the forest, and it worked. The tanks could climb all right with that. When we got into the forest we invented a new method of getting through. We'd wrap up the branches from these trees and wire them up and lay them down on the ground for tanks to pass over them, and it worked. Another thing that doesn't get heard about is that the 3rd Division and the 4th Division got firing at one another. That lasted for a couple of hours.

W.J. O'Callaghan and R. Nis hanging their washing on the barrel of their Honey tank in the Hochwald Forest.

Jim Parks, Royal Winnipeg Rifles

In the area of the Hochwald Forest we lost one of our guys called Reese — he was a driver of the company commander. I look back and I understand that around the Hochwald our casualties were about 190, with 30-some-odd killed, the rest were wounded.

George Mummery, Highland Light Infantry

Good story from the Hochwald Forest — that was the first time I seen a dentist since we left England. And they brought up these trucks with the trailers and the dental labs and we were going to cross the Rhine. My front tooth had a cavity, and I'm sitting in the dental chair, and this guy — I said to him, "Christ, are you just out of college?!" He said, "Who are you with?" I said, "I'm with the HLI."

"Oh shit," he said, "you guys are going to lead the attack." And I said, "Oh, I don't know if we're going to lead, but I know we're going over."

"Oh well," he said, "no sense in filling the goddamn thing, you won't even be here by the end of the week." He said the quickest way is to pull the goddamn thing out, and he did. I laughed when I got home because I had to go to this dentist down at Bay and Avenue Road for about six months to fix up the devastation this guy had done.

The city of Xanten dates back to Roman times, and it is the home of many archeological sites.

On March 8 the Canadians attacked Xanten, capturing the high ground south of the city, sending in the Black Watch and le Régiment de Maisonneuve together with the Sherbrooke Fusiliers. The area was cleared, then the attack was put in on Xanten. The town was captured, and the key to the German defence in the area was in Canadian hands.

Doug Shaughnessy, Royal Hamilton Light Infantry

We were in there a month when we got through to Calcar and Goch and we were on our way to Xanten. I was due for leave on the twelfth of March 1945. Boy I was counting down the days

Wreckage and rubble was all that was left of many towns that got caught in the path of the advancing Canadian Army.

A Canadian soldier surveys the ruins of a German town in the Rhineland.

— if I could make it for five more days … four more days … three more days … and so I made it out of there just as we were going into Xanten. I was on leave for two weeks, and I thought, *They should be across the Rhine by the time I get back*, and the thing was they had gone into a state of rest, and there was another river to cross.

Charles Barrett, Highland Light Infantry

A sort of an amusing thing that happened at Xanten, I don't think it was very amusing for the colonel who was involved. They had taken the position at Xanten and the colonel — I think it was of the Royal Regiment — had finally lain down to get some rest. Commanding officer of infantry companies is probably one of the most arduous jobs in the army in my opinion, they were up practically all of the time, a lot of responsibilities, and it took up one after another to battle fatigue. But this one had finally got to sleep and it was behind the bank building. In the meantime some of his men had gotten around to the front of the bank, and they became very interested in the fact that there was a large vault sitting there. So they were trying to examine how they could get into the vault and they pulled up an anti-tank gun with armour-piercing shell loaded in it and fired it through the front door of the bank into the vault. Well, it didn't really do much good. It certainly penetrated the vault and burnt everything in it, but it also knocked the wall out, the rear wall of the bank, which landed on the colonel, and he was not pleased at all, the poor fellow. There are these crazy things that happened.

The Germans were in retreat, and on March 10 they blew up the bridges over the Rhine at Wesel and withdrew to the east bank. Canada was occupying the left bank, and the Rhineland Campaign was over. It had been a vicious month of warfare, and the 1st

THE RHINELAND CAMPAIGN
February 8–March 11, 1945

Canadian Army lost 15,634 men (killed, wounded, or missing), of whom 5,304 were Canadians. It was estimated that the Germans lost 90,000 in the desperate attempt to halt the progress of the Allies. The Second World War was in its final months, and the Germans were down to their last major line of defence. The success of the Rhineland Campaign was pivotal in the war, and the success of the Canadian soldiers was duly recognized by General Dwight D. Eisenhower in a letter to General H.D.G. Crerar on March 26, 1945:

> The purpose of this note is to express to you personally my admiration for the way you conducted the attack, by your Army, beginning February 8 and ending when the enemy had evacuated his last bridgehead at Wesel. Probably no assault in this war has been conducted under more appalling conditions of terrain than was that one. It speaks volumes for your skill and determination and the valour of your soldiers, that you carried it through to a successful conclusion.

TOP: *Free beer for three Canadians, courtesy of the proprietor of a pub.* BOTTOM: *After an exhausting campaign, a Canadian soldier catches up on some sleep.*

With the end of the Rhineland Campaign, the Allies were poised to launch the final phase of the campaign in northwestern Europe. The British and Americans would battle across Germany, while the Canadians were given the task of pushing west through the Netherlands to liberate the rest of the country. A large number of German troops were tenaciously holding onto the Dutch provinces that they still occupied, and it was not going to be an easy task.

On March 13, 1945, Queen Wilhelmina returned to the Netherlands, almost five years after escaping the clutches of the Nazis. Arriving at Eede, Zeeuws Vlaanderen, Her Majesty Queen Wilhelmina was finally home again.

Ten days later, on March 23, the British crossed the Rhine (at Rees and Wesel), taking the war to Germany. As a part of the airborne segment of that crossing (Operation Varsity — the largest airborne attack in history up the that time), the 1st Canadian Parachute Battalion dropped behind enemy lines and secured strategic positions near Wesel.

Jan de Vries, 1st Canadian Parachute Battalion

This was ten o'clock, broad daylight, a bright sunny day — but the Germans knew we were coming and they just shot the heck out of us. When I was coming down the field was covered with bodies — some wounded and some killed. Our colonel was shot coming down.

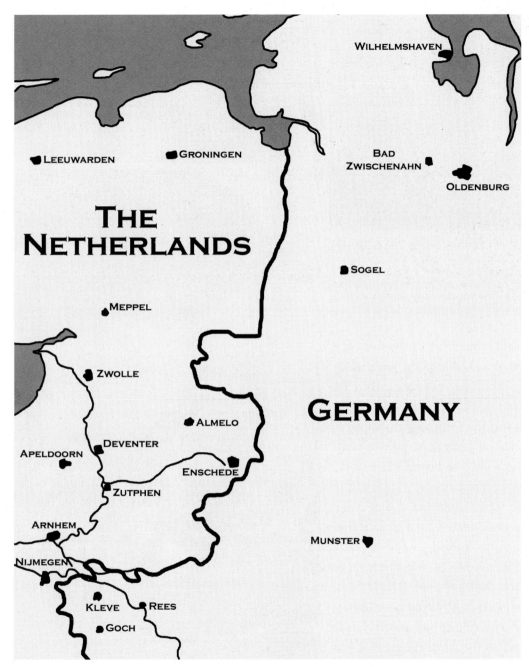

Germany and the Netherlands: major sites of the final phase of the Second World War.

ABOVE LEFT: *The Rhine River – the next obstacle lying in the path of the Allies.* ABOVE RIGHT: *A massive armada of Dakotas prepared to carry out the largest airborne operation in history.* RIGHT: *Touching down in Germany, a Canadian paratrooper lands amongst other members of his battalion. It was a stunningly accurate drop, leading to an extraordinarily successful operation.*

An interesting situation there was we were to drop at ten o'clock sharp. The air armada arrived there about ten minutes early. The artillery that was on the other side of the river was to knock out the German gun emplacements. So they were going to keep firing right up until about a minute before ten o'clock, and they counted on knocking out all of the gun positions. What happened in fact is the German general decided by ten o'clock that there were no paras coming, so he was going to send some men down to help them out at the river, which makes it sound like it's easy for us. On the other hand because we arrived early, the artillery had to cut off and they hadn't knocked off all the guns so I guess it was about equal.

In the air I looked up, I could hear these bullets going by, and I was just wishing to get down fast. I looked up and my chute was full of holes. A gust of wind carried my chute over and I came down through the trees. My chute got caught up in the top and I came charging through the branches, and then about seven feet off the ground I came to the end of the line and the harness jammed up. Now I had all this equipment in front of me, I couldn't get my leg up to get my knife to cut myself free, so there I hung with my helmet jammed halfway over my eyes and watching and hearing these bullets go by and the branches dropping. The Germans were sweeping the field on a steady basis, and I was just at the edge of the field. I don't know if they saw me or not — I doubt it or they would have got me. They were just firing at random at everybody on the field still. So it was a pretty hot bit of action — that's where a couple of fellas won medals as well as Topham, who won the only VC in the division. It was a good day, and a lot of action.

LEFT: *Frederick G. Topham (1st Canadian Parachute Battalion).* ABOVE: *Frederick Topham's Victoria Cross medal, the highest honour for gallantry.* BELOW LEFT: *Inscription of the Topham monument in Etobicoke, Ontario.* BELOW RIGHT: *Members of the 1st Canadian Parachute Battalion Association at the dedication of the Topham monument in Etobicoke, Ontario.*

Frederick Topham of the 1st Canadian Parachute Battalion took part in that operation, and his heroics as a medic earned him the Victoria Cross. (Topham lived in Toronto after the war and passed away on March 31, 1974.) It was the second-last VC ever awarded to a Canadian.

The 9th Canadian Infantry Brigade was also involved in the Rhine crossing at Rees. The 1st Canadian Parachute Battalion spearheaded the drive across Germany until they met up with the Russians in Wismar, on the Baltic Sea. They were the only Canadian unit to hook up with the

CORPORAL FREDERICK GEORGE TOPHAM, V.C.
1917 - 1974
Born in Toronto, Topham was educated here before working in the mines at Kirkland Lake. He enlisted on August 3, 1942, and served at home and abroad as a medical orderly. On March 24, 1945, while serving with the 1st Canadian Parachute Battalion, he defied heavy enemy fire to treat casualties sustained in a parachute drop east of the Rhine, near Wesel. Rejecting treatment for his own severe face wound, he continued to rescue the injured for six hours. While returning to his company, he saved three occupants of a burning carrier which was in danger of exploding. For these exceptional deeds, Topham was awarded the Victoria Cross, the highest decoration for valour in the British Commonwealth.

Erected by the Ontario Heritage Foundation, Ministry of Culture and Recreation

TOP LEFT: *Rees, Germany – site of the Canadian crossing of the Rhine River.* TOP RIGHT: *Bailey bridge being pushed into position.* BOTTOM LEFT: *Two tanks cross a Bailey bridge.* BOTTOM RIGHT: *A tank climbs onto a Bailey bridge for a crossing.*

Russians, and that was in May, at the end of the war in Europe. The Americans crossed the Rhine on March 26 at Worms, and from there the Allies crossed Germany until the Third Reich surrendered.

Jack Martin, Queen's Own Rifles

We crossed the Rhine at another spot farther into Germany. I can remember going across this Bailey bridge that they put in — in fact it was just a bunch of pontoons laid across and a surface for us to travel across. The Chaudières in the meantime were on our left, and there was a report there that they had come to a canal and that there was no way of getting across the canal — this came over on the wireless. They said, "We are going to build our own bridge." Of course they're speaking in broken English, and later on they said, "Well, we have finished our bridge, we are about to start across. There goes the first flamethrower." And then there was a long pause, and then they said, "Oops! It didn't work. The carrier went right down."

Operation Varsity: the skies filled with paras.

The temporary grave of Colonel Nicklin (1st Canadian Parachute Battalion) in the area of the Operation Varsity drop.

Colonel Fraser Eadie (1st Canadian Parachute Battalion).

Lockhart Fulton, Royal Winnipeg Rifles

We crossed on Bailey bridges. The way they got across the Rhine they put 9 Brigade in assault craft and they captured a large area and then the next morning they dropped the airborne, there was an airborne attack. When we were crossing on the Bailey bridges the airborne attack was just overhead, just going in ahead of us. Then we could see the drop zones. The reason why we were always concerned, the airborne battalion was commanded by Jeff Nicklin, who had trained with us. We knew Jeff, and some of the Blue Bombers that he played with were in our battalion, and Jeff was killed on that drop. Fraser Eadie took over from him, Fraser was also from Winnipeg, he had been with us in the early going.

John Honsberger, 4th Canadian Armoured Division

We went across the Rhine. We went across in the middle of the night. My impression was that the infantry had gone across and established a bridgehead, and they had done it early enough for the engineers to come up and make a bridge across. It was called the Black Friar's bridge, and the engineers must have been well-prepared for this as the bridge consisted of maybe twenty boats, somewhat larger than a rowboat, but anchored in a row across the river, and then there were two planks that went from one boat to the next boat that all of the vehicles drove across. That was

The boardwalk along the Rhine at Rees, 2004.

Pontoon bridge across a river.

The remains of a glider that crash-landed.

kind of scary when you only seem to be about fifteen inches above the black waters swirling underneath you, and to say that two or three o'clock in the morning we went across and the drivers had to keep on these two planks. As far as I know nobody had any problems. We went across that night, and a big barrage was going on.

Russell Sanderson, Black Watch

We had to relieve the British paratroops. A lot of those poor souls were still in some of their aircraft — the bodies. When the gliders came down, the Germans opened up on some of them with machine gun fire and killed all the poor souls sitting in the jeeps and the pilots, and they were sitting there dead in their equipment. Before the British pulled out, they booby-trapped them, then the Germans booby-trapped it. Then there was another phase in the operation where the British were moving around — they booby-trapped it again. I wouldn't have wanted to be with the engineers to go in there and try to clean that stuff out.

John Honsberger, 4th Canadian Armoured Division

As soon as we got across we went straight north to Wilhelmshaven (which was the important German naval base), and it took two and a half months to go there. The 4th Armoured Division was on the extreme right flank of the army, which meant with the indentation of the frontiers between Holland and Germany we would often be a couple of weeks in Germany and move up into Holland again.

Dark times: a town prays together.

Canadians taking control of a German town.

Elly Dull

The Allies had pushed through and had gone across the rivers, and we were soon very, very encouraged. We were greatly exaggerating all the good things that they would have and how soon it would come.

Jack Heidema

I escaped twice from the Germans. I was in a factory in Borken, and there was a German infantry soldier at the door and he had walked away to the next corner and he was talking with some civilians. We just simply walked out the door, went around the corner of the building, and started running. Then we got to the Dutch border, it was about seventeen kilometres, and we were promptly picked up by the German military police. I was sent to a different camp.

Canadians taking prisoners.

The second time I was in Bucholt. We had to clear rubble, that was our daily lot. Sleeping on straw, with little or no food. The Flying Fortresses came over the city of Bucholt — it was about twenty-five kilometres across the Dutch border. They bombed the hell out of that city. We had a direct hit on the house that we were in, we were in the basement, there were twenty-five of us, and we spent about twenty hours in that basement. We were dug out and taken to a farmhouse outside the city, and the next morning we were sent back in to clear more rubble. We opened up the roads for the German army. This lasted another week or ten days, then one night we were in no man's land and we didn't realize it. Artillery fire would come in from both sides, the Americans from the north and the Germans retreating. One of the guys went out for a pee, and the German guard was gone and we just walked away across the Dutch border. We had no transportation. I was about three hundred kilometres away from the city of The Hague and walked seven days. We walked in the night and hid in the daytime because of fear that you would be rounded up by Germans — it would be back on the train and back to slave labour in Germany. I came back and found that my mother had disappeared. When my brother was shot my mother was taken by the police and saw my brother die and then disappeared because the Gestapo was after her again. So when I came back after my escape from Germany I went underground again, and the funny thing is that my comrades in the Resistance would not talk to me because I came back. If you came back from Germany you must have talked. So they didn't trust me. It lasted about two weeks. In two weeks' time nothing happened — no raids, no arrests — then they started talking to me because obviously I was clean.

Helena van Doren

They picked up the men at the home and take them for a work detail. One time they took them all to a big place where the boats took the supplies to Germany. There were over a thousand people in there, and they picked up my husband too. I had to go get him back, so I went to the Germans, and they stood there with two rifles and they said, "What are you doing here?" And I said, "I want to speak to the boss," and they said, "Go in." I went in

Dutch women with bicycles in the country.

there and my heart was pounding. I had to go through the office, and it was filled with Germans with the big moustaches, and they said, "The hell with your husband" — and they took bundles of money out of their pockets — "you stay here with us and we'll take you out and we have money and we have food." I said, "I want to talk to the boss and that is all that I want." I was shaking because I was so nervous, and they said, "He's walking his dog." He was walking with a great big German shepherd, and he came sniffing me, and he called the dog back. "What is it?" he asked. I said, "Well, you made my husband work for you, he was fixing the houses that got bombed, now they took him, they want to send him to Germany." He said, "You go home, and he will be home tonight." I had to go three times, and it was thirty-two miles, and I went on a bicycle without tires and I just had my baby. I went back the next day, and he said, "He's not home?" And I said no. "Go home, he will be home tonight." I went home again, and nobody came. I went back again on Thursday, and he said, "Go home, he will be there tonight."

He was in the big building where the people were waiting to be transported to Germany, and when they called his name they called four other names, and those people were not there, they were underground or they were already in Germany. And he said to a guy beside him, "Why don't you go? They don't know your name, they don't know the people." He said, "I'm so scared." Peter said, "C'mon, they called three more names and they called one name and nobody showed up." He said, "You take that name." But he was too scared. Well, they were all killed who were in there.

I waited, and my neighbour said, "Come in here, Helena, don't sit alone there waiting." It was after eight, and the boys said, "Take a look who it is, it's a beggar." It was my Peter, he looked so bad, he had to walk thirty-two miles on his bare feet because he was not allowed to go on the train. So he came home, thank goodness, and he worked for the rest of the war there.

Zenderen, near Almelo.

Jack Heidema

I found my mom. She was in hiding with another family, and I joined her in that particular house after my escape from Germany. I felt hatred for the Germans. Because my mother was a physical wreck. She spent a year and a half in a prison camp, then when she was released they had killed my brother — I was just burning with hatred. I think I lived on hate. I think we all did.

Tanks of the 4th Division crossing the Rhine River on a pontoon bridge (near Almelo).

On March 28 the Canadians crossed the Rhine and battled for three days to take Emmerich in Germany. Once they had succeeded, they re-entered the Netherlands.

As the 1st Canadian Army went into action to liberate the Netherlands, they were joined by the 1st Canadian Corps from Italy. It was the first time in history that two Canadian Army corps fought side by side. The two Canadian corps were given their tasks: the 1st Canadian Corps would liberate the western Netherlands north of the Maas River, while the 2nd Canadian Corps would liberate the northeastern Netherlands and clear the coastline of Germany up to the Elbe River. Also key to their mission was opening the supply route to the north through Arnhem.

Sydney Frost, Princess Patricia's Canadian Light Infantry

The move from Italy to Holland was called Operation Goldflake. We heard about it when we were in the winter line, we had been there about two or three months, it was February. All in great secrecy, of course. We left there by lorry, cut across the Italian peninsula to Leghorn, boarded the ships, and went to Marseille. Then from Marseille by truck right up into Holland. The Germans hadn't a clue where we were all that long time, and that was very important. They didn't realize that we were in Holland about to attack.

John Drummond, Regina Rifle Regiment/Saskatoon Light Infantry

I started out with the Regina Rifle Regiment, I went overseas with them and I spent about two and a half years with them. When they planned on the invasion of Sicily, I was transferred to the 1st Division and I went down to the Mediterranean area, Sicily and Italy, and I spent a year and eight months in that area. I was trained as a signaller with the Regina Rifle Regiment, and then I was with the Saskatoon Light Infantry in the 1st Division, and also an artillery unit, and at the last I was with an infantry group that was made up of ack-ack and army service corps and recce. They were just so desperate for infantry, just overnight they turned recce reconnaissance — I think two regiments, one anyway, and a regiment of ack-ack, they turned them into infantry. Then the powers that be wanted the whole Canadian Army to get together for the push into Holland.

Harry Fox, Hastings Prince Edward Regiment

We were pulled out of action at the end of February, and then the brigadier told us we were going to the Western Front. And of course we all give a cheer. Then we went on an American ship, changed to landing craft at Marseilles, up through France by truck into Belgium, and we stayed two or three weeks in a monastery there. We got new weapons there and a little bit more training and then went into action.

Al Sellers, Governor General's Horse Guards

I was with the Governor General's Horse Guards — a Toronto-based tank regiment in the 5th Canadian Armoured. We left Italy, we came by a liberty ship, moved the tanks on by rail into Belgium, then we drove the tanks into Holland. What a difference. All the difference in the world in topography and the attitude of the people. The Dutch to me were a stubborn people, and the Italian people — some in Italy were very, very poor. There's no comparison between the two, when we got to Holland I found that the people were as happy as heck for us to be there despite us shooting up their towns and making a mess of the terrain with tanks and whatnot.

Gordon Mortensen, B.C. Dragoons

I recall going along the road one day when an English chap came out of the side of the ditch, and he had on dirty clothes and he said he had been hiding out from the Germans since Operation Market Garden. So I said, "Well, prove it to me that you are an English soldier," and he took off his blue outfit and of course he had his uniform on underneath. So we filled him up with a cup of tea and sent him back to our headquarters to be interviewed, and I don't know what happened because we went on.

Almelo on deliverance day.

A joyous crowd greets the Canadians at Albergen.

The 2nd Canadian Corps gathered momentum moving north. They were greeted at every town and city with a massive outpouring of joy as the Dutch revelled in their newfound freedom. Liberation was sweet, and the Canadians enjoyed the benefits of being the ones to deliver it. They moved quickly as German resistance crumbled before them, and the list of towns being liberated grew at a dizzying rate: Ruurio and Oldenzaal on April 2; Didam, Lochem, Zevenaar, Borne, and Holten on April 3; Delden (after some stiff German resistance)

TOP LEFT: *The Fusiliers Mont Royal's A Company moves north in the area of Laren, Netherlands.* ABOVE: *Men of the North Shore Regiment's C Company cross a canal in Zutphen.* BOTTOM LEFT: *Men of le Régiment de la Chaudière cross the Ijssel River in rubber rafts near Zutphen.*

on April 4. As the 2nd Canadian Corps moved further north, the Germans in the western provinces were quickly being cut off.

The 4th Canadian Armoured Division crossed the Twente Canal on April 5 and proceeded to liberate Almelo. They then moved east into Germany to continue the advance. Elsewhere, Canadian troops were liberating Warnsveld, Albergen, Tubbergen, and eventually Wierden after a bitter defence by the Germans. Some Canadian units that had entered Germany came back around to capture Coevorden and free the Dutch civilians there.

The 2nd Canadian Corps advanced to the north in three columns. The 2nd Division moved up the centre, crossed the Schipbeck Canal, and moved quickly towards Groningen in northern Holland.

Al Armstrong, 14th Canadian Hussars

Going through France and Belgium these people would climb all over your vehicles, the French Underground, and in Belgium it

180

LEFT: *C Company of the Highland Light Infantry passes by a windmill in Dalfsen.* ABOVE: *Dutch citizens greet the Highland Light Infantry as they cross a river by barge.*

was the White Brigade. They'd be there all over your vehicle and you got to the outskirts of town and there are a few shots fired and they were gone. The Oranje Brigada, which was the Dutch Underground, didn't work that way. They would meet your vehicles on the edge of town as you came into the village and they would meet with our leaders and say, "No, no, no, don't put your men that way, don't send your vehicles down that way, we'll send a man with you." We found them very accurate. A lot of our intelligence officers didn't believe them, but it turned out, in my estimation, the Dutch were accurate and they were fearless. They were good people.

The 3rd Division marched along the left flank. The area over to the Ijssel had to be cleared of German troops, then the Canadians laid siege to Zutphen, where the German 361st Infantry Division and an airborne training battalion (made up primarily of teenagers) put up a tough fight. The battle for Zutphen was drawn out for several days.

A Canadian soldier who was wounded by a German sniper while crossing the southern dike of the Afwalnings Canal.

Leading sections of the Black Watch moving through the forest south of Ommen.

Elsewhere the Canadians were rapidly liberating towns: Daarle and Hellendoorn on April 6 and Dedemsvaart on the April 8. That same day they started to scout the outskirts of Meppel, which was heavily fortified by the Germans. In the meantime, the Dutch Resistance was launching attacks of their own, stopping the Germans from destroying bridges in an attempt to slow the Canadian advance. On April 10 battles raged in Deventer, but by the end of the day it too was liberated.

The next day the advancing troops crossed the Ijssel and pushed towards Wilp (east of Apeldoorn).

Sydney Frost, Princess Patricia's Canadian Light Infantry

It was a neat manoeuvre, here we are, the 1st Division is coming up from Marseille through Kleve, right into a place called Gorssel, on the east side of the Ijssel River. In the meantime the 5th Division had also come from Italy and it was poised to strike across the river down at Arnhem.

So the plan for the crossing of the Ijssel River, it was a great honour, I had just been made a captain commanding D Company in that assault. The Patricias and the Seaforth were the first Canadian soldiers to enter western Holland, and I was one of them. I am tremendously proud of

that. H-Hour came up, eleven o'clock, and we assaulted across the river in Buffaloes. We went across the river and then crawled up the other side. Well, the Germans finally woke up, and they had tanks and mortars and artillery, but nevertheless we captured Ness and knocked out a tank in the process. Then we moved on to another place code-named Byron, which had previously been attacked and captured by B Company. We turned north into Winchester, and there we had quite a battle because the Germans had mobilized several battalions, and they came down the road at us with three or four tanks, one hundred or two hundred infantry, and so we had quite a battle there. When we finally got into Winchester and got into a rough defensive position, we could hear the tanks coming. I thought, *Well, I'll get on the wireless and get some anti-tank guns*

TOP LEFT: *The Black Watch in their slit trenches at Holten.*
TOP RIGHT: *Members of Princess Patricia's Canadian Light Infantry and a Buffalo amphibious vehicle used to cross the Ijssel River.* BOTTOM LEFT: *Collaborators in Deventer pay for their deeds after the city is liberated.*

across the river to us. Then a small chill went down my spine because I realized that the engineers were having trouble erecting a bridge and there would be no anti-tank support. So here I am faced with three or four enemy tanks coming at us with just these little hand-held anti-tank projectiles. The men were wonderful. It was pretty nip and tuck for a while there, whether they would overrun us or whether we would stop them. The Germans panicked and went past

Personnel of the King's Own Yorkshire Light Infantry crossing the Ijssel River en route to Arnhem.

Two vehicles hit a mine. Canadian casualties continued to rise as the war wound down and the Germans retreated.

Buffaloes coming ashore with members of the King's Own Yorkshire Light Infantry after crossing the river Ijssel.

Fire and explosion across river during attack at Westervoort.

my company down to the other company we had on our right, and they put up a good fight. The Germans turned around and came back, and we were ready for them. We just finished them off, and Wilp was secure. There wasn't any Germans left standing, they were either dead or a prisoner of war. The crossing of the Ijssel River was really the beginning of the end of the war. The Germans then realized it was hopeless, and they started to flee and surrender in droves.

It was a great strategic move because the 1st Division attacked from the Ijssel River going west while the 5th Division from Arnhem attacked going north. If you can visualize that, we were creating a pocket of Germans. We put a whole bunch of them in the POW cages, a hundred thousand of them. They had nowhere to go. It was a brilliant strategic move.

Infantry of the 1e Régiment de Maisonneuve moving through Holten to Rijssen.

W.J. Trump and W.H.G. Ritchie of the Fort Garry Horse give chewing gum to a child after the liberation of Rijssen.

Al Sellers, Governor General's Horse Guards

We went through Nijmegen and into Arnhem and then went north. German resistance was very spotty. I would say the 3rd Division had the greatest opposition. You see the 5th, we were working with Americans and British — mostly the British. The Poles worked on the left, they went up with the 1st Division, up through Apeldoorn, and we were on the east side. Our tanks would carry the Irish Regiment, the Perths, the Westminsters were a motorized regiment, so they had their own vehicles. We also carried the Cape Breton Highlanders. So we were always on the flank carrying infantry with us. The Horse Guards were a fragmented regiment — there was always a squadron with one of the infantry regiments. Like we had three fighting squadrons — A, B, and C — so A would be with one infantry outfit, B would be with another, and C would be with another one.

Wet weather cannot dampen the spirits of the Dutch as Tobergen welcomes the Canadians.

After battling for several days, the Canadians overcame the German defence at Zutphen, and the town was liberated on April 12. The victory was a sobering affair as the Canadians discovered Stalag VI C near Zutphen. It was a POW camp for soldiers captured along the Russian front. The Nazis were particularly vicious with Russians prisoners, and the conditions in Stalag VI C were horrible. Like the liberation of concentration camps elsewhere, the experience steeled the soldiers' resolve, knowing that their cause was just.

Doug Shaughnessy, Royal Hamilton Light Infantry

The thing about our section of the front was that we ran into several camps of Russian troops who had served in the German army, and they couldn't go back to Russia because they would have been shot. The Germans didn't want them, and there were thousands of men in a camp and they had nothing to eat. I don't know whatever happened to them.

Helena van Doren

I was going home, it was just before eight o'clock and I was in a hurry. Up came a young German soldier and he wanted to talk to me, and I said, "Leave me alone." We were in a ditch. He laughed and he touched my arm, and I said, "Leave me alone," and I shoved him. We were right by the canal and he fell in. I started running, and he started calling, I don't know if somebody got him out. The wall was too high for him to climb out, and I ran home and I told my husband. I said, "I didn't do it on purpose and I couldn't help him." I didn't want to help him either, but if I wanted to help him it was too high. So what happened to him, I don't know. Nobody knows. I ran home and that was it. But it was a horrible feeling, that I maybe killed somebody. They never said anything like that in the papers, so I don't know. I never heard anything about it. I don't know if he got out or not.

Also on April 12 the Canadians launched the second battle of Arnhem (the first was Operation Market Garden). The air force bombed the German defences, followed by an artillery barrage all night. At the same time Canadian troops were crossing the Ijssel at Westervoort and liberating Hooghalen. The men of Number 7 Troop of the 8th Canadian Reece Regiment (who were preceding the South Saskatchewan Regiment) came upon a dreadful scene that day. While clearing the area in the north they liberated Westerbork camp. There were 876 inmates there, 569 of whom were Dutch nationals. They had survived the savagery of the Nazis, something that over one hundred thousand other Jews from the Netherlands had not.

John Drummond, Regina Rifle Regiment/Saskatoon Light Infantry

I think the condition of the people really hit most of us. The further west you went the more starvation there was. We would see hundreds of civilians just without anything, just the clothes they have on. You do become hardened to that, but when you see people starving and children just so thin and hungry looking, even a hardened soldier feels it. I remember one time we had some canned food and we were heating it up, and you know the smell of bacon and how it travels for a long distance, and some of the people were crowding around there when they smelled the bacon, and people were fainting from hunger. We gave them what we could, but being front-line combat soldiers, you don't have much with you.

Corrie Schogt

You were in this situation and had to try to stay alive, and liberation was so far away although it was so close by.

Henry Schogt

It was very close by, and for Corrie, she knew the area where they were fighting very well.

Corrie Schogt

Snippets came through, horrific things were happening because the Germans at the end out of desperation flooded areas so that the Canadians couldn't advance, and people were drowning, just children and people who were living in that area.

Henry Schogt

And for instance there is an artist in Groningen who made beautiful illustrations for Hasidic stories, and he was arrested visiting friends. He was executed four days before the liberation. Just out of spite.

Aerial photo of the flooding in the north where Germans had blown the dikes.

Groningen – a city of canals, difficult to liberate.

Members of the Fusiliers Mont Royal move up one of Groningen's canals. The combination of canals and narrow alleys led to extensive street fighting.

While the 2nd Canadian Corps advanced to the north, the 1st Canadian Corps under Lieutenant-General Charles Foulkes moved into the western area of the Netherlands north of the Maas River. This campaign included the large cities of the country, including Amsterdam, Rotterdam, and The Hague. These large urban centres, as well as the isolated (due to flooding where the dikes had been) communities to the west, had suffered through the hongerwinter, and they were desperate for aid. Slowly it was coming, but the Germans yet again stood in the way.

The number of liberated towns in the Netherlands continued to grow with every passing day. Assen and Sneek gained their freedom on April 13, and the 2nd Division of the 2nd Canadian Corps arrived in Groningen in the north. The liberation of Groningen was not easy: the Germans hid snipers on rooftops and employed ambushes with hidden machine gun nests as well as dressing SS members as civilians. It would take several days to completely clear the city.

Russell Sanderson, Black Watch

It was just a matter of forcing them out and making them retreat to another position. For the most part they had secondary positions pretty well prepared. Driving them back was quite a fight until we got up to the city of Groningen. It was a big and beautiful city. The Maisonneuves and the Calgary Highlanders were going to go into one area, and we were to follow through them. They got stopped up, so we veered off to the north to go through the city. I know that a couple of us went across on a rowboat and there was a barge. That was one of the first crossings. There are so many canals in that area, and it was so heavily defended. There are sections of that city, the one street that was taken by the FMR Fusilier Montreal, and my friend Elmo was the company commander, and Elmo fought in this one area with his men; there are pictures of Elmo's men fighting in front of these buildings shooting down into the basements areas. We went down that street, and in certain areas tears come pretty easily. You remember what happened and how bad it was.

We made several moves, and the tactical headquarters moved up to a yellow brick schoolhouse. George Ewan and I got called in, and ahead of us was a large park. We were shown a map of the park, and the intelligence officer said, "Go in there and find out where they are, how many there are, and what they've got." So George and I left, and we had to go through side streets until we got to the edge of the park. We made our way through the park. We crawled in places and ducked from tree to tree and behind bushes and stuff like that until we got to the far side of the park.

The battle for Groningen: a Sherman tank, burning buildings, and onlookers on one of the main streets.

Bringing in German POWs on the outskirts of Groningen.

There was a line of houses on one side and a side street and a bunker on the left. George and I were on the ground on our bellies below this sparse hedge, which was only about twenty inches high, and we're lying there thinking, *Hey, this is a hedge, nobody can see us!* You could see everything through it, you could read a newspaper through it! But you've got faith. So we lay there and we're watching this bunker, and by God we see movement. There was a couple of Jerries outside the bunker. Pretty soon there were more. This was getting ridiculous. There were more and more of these guys — we had to get the word back. George — he takes off back to tac headquarters through the park.

Now the houses were built right out to the sidewalk and they're all joined together. There was nobody at the house on the corner. There was a lady and a little girl in the first doorway, the next one there were two ladies and two little girls, and at the third house there was a lady and a couple of children there. At one point the Germans disappeared from my view behind the bunker and I thought, *This is it.* I jumped the hedge and ran right across the road to the first doorway, and as I run in I asked the woman if there are any Germans inside. No — no Germans here. So I went past her and up the staircase, and ahead of me at the end of the hall is the bathroom. There was a window. The building on the corner was not as long as the house I'm in, and I'm looking out the bathroom window and I'm looking down right on the bunker and all the Germans outside the back of it. I thought, *Jesus — this is not a very good place to get caught. If they decided to occupy these buildings to defend them I'm going to be up here*

Tanks blasting buildings in Groningen.

Men kneeling and lying in ditch to avoid fire from snipers along road into Groningen.

all by myself and thirty or forty Jerries are going to be the tenants. You make a snap decision — I don't know why, but I ran down the stairs and right out into the middle of the street. I hollered in German for them to surrender, with a few obscenities. At the same time I'm directing imaginary troops who aren't there: "Get that machine gun over there, bring that Bren gun over here, you guys go there!" There's no one there — I'm alone, standing in the middle of the street like an idiot. The platoon officer turned around and looked at me, then I hollered at him to come here and surrender. He turned away from me and I thought, *Uh-oh — this is it! I'm going to catch it now.* So I'm still shouting instructions and obscenities at these non-existent troops that are with me. The officer turned around again, and I hollered at him to surrender and get over here. He turned back to the men, and I saw this gesture, and they laid their weapons on the ground, much to my relief. They started to come out and got lined up, and I told them to run. We started a jog down the road. Six or eight were dragging back — maybe health or wounds or whatever — and I thought, *I need some help here,* so I hollered, "Do any of you bastards speak English?" Then a voice said yes, and I said, "Well, get out here." This young fellow came out, and I said, "Those men at the back are dragging back, and I can't take a chance of them getting amongst the civilians and somebody getting hurt. You go back and keep them up or they're going to have to be shot." He went back and he kept them up. Now I ran these men from that bunker around the ring road in the park to the first exit. At that exit there are two Bren gun carriers at the entrance to the park, and a third one behind them. The guys stood up in the carrier and said, "What have you got, Sandy?" I said, "I don't know, but I got them."

"You want some help?"

"You're damn right I do." So a few of the carrier men jumped off with their rifles and ran with me. I ran them back to this yellow brick schoolhouse, and there was a small courtyard in front of it and I lined them up there. The rest of the scout platoon comes out and all they can say is, "Oh, can we help you gentlemen? What do you happen to be carrying?" And the search was on. I said to the one fellow, "Where did you learn to speak English?"

"I lived in America."

"Okay, where in America?"

"I lived in Buffalo five years and I lived in New York City two years. My mother and father are both German and they are doctors in Buffalo, and my father sent me back to Germany in 1938 to study medicine. Then I was drafted into the German army."

I said, "If you lived in Buffalo, what do you know over in Canada?" He said, "A large amusement park — Crystal Beach … Ridgeway … Stephensville … Fort Erie." Now he lived there. I told him when I left there was a prisoner of war camp for German troops in Niagara Falls. I said, "You SOB, you'll probably get back to Niagara Falls before I will!"

"That would be funny," he says! We had a laugh over it.

Infantry running down Coster Street, Groningen.

Liberation at last in Groningen: a patriotic Dutchman throwing small flags to crowd below.

John Drummond, Regina Rifle Regiment/Saskatoon Light Infantry

Our equipment certainly didn't come up to the standards that the Germans had. They had been getting ready for it for years. Our wireless equipment was pretty terrible. Very unreliable. We usually had to rely on field telephones, and if we had time to set up a system — a lot of time those Number 18 wireless sets wouldn't work.

Harry Fox, Hastings Prince Edward Regiment

The CO got cheesed off [at the lack of communication], so he took one man as an escort and went up to see the forward companies. For some reason we had been restricted to two vehicles, one was a hospital jeep and one was a truck that was our battalion headquarters — that one vehicle. I was there when this one soldier comes running to me and says he's lost the CO. I said, "Holy crow, how did that happen?"

"Well," he says, "a flight of mortar bombs come in, and of course I hit the grit, and when I got up the CO was gone." He said, "I looked around and couldn't see if he had been wounded or anything." We belted up the road and found where the mortar bombs had come in. You could see the craters, fresh ones, and smell the explosives. Then I thought, *Where's he going to go, the nearest company is Charlie Company, let's move off towards Charlie Company.* So we had gone I guess about a quarter of a mile when we came into a little clearing, and there's the CO with his pistol pointing it at a German prisoner. He told me later that he was in a quandary: he didn't want to shoot a helpless man, he couldn't take him with him up to the forward area, he couldn't very well go back with him as a prisoner because he wanted to see what was going on, so he was making up his mind to shoot him. The Jerry knew it and he was shivering, and the CO was shivering just as bad. I took the prisoner back.

The Germans were committed to a fighting retreat. Some towns were heavily defended, while others were simply evacuated. For the advancing Canadians, they had to be very careful to ensure which defensive plan was in effect by the Germans. Now more than ever, it was important to be on one's toes. The Germans pulled out of Zwolle on April 14, and the Canadians moved in.

Jim Parks, Royal Winnipeg Rifles

Zwolle was a different sort of thing, a cautious thing, and I remember the Dutch were becoming free and easy. We were in the outskirts, and I went back to get some rations, and there's this big commotion. All these girls that had been collaborating with the Germans — they were shaving their hair. One of the girls ran away and she ran into the building and she jumped off the fourth-storey roof. She got up to the top and jumped right off and killed herself. It's kind of a sad thing, but they said these people collaborated with the German soldiers and this is their punishment. Shaving their hair.

Heerenveen and Dokkum were liberated, as was Arnhem after several days of fighting. The people of Arnhem, who had had their hopes for liberation raised in September, could finally enjoy freedom! On the same day the Germans attempted an amphibious landing in the harbour of Anjum, but the Canadian troops and the Dutch Resistance turned them back in a hail of bullets and artillery.

John Drummond, Regina Rifle Regiment/Saskatoon Light Infantry

We went into Arnhem, and it had devastation. As we went further west we came across a lot of hungry people, starvation, that's what impressed me most, the condition of the people. It was pretty bad.

Joy spreads throughout the Netherlands: a crowd welcomes the Stormont, Dundas and Glengarry Highlanders to Leeuwarden.

On April 15 there was action all across the Netherlands as the Canadians continued their assault on German positions. That day they reached Waddenzee (at Zoutkamp), battled all day to liberate Woudsend, and began the assault on Apeldoorn. Elsewhere units were beginning to clear southwest Friesland, and the 3rd Division of the 2nd Canadian Corps arrived at Leeuwarden, bringing them within fifteen kilometres of the North Sea.

Lini Grol

We were in Friesland and our friends had a radio hidden, and you could hear Churchill say everything is fine, we are progressing. Every time you had hope that the end is coming soon. At a certain point we heard they were already in Zwolle and thought it must be getting close, and then they were in Meppel. City after city we could hear that they were there and so we waited. We had heard every time the Germans would blow up bridges before retreating, and we were very close to the bridge in our town. We expected the bridge to go before the Germans went, so we were really afraid and sitting in the basement. It was a strange quiet, and we thought at any moment — but no. Then finally we went out and we heard something like a rumbling and here came the tanks from the Canadians. People came out of their houses running. Well, the bridge is still there, the Germans haven't blown it, and they are gone. So we were lucky. Then everybody ran out of the house, and then the Canadians said, "Go back!" Everybody started coming with flowers. They really had to push the people away, they didn't know that the Germans had left, because they knew there was a bridge, so they expected the Germans to fight for the bridge. Quite peacefully they came into that town and they quietly went through it. That's when the Canadians went over the bridge and we knew we were free! Everybody went berserk!

The Perth Regiment advances through the streets of Arnhem.

As the 1st Canadian Corps moved north into the western region of the Netherlands, the men saw evidence of the hongerwinter. The further they went, the worse it got. The impact was devastating, as starving civilians mustered all of their strength to greet their liberators. Gaunt and desperate, they welcomed freedom and looked forward to the aid that came with it.

Gordon Mortensen, B.C. Dragoons

Oh, they were very, very receptive. We got great greetings. After the war we stayed over there for another several months, and we were staying in a town by the name of Veendam, and we made terrific friends in that particular area because all our men were billeted in various homes. I think Veendam became the sister city of Kelowna.

Gert van't Holt

I was five years old as the Canadian tanks came into my town. I still remember the smell of the diesel oil of the tanks. The tanks were stopping just before our house and out of the tank came a soldier and he came up to me — I was standing there with ten or fifteen children, and we got the first chocolate from a Canadian soldier. I still remember that because it was in April and it was a sunny day and I had a piece of chocolate in my hand and suddenly the chocolate was melting. I didn't know what it was, so the Canadian soldier said to me I had to lick it, and it tasted very sweet. My hand was totally brown. Suddenly out of the tank came a Negro soldier, and I had never seen a Negro, and I said to my sister, "Wow! The whole tank is full of this stuff!" That was my first memory of the Canadian soldiers.

John Honsberger, 4th Canadian Armoured Division

You'd see their orange banners, mixed with their flags — it was beautiful, they were ecstatic when we got in there. They were very hungry. That spring as we came through, the Dutch were really starved. You were a liberator for a few days or so and then we went into Germany and instead of seeing the Dutch orange banners there'd be sheets hanging out of the windows.

Mervin Durham, Royal Canadian Engineers

Oh my God — they'd make saints out of us all! They couldn't do enough for us. I felt I fought in two wars: the war of liberation, then the war of occupation. When we were in Holland we were liberators, when we got into Germany we were occupiers. It was a different situation entirely. We didn't get any welcome meals in Germany, which is understandable. But we certainly were well-treated in Holland. We passed through this little town. People were out cheering us, they hadn't see Canadians before. This Catholic priest came out of the church and he had two eggs in his hand — he wanted to know if we wanted an egg. But they were starving to death. I happened to be a Catholic, and I asked the priest if he could understand me, and he said somewhat, so I went to the confessional booth.

Al Sellers, Governor General's Horse Guards

We'd drive through and the people would follow us. We didn't see much of the celebrations, but the fellows who came behind us they saw everything, the Dutch were out there cheering them on. We would share our tank rations with them, personal parcels — give them away, no question. The Dutch people were so appreciative. For the kids, it was great. They loved chocolates, and of course everybody wanted cigarettes, which we always got in our parcels. Apart from that, they took us in — it was so nice to be sleeping in a house for a change.

Freedom and food: the Canadians delivered liberation, and then food. Here soldiers pass out biscuits to the children in Putten.

Many Dutch citizens were forced to find temporary shelter in basements, shacks, hen houses, and so on, due to German bombing.

Lini Grol

We were liberated on April 15, and the seventeenth was my father's birthday so we stayed until then, and on the eighteenth we cycled back to Nijmegen from Friesland. There were still Germans everywhere and they were still trying to fight. Little pockets of resistance. So we had to go around every time we were warned don't go there!

When we got to Nijmegen it was terrible. The heart of the city was completely destroyed. My father's house used to be there in the heart of Nijmegen. There were no houses to be had, there were no apartments or anything. I was just lucky I knew someone whose parents lived in the north. When I got into my hometown I thought, *I'll go tell her that her parents are all right since she can't reach them.* There was no telephone, there was no post. So I went to her and said, "Oh, your mother and father are fine, I saw them. I am going back, if you write a letter I can take it with me." I said, "You have a lovely house." She said, "It's rather big for us, we can't afford it." I said, "Can I see it?" She showed me, and this was really three small rooms and a bathroom in the attic, and I said, "Rent it to me." She said, "You can't get a permit." I said, "Oh yes, I've got a permit, but I can't find a house." And she said, "You can't live here, there are no windows, and there are holes in the roof, so how can you live here?" I said, "Well, my brother-in-law can take care of that," and he did. So because I went to help them, I got a house for my parents.

LEFT: *Dutch civilians filling holes in the road to allow Allied vehicles to enter Doesburg.*
RIGHT: *The 1st Canadian Division marching through liberated Apeldoorn. After five years of occupation, there could be no greater joy for the Dutch.*

On April 16 the 2nd Division of the 2nd Canadian Corps had finally cleared Groningen, and it was safe for the populace to celebrate. Elsewhere, Hattem, Afsluitdijk, Harlingen, and Franeker were liberated, while the troops shelled Lemmer to rout the German defenders there. In the eastern sector of the Netherlands, the 2nd Canadian Corps

196

Apeldoorn, 2004.   *Members of the 1st Canadian Division after the liberation of Apeldoorn.*

Dutch children with flag marching through the streets of the liberated city of Apeldoorn.

began clearing their sector, all the way to the German plains. Upon entering every town and city they were greeted with an overwhelming response. The cheers and kisses bolstered the spirits of the Canadian soldiers who had spent nearly a year in hard combat. For the Dutch, the arrival of the Canadians signalled the end of the darkest period in their history.

Freedom was spreading across the Dutch countryside. Apeldoorn, Lunteren, and Wageningen were liberated on April 17, Ermelo, Putten, the Ijsselmeer, and Makkum on April 18, and Loppersum on April 19. In a futile attempt to slow the Canadian advance, the Germans flooded Beemster and Schermer, north of Amsterdam.

John Drummond Regina Rifle Regiment/Saskatoon Light Infantry

I can remember the Royal Palace in Apeldoorn. The story was they had wild pigs in this fenced-off area belonging to the royal family, so a couple of guys got their rifles, got over this fence, and shot a wild boar. We got it out of there and tried cooking it, but it was a little too tough to eat. The 1st Division liberated Apeldoorn, and there's a lot of memories in that area.

Douglas Lavoie, Fort Garry Horse

Once Groningen was finished it was into Germany, a little town here and there, and we ended up at Oldenburg where we just about got killed. We were at a crossroads with a bridge that goes across the canal, and our job was to protect that crossroad. On the other side of the canal were a line of buildings that were two and three stories high, and we're just sitting there watching, and I could see these men running inside the buildings. I could see through the windows, and they were German soldiers. I said over the intercom, "You realize that there's Germans across there in those buildings?" And the commander said, "Yeah, yeah, yeah, I can see them." Well, we didn't do very much until a bazooka came out of one of the windows and it came across and landed right in front of the tank. And I said, "What are we going to do?" Well, he didn't do anything. I knew the gunner had an HE in the breach of our 75, so I just reached back as the driver can do, you can reach back and you can touch that solinoid switch that fires that gun, and that's what I did. The gun went off and there

Perth Regiment and Lord Strathcona Horse Unit tank loaded with Dutch children in Harderwijk celebrating liberation.

was dust and rocks and bricks flying out of that building, but no more bazookas. All I could hear was some yelling up in the turret, the crew commander giving the gunner hell for firing the gun. I never said a word after that.

Bill Clifford, RCAF

I did my last operational trip on April 20. That same day we moved to Celle, just west of Hamburg. Our aircraft were all shot up, and I led the squadron to the new base. The sun was setting and there was a forest fire blowing smoke across our landing strip, and we were going into another grass field. On April 22 the squadron was scheduled to fly to Warmwell in

England for an air firing exercise and a bit of rest for three weeks. During the short stopover at Celle we witnessed the liberation of Bergen-Belsen concentration camp. Anne Frank had died there less than a month previous.

I flew ninety-two trips total completing my tour of operation, most of which were done from Eindhoven. Fifteen of my fellow pilots were killed during that period, and three of them were retrieved and buried there.

The Hastings Prince Edward Regiment (of the 1st Canadian Division) in the bush.

The Germans were increasingly cut off and being squeezed into a smaller and smaller amount of occupied territory. On April 21 the Germans defending Appingedam were under attack. Two days later the town was free.

On April 23 the Battle of the Delfzijl Pocket began. For ten days the Canadians engaged the Germans around the Dutch port of Delfzijl, where the Nazis had built a naval fortress. The defences were formidable. Huge coastal gun emplacements, minefields, and a determined naval garrison awaited the Canadians. The Perth Regiment cleared the northern approach to Delfzijl, taking eight hundred prisoners. It was a desperate, last-ditch effort by the Germans. With the defences breached, the final assault on the port occurred at the beginning of May.

Delfzijl, Dutch port on the northernmost coast of the Netherlands. The German base at Delfzijl was one of the last major that the Canadians encountered in defences in the Netherlands.

Jim Parks, Royal Winnipeg Rifles

So there were a lot of skirmishes when we went up to Groningen and then we went along the coast and we ended up around Emden, which is across from Delfzijl — it was a little rough there. We were set up behind this house and they started firing a 75mm. Somebody said, "Let's get the hell out of here!" So I ran like mad to this window and just got my foot in the window and that's the last I remember — I saw orange flame. The guys were inside already and they came flying across the room. Those Dutch houses, they have the beds in the wall, you pull it apart and there's room underneath. I went flying underneath there, and when they eventually yanked me out, I was unconscious. I was evacuated by jeep, they dropped me off at the RAP centre. They could find all kinds of little stones on my face and on my back — you know, gravel. My ear — everything was hollow, like talking in a barrel. This is the fourth time this had happened, and the doctor said it would all come back. I was in a hurry to go back to my unit because I didn't want to get shipped back to the hospital. I went back, but the hearing never came back. I remember sitting in a yard that had a fence and what they were doing was sending airbursts over. I couldn't hear them. I had the phone up to one ear and the other ear was no good. I could see these little puffs of smoke — dust coming off the fence. I just dropped everything and headed back into the barn to get out of the way.

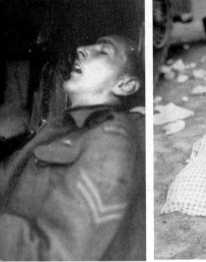

Lockhart Fulton, Royal Winnipeg Rifles

The fighting was sporadic. The Germans would occasionally stop and fight; the next time they would pull out before you got there. We had some fairly difficult times and had some casualties that were very hard to take. One was a company commander by the name of Brian Robertson. When I had commanded the carrier platoon he had been my second-in-command, and he was a very fine officer. We thought all we had to do was take over the guns on the Ems River. We were told it was just a question of them surrendering, and I sent Brian with his company to take their surrender. When he got there he found that they weren't about to surrender. He had set up his headquarters in a house and he was getting an attack lined up when a burst of machine gun fire came through the window, and he had his hand in his pocket and the bullet went through his hand and through his stomach just at the lower part of it. He was badly wounded. He was brought back as quickly as they could to the regimental aid post and he was just touch and go when they got him there, but they kept putting blood into him and he recovered. Once I put the battalion on the move, myself and the adjutant and my third company commander, the three of us went back to the forward medical station that Brian was in just to see him because we thought

TOP: *Far from the comforts of home: J. Harris uses an open-air latrine.* LEFT: *Fast asleep after an exhausting campaign.* RIGHT: *Every opportunity to catch up on sleep had to be taken.*

so much about him. He seemed fine, and I will always remember talking to the doctor when I left, could he tell me for sure that Brian would be all right. "Yeah," he said, "he'll be okay, we'll send him back to England shortly."

By April 28 the Germans had been backed into an area bordered by Wageningen to Amersfoort and by the coastline. The situation for the Dutch civilians trapped in the occupied territory was beyond desperate. For the Germans, there were two camps: professional soldiers who did not desire to see civilians suffer and soldiers who were concerned about how they would be dealt with for their actions during the war. The result was a truce with the Canadians, and arrangements were negotiated for the delivery of food to the civilians. On April 30 Operation Manna was launched. Four drop zones were agreed upon, and Allied bombers ran missions over the Netherlands dropping food instead of bombs. The next day the operation was expanded to eleven drop zones, and in total 5,356 mercy flights were made, dropping 10,913 tons of food. The relief was incredible for the starving Dutch people. Also on May 1, German and Canadian envoys met in De Nude to negotiate Operation Faust, while telephone links were wired up between the headquarters of both sides for closer coordination of the relief efforts.

Sydney Frost, Princess Patricia's Canadian Light Infantry

We got as far as Achterveld. We arrived there just in time, the Germans were about to blow up their very sacred church. It's a beautiful church, it's been there for centuries. Those Germans were going to blow it up just for spite. We got there just in time and saved the church, and the Dutch have never forgotten it.

There is a plaque that the Dutch erected in 2000 to honour the Princess Patricia's Canadian Light Infantry, who had saved their church. It says, "Canadian soldiers from Princess Patricia's Canadian Light Infantry prevented the destruction of the parish church of Achterveld used as an observation post. We thank these soldiers who saved the heart of our village." Isn't that a touching thing? That is now enshrined as a monument, and we had a big parade in the year 2000 and they presented this plaque to me as well.

The church at Achterveld that was saved by the Princess Patricia's Canadian Light Infantry from being blown up by the retreating German forces.

Plaque honouring the PPCLI for saving the church at Achterveld.

Building where the Food Truce negotiations were held in Achterveld. The negotiations for the distribution of food to the Dutch population eventually led to surrender talks.

Al Armstrong, 14th Canadian Hussars

When we got farther up into Holland the situation became desperate, and a German commander came out because we were on their tail all the way up and asked for a truce. So our commander spoke to him, and he said, "What you're going to find as you advance north of here, I'm not responsible for." The Canadian commander said, "You are responsible, you conquered these people and it's up to you to feed them." The upshot of the whole thing was they called a seven-day truce and the war stopped.

Sydney Frost, Princess Patricia's Canadian Light Infantry

On April 30 the bigwigs from the German Army, including this Seyss-Inquart and his chief of staff General Blaskowitz, and all the Allied representatives from Montgomery's army, from the Americans too, Bedell Smith was there, and even a Russian colonel, they were represented. They signed the food truce, and the supplies started going in immediately. Now where they signed the food truce was right in my company area, a schoolhouse, and today it's a shrine. Prince Bernhard was there too, and he drove a Mercedes Benz that Seyss-Inquart had driven. It had been captured by the Allies, without Seyss-Inquart, about two or three months earlier, so we presented it to Prince Bernhard. He was the first up, and he drove right up to this schoolhouse door and stopped so that when Seyss-Inquart arrived a little later, he had to hobble around his own Mercedes Benz to get to the entrance. Oh, he was annoyed! Miserable little man, he was subsequently hung for his crimes. He was one of the war criminals. He did terrible things to the Dutch. So all of this happened in my company area, and I'm very proud of that.

The Allied air force dropped 11 million rations into occupied Holland. Each day sixteen hundred tons of provisions by truck were sent through the lines into western Holland, and that saved the Dutch.

We had guards and armed soldiers accompany the trucks, and we made darn sure it went to the Dutch and not to the Germans. The

LEFT: *Statue erected in Achterveld commemorating the Food Truce.* ABOVE: *Bombers refitted for dropping food instead of bombs made the flight over the Netherlands without a shot being fired. The sight was a huge relief for the Dutch.*

Germans couldn't do much about this. It was weird because they were fully armed, we were fully armed, and in many cases the Dutch were armed, and everybody was just glaring at each other, just waiting for the first guy to shoot somebody and there would have been a complication. It didn't happen. So they got their food, oh yes, they got their food.

Corrie Schogt

In April '45 the Allied forces were allowed to drop food — fantastic. We had a flat roof and we were standing there and the bomber's doors opened — they were very close to us.

Henry Schogt

In Amsterdam it was the same.

Corrie Schogt

And the food came out. I mean bags, and it was not very well protected so a lot of it smashed, we could sort it out, much could be salvaged.

ABOVE: *An Allied bomber dropping food during Operation Manna.*
BELOW: *Drop zones had been negotiated and the supplies were quickly collected to be distributed to a desperately starving population.*

ABOVE: *A food drop at Duindigt racetrack near The Hague.*
BELOW: *The collection of food crates at Schiphol Airport, Amsterdam.*

Elly Dull

It's just outside of Amsterdam they dropped things like corned beef, white bread, margarine — basics. It was incredible to see that in the stores the next day. I remember being ill because I couldn't tolerate milk products or bread made with milk. That really upset our digestive system because we hadn't had it for so long. It took away some of the joy, but we really, really had too much of it at the time. And then it was party time.

On the dikes in the northern region of the Netherlands.

Royal Winnipeg Rifles War Diary, May 1 1945

At 2230 hrs the BBC reported that the German News had stated Hitler died in Berlin today.

As negotiations went on in the northwest for aid, the Battle of Delfzijl was heating up. With the main defences breached, the 5th Armoured Division battled the Germans to take the northern port. For the Cape Breton Highlanders it was some of the toughest fighting they faced in the entire war. Thousands of Germans surrendered, but a fanatical few fought to the end, bitterly trying to kill whoever they could before dying themselves. On May 2, after ten days, Delfzijl was secured when the Germans surrendered to the Irish Regiment of Canada.

That day Operation Faust had Canadian truck convoys cross the German front line at Rhenen. All was quiet with the ceasefire in place, and the convoy reached the starving communities in the occupied zone. May 2 also saw Queen Wilhelmina and Princess Juliana return to Breda. For Princess Margriet it was the first time she had been on Dutch soil. It was a grand moment for the Netherlands.

Royal Winnipeg Rifles War Diary, May 2, 1945

The day was spent in cleaning weapons and getting equipment into shape. In the evening, T.F. Cox put on a show, which everyone enjoyed. At 1900 hrs we heard over the BBC that the German Army in Italy had unconditionally surrendered and later on that Berlin had fallen. The general feeling is that it can't last much longer now.

Sydney Frost, Princess Patricia's Canadian Light Infantry

We were still, of course, armed and waiting for the truce to end and the fighting to begin again. So we didn't do much fooling around and we stayed where we were at our outposts. We let the service corps deal with the food distribution. I must say that they did it awfully well. The organization — can you imagine? The moment the truce was signed the trucks started to roll right through day and night. The Germans just couldn't believe it, this armada if you will of trucks — by that stage they had no trucks, and that told the Germans they were finished.

ABOVE: *Operation Manna. A convoy of trucks filled with food moved to German-occupied territory in western Netherlands.*
RIGHT: *Canadians posing in front of a windmill.*

On May 4 the war was clearly ending. Field Marshal Montgomery called on the Dutch Resistance to refrain from military activities, even though they continued to provide temporary civilian authority until the country was back on its feet again. Negotiations were underway for the surrender of the Germans in the Netherlands. The Second World War was about to end for the Dutch and, in the following days, for all of Europe.

Mervin Durham, Royal Canadian Engineers

I was in Germany, and we were building a bridge. We were in the middle of a battle, actually, when a dispatch rider came up to my troop and he handed me a note, and it read like this: "As of 0800 hours May 5th 1945 hos-

tilities will cease forthwith. All troops standby until further orders." We had a man killed that night, which should never have happened. They postponed the date on this ceasefire order since the Germans had no communications. One outfit can't stop the war and another one keep going, so today they set up for tomorrow morning.

Lockhart Fulton, Royal Winnipeg Rifles

We were in a position in Germany, and I had been told that I was to attack the city of Aurich the next morning. There was a canal around the city, and they had blown all the bridges. So I was looking to see how in the world we were going to get across to fight this battle. There had been some talk on our radio in the scout car as we were coming up there that there was a big session going on, and when I got back I was told that the Germans had asked for an armistice, a ceasefire. We were to stay put where we were and to take no further action. Which were the most pleasant words I ever heard in my life! Eventually a message in writing came down that the ceasefire would be at 0800 the next morning. At the same time another message was included that Brian Robertson had died of wounds. What had happened was that they didn't have the kind of antibiotics to work outside the circulation system and infection started and it grew fast and he died. One of the messages we had looked forward to for about a year, and the other was the worst thing that could have possibly happened. Your finest company commander has died of wounds. Brian was twenty-four years old and is buried in Holland at Holten.

TOP: *Canadians in the Netherlands.* BOTTOM: *The grave of Brian Robertson of the Royal Winnipeg Rifles at the Canadian War Cemetery in Holten.*

John Honsberger, 4th Canadian Armoured Division

The message came through that at eight o'clock there'd be a ceasefire. Here we were suddenly unemployed. I remember the war was over, and we were kind of standing around in the front of this house and discussing what would happen next. Then about eleven-thirty that night, geez, I thought the war had started all over again. There was a tremendous barrage that seemed to be almost on top of us. We did find out that what had happened was that this Polish division that had been coming up on our left flank had got right beside us and they received the same order that there would be a ceasefire at midnight. We heard afterwards that the Poles had decided as a point of honour that they would not enter into the ceasefire with any unused ammunition. They fired everything they had at eleven-thirty at night to comply with the terms of the ceasefire, and it was all over at midnight.

CHAPTER SEVEN

DE BEVRIJDING
May 5, 1945

Representatives of Germany had negotiated an unconditional surrender for northwest Germany, Denmark, and the Netherlands with Field Marshal Montgomery on May 4 and then signed the document of surrender dated May 5, 1945. Orders were sent to German General Blaskowitz (who stubbornly insisted on excluding western Netherlands from the surrender) to commence with separate negotiations. On May 5 Blaskowitz met with Allied negotiators at the Hotel De Wereld in Wageningen. Included in the Allied group were Canadian Lieutenant-General Foulkes and Prince Bernhard of the Netherlands. Meanwhile, on the other Canadian front, General Simonds accepted the German surrender at Bad Zwischenahn. Negotiations with Blaskowitz dragged on, and eventually he signed the documents of capitulation.

The Second World War was over for the Netherlands, and an uproar of jubilation resounded across the country. The news was greeted with a mixture of relief and joy. For many, freedom meant the chance to eat again. The streets were crowded with a proud people — maybe starved and beaten, but never defeated.

Ada Wynston

I was just north enough not to be liberated in September 1944, my sister and brother were, they were in the extreme south. We weren't liberated until May 5, 1945. I did see Canadians, although I didn't know who they were. They were screaming in the house the war was over, so I ran out of the house. I went up the bridge and I stood by the

LEFT: *Accepting surrender at Wageningen, on May 5, 1945.* RIGHT: *Lieutenant-General Charles Foulkes (left centre) accepts the surrender of German forces in the Netherlands from General Johannes Blaskowitz.*

Dutch girls walk arm in arm with Canadians. The joy of liberation and the relief of the war ending made for a heightened level of emotions that lasted for a very long time.

church and I saw a bunch of young men in uniform, and I knew they weren't Nazis because they didn't have the helmets and the stern look. They were sort of tired and worn out because they had a long trek, and those were the first Canadians that I ever saw. I wasn't afraid of them, they looked different than the Nazis, and I thought, *Well, now I can go home. Holland is free now.* We were the last to be liberated.

Elly Dull

I think there were some British and Polish troops that I remember seeing, but mostly the Canadians. We lived in the south of Amsterdam near the only skyscraper, twelve storeys high, and they came right across the Amstel bridge, and I remember standing there as a child. I still vividly remember standing on that certain spot, trying to reach them, and the people were so fanatical about being close to them, so hysterical about seeing them. The Canadians had hands full of cigarettes and chocolates, and they just threw them off so that the people would disperse for a moment so they could advance another two or three metres. I was so desperate to get to this truck and to find some chocolates or cigarettes or anything, then somebody very, very thin picked me up and put me in the cabin of this truck, right on the lap of the guy who drove. There I was, it was just a phenomenal experience, I was right front and centre, higher than anybody else. They gave me chocolates, and I drove in that truck with them out of Amsterdam halfway to Haarlem, and that town is called Halfweg, and eventually they put me out on the street and I walked back to Amsterdam.

Gert van't Holt

Oh, it was a lot of days of joy, festivities. I saw my sister dancing with the soldiers in the market, a fairly big crowd of people cheering and waving the Dutch flag. I was too young to know what it was all about.

Liedewij Hawke

I remember clearly the mood of total excitement, exhilaration, the release of joy. There were many celebrations in different parts of the village of De Bilt and Bilthoven. There were parades, there were costumed people, there was an enormous feeling of togetherness. Great friendliness and delirious relief. Great, enormous joy. That mood was just beginning. On the seventh of May the Polar Bears arrived in their tanks, and Prince Bernhard was among them. He happened to be on his way to the west. My father lifted me onto his shoulders, and I remember seeing all those tanks and the enormous joy. Those were the Canadians who liberated us.

Lini Grol

We were elated! On cloud nine — all the time. We were all running around. That first moment when the Canadians went by and they went over the bridge we knew that we're free. Then we ran out, and everybody hugged everybody and kissed everybody, and then they said, "Let's go to church." We all went to church to pray and thank God that

While the war ended on May 5th, numerous Dutch cities had to wait several days to welcome the liberators. The liberation of Utrecht came days later.

The roundup of the Dutch Nazis and SS by the Resistance in Amsterdam. Trials would be held, some would be executed, and many would be imprisoned for their crimes.

Children celebrating the liberation. Joy of unprecedented levels enveloped the country.

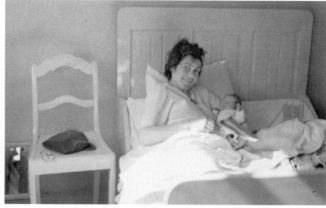

Albert Johan Maria Spook, a child born during the 1st Canadian Division artillery bombardment of Apeldoorn (April 14), with his mother.

Liberation day in a small Dutch town.

A Canadian armoured car on Dam Square in Amsterdam surrounded by a crowd of joyous Dutch citizens.

we were free. Catholics and Protestants in the Catholic church. The Catholic church was always open, that was the difference, of course. We had a Protestant church, which was open later on, but that first moment everybody said the first church was all right! The Jews that came out of hiding came to pray too.

Jack Heidema

Liberation came, church bells were ringing, and my mom and I stood on the sidewalk and we held hands and cried. There was no joy. The joy came later on. We had gone through too damn much. Seen too much. And had too much pain and suffering. When liberation came, a lot of people went wild — we just didn't have it.

Rationing continued well after the liberation as a regular supply of food and materials had to be established. Here two girls write down the ration amounts available.

For the Canadian soldiers, the exhilaration of the reception was buoyed with the knowledge that the war was over. It seemed almost unreal for many of them. The realization was sinking in that they had indeed survived and would soon get to go home again. That was a reason to celebrate in itself. Victory was sweet, but home was even sweeter.

Sydney Frost, Princess Patricia's Canadian Light Infantry

We fully expected the war to start again after the food truce, with this crazy nut Seyss-Inquart, we were ready for it. In the meantime, Hitler shot himself and the German Army under Blaskowitz surrendered in Holland on May 5, so our war was over on May 5, and to this date it is celebrated in Holland as liberation day. Not May 8, because that was the official day of the surrender of the entire German Army, not just the ones in Holland. So they make that distinction and they are very proud of it.

Doug Barrie, Highland Light Infantry

The Canadians were well-regarded and well-treated and certainly well-liked because we were able to liberate a good part of Holland. We could do no wrong, they couldn't do enough for us! They were wonderful. They had no food, and we were able to pass on food to them, and they've never forgotten us.

Norman Edwards, 14th Canadian Hussars

We were in Groningen on May 5. We lost an armoured car the night before the ceasefire. That was a very traumatic experience. We were just pushing ahead and I guess somebody was exposed and there were three men killed. So instead of celebrating on the next day, we went to a funeral. That's an experience that you remember.

Harry Fox, Hastings Prince Edward Regiment

Well, I was going back to England on leave that night, and I wondered what the heck was going on — I could see mortar flares going up all over the place. So when we got off the train we were told that the war was over, that the

Bonds of friendship: young girls offer fruit to a Canadian soldier.

General Simonds addressing the men about going home at Bad Zwischenahn.

Germans had surrendered. So I was on my way to England on leave at that time, I had ten good days!

Doug Shaughnessy, Royal Hamilton Light Infantry

I can remember I was on guard duty at the front gate and the war had ended the previous day and all of a sudden down the road came a big Mercedes Benz, and out came about four German officers, and this guy came up to me and he clicked his heels and he said, "We wish to see your commanding officer." So I said, "Just wait here," and I went over and I got the colonel. So he was a little sleepy and came out, and the German officer said, "We want to have some benzine," that's gasoline, of course, and he said, "What the hell do you want gasoline for?"

"Well, we're going to Berlin." And the colonel said, "You go back to where the hell you came from and I'll tell you when you can go to Berlin!" So they had to go back.

Mervin Durham, Royal Canadian Engineers

We were in Germany, and we checked into this place to have a little celebration, we had quite a bit of liquor on hand. Not to the extent of getting rowdy and so on, but anyway it was quite a celebration.

I got word that night from Major Leggett, he said, "Sergeant, you have one more bridge to build." He said there was something like thirty thousand troops coming in from the south. I said, "Sir, if you can find sober men in this outfit, we'll build it right now." So he got serious: "You haven't got time for that. You have that bridge to build at eight o'clock in the morning." I said, "If you can find a sober man we can build it tonight, sir." He said, "You'll build it at eight o'clock in the morning." It took us three hours to build a bridge that we would normally build in twenty-five minutes.

Sydney Frost, Princess Patricia's Canadian Light Infantry

The people went absolutely berserk. The Dutch are supposed to be stolid, calm people … they climbed all over our cars and our trucks and they kissed us and embraced us. We had some great parties, I'll tell you. It was a wonderful time to be with the regiment, a wonderful time to be alive. Not many people had that thrill, but I did, and I'll never forget it. Many times I'm asked, "What was the most important part of your service?" That was it, right there. It all seemed worthwhile, all the wounds and the suffering, suddenly it seemed very much worthwhile.

With new friends on Marken Island, July 1945.

Crowd celebrating the liberation of The Hague, almost five years to the day after the Germans invaded.

On May 8, VE Day was being celebrated throughout the Allied countries as the Germans finally surrendered. The Second World War was officially over in Europe.

That same day the Canadians entered Rotterdam. The welcome was emotional, and it was repeated in Amsterdam and The Hague.

Lockhart Fulton, Royal Winnipeg Rifles

There were no ships for us to go home. The war ended for us on the fifth of May, and we didn't get out of Holland until August. So we spent months in Holland trying to keep order.

Charles Barrett, Highland Light Infantry

We were up in the north of Holland at the end of the war. The day after we were at brigade headquarters and a couple of vehicles arrived and a German officer was escorted in. He was introduced as Colonel Schilling. We had been hearing about Colonel Schilling all the way up the coast from Boulogne, Cap Gris-Nez, up into the Scheldt, and he always disappeared. He was never there when we took the area, somehow he got out. We were talking to him, we weren't supposed to do this because you were supposed to let intelligence interrogate him at a higher level. But the war was over and I suppose we were relaxed.

We were talking, and I asked him what he thought was our most effective weapon, and it was our Typhoon bombers. I asked why is that? He said when he was in

TOP LEFT: *The aftermath: death permeated the larger cities as reminders of the dreaded hongerwinter.* ABOVE: *Headquarter of the 8th Canadian Field Squadron of the Royal Canadian Engineers.* BOTTOM LEFT: *Canadian soldiers visiting Amsterdam in July 1945.*

this position across from us in northern Holland he had called his commanders in to a little farmhouse that was very isolated. He gave strict instructions that said not to approach in any vehicle whatsoever, he didn't want to leave any tracks that would show from the air. It was an inconspicuous little house, and he thought he was quite secure there. So he is sitting with his commanders in the front room of the farmhouse and discussing the situation. He went back into a rear room to get some maps, and while he was there, there was a big explosion and the front of the farmhouse was gone. He lost all his commanders. He said at that point he realized the war was over as far as he was concerned.

Well, apparently this was a Typhie attack that we organized. I remember very well that it was a clear sunny day in the north of Holland and we were getting prisoners coming in and we kept having them interrogated to find out where their command post was. Several of them pointed this place out on our map. Finally after we got enough of them who said this was their command post, he thought, *Well, maybe this is it in fact.* It was a beautiful day, and we had a group of Typhoon bombers that were circling above us waiting for instructions. I went to the air liaison officer and I gave him this coordinates on the map. So we watched these Typhies straighten out over ahead of us and vectored down and fired the rockets, and I think this was the occasion that ended the war for Colonel Schilling. It was an interesting meeting with him when it was all over.

Mervin Durham, Royal Canadian Engineers

On the thirteenth of May I had a letter to all troops, and here's basically what it contained: They wanted volunteers for the Pacific and you get home immediately, and I took the hook. I volunteered for the Pacific along with about ten of the other guys, and it was another six weeks before I got back to Canada. So they fooled me on that. Some of the boys joined up for the army of occupation, but I joined up for the Pacific.

Ada Wynston

The feeling was, "I want to go home. I wonder where my mother and father and brother and sister are." By then I was not nine yet, and the Dutch family that hid me kept me there for a while. My father showed up, which is a horror story because I didn't know who he was. I saw somebody coming up the drive on a bicycle without tires. They always told me during the war if you see somebody you don't know, you know where your second hiding place is, and this is exactly what I did, four months after the war was over. I crawled under the table because I didn't know who the man was. I didn't come out. He had to go back, and he came back in another month, two months later, and they dragged me out. He had my doll with him, and that was the only way that I would trust him. He had been given the addresses of my brother and sister, and he told us he couldn't take us home because he had no wife. So from that point on my war parents said, "Maybe you should go and visit your brother and go find him." So I ended up at my brother's, who was in the extreme south of Holland. He was this little blonde-haired, blue-eyed boy who was six years old by then, a devout Roman Catholic — he had been hidden by Roman Catholics, and of course he had to be the same as they were. They loved him, they had no children. I showed up there, and they told me if I want to stay, I'm welcome, but you've got to learn to pray the Roman Catholic prayers. So there I learned everything about Roman Catholicism for the three months that I could muster, and then I said I want to go and visit my sister. She was only fifteen minutes away. So I said goodbye to my brother, who had no idea he had sisters. I went to visit my sister, and this was 1946, and I stayed there for a year and a half. We stayed together until my father came and said that he had found somebody to marry him and we had to go home. To my sister and my brother, and to me only partly, this was the worst part of the war because your war parents were good to you all these years and you had to leave.

The war was over, but there was still much to do. Aid kept pouring in with food and medical supplies. Germans were still being disarmed. On May 8 eighteen thousand Germans defending the coastline were taken prisoner. On May 10 the 34th SS surrendered to the Canadians, and the next day there was a surrender of holdouts at Ridderkerk. Here and there pockets of resistance held out until June, but once they were cleared the Netherlands was safe again.

While celebrations and parades gave the Canadians and Dutch a chance to enjoy their victory, there was a country to recover. Canadians cleared mines and rebuilt bridges across the Netherlands. Operation Eclipse saw the repatriation of 120,000 German soldiers. War criminals were weeded out and put on trial. The evil of the past five years was coming back to haunt its perpetrators.

Caught up in the joy of De Bevrijding, many young Canadian soldiers and young Dutch women found each other irresistible, and the result was an astonishing number of Dutch war brides. As the stay of the Canadian soldiers extended for months, the number of unions increased, as well as the number of children being born to Canadian fathers. In August 1945 the Canadian Embassy responded by opening the Bureau of Dutch Spouses. In total, 41,351 war brides moved to Canada after the Second World War, made up primarily of British and Dutch nationals. In addition, 19,737 young children went home to Canada with their fathers in uniform. The bonds between Canada and the Netherlands were being drawn tight through marriage and family.

Canadian soldier with a Dutch woman in Volendam.

Martin van Denzen

Even now with the Dutch radio program that I do ... sometimes I get in contact with Dutch war brides that married Canadians. They sometimes talk about their experiences, how tough it was. What they went through, it was very hard on them because they hardly spoke English; you know love is a universal language, but then when the things all settled down it was very tough for them sometimes when they came here.

Elly Dull

I remember the next Christmas some people had Canadians as houseguests. It's the fifth of December when the saint comes from Spain, it's very different, it's not Santa Claus from the North Pole — our Santa Claus comes from Spain and he's a bishop and he comes on the fifth of December. If you could get your hands on a liberating soldier and invite him into your home, that was a real prestigious thing to have. Many girls who were older than I was, they went out with Canadians, and we kept hearing that they were leaving, that they were marrying, that they had babies.

LEFT AND RIGHT: *Canadians helping to rebuild the Netherlands.*

Canadian soldiers enjoying some sightseeing during the wait to go home. RCE members shown: Hancock, Dolan, Black, and Neely.

Canadian soldiers visiting the first locks.

By October 1945, 110,000 (of 282,000) Canadian servicemen were able to return home as more and more transport ships became available. The welcome of the war heroes was warm and heartfelt, but nothing matched the emotional outpouring of the liberation of the Netherlands. The bond between liberator and liberated was such that nothing else could compare.

John Honsberger, 4th Canadian Armoured Division

I think we were all pretty stressed out. We were exhausted, tired, and that lasted for sometime. It had a long-term effect. I remember being back home months later and going up University Avenue at noon hour and a car backfired. I just

At long last! A Canadian soldier returns home to his family after many years serving his country.

Amsterdam 1945.

Canadian soldiers posing on the North Sea. Left to right: Auld, Black, Dolan, and Hosler.

threw myself on the sidewalk. People were staring at me. That's how you responded in the war — you just hit the ground. But here I was doing this six, seven, eight months later.

John Drummond, Regina Rifle Regiment/ Saskatoon Light Infantry

In fact when we first came home when the war was over it seemed that no one was interested. No one asked questions where you were, what it was like. It was just like when you come home, okay, get on with your life, get married, get a job, raise a family, and it wasn't until after we retired that a lot of us, the combat vets, realized that it was common amongst us that after you retired, this all came to the front again. It was almost like you put the whole thing into a compartment in your brain and it comes out after you're older.

On January 3, 1946, General Simonds returned home to Canada, and by May the Canadians had closed their headquarters in the Netherlands. Canada's military role in the country was complete, but the bonds would last longer than anyone could have imagined at that time.

DE BEVRIJDING
May 5, 1945

Canadian servicemen relaxing and enjoying the Dutch scenery.

During the Second World War Canada committed more to the war effort and the cause of freedom than could be expected. In relation to population, no other country gave more. Of a population of 11 million people, an incredible 10 percent served in uniform. In only six years, Canada was able to build the world's fourth largest navy, a powerful air force, and a formidable army. The importance of duty and the fight for freedom was so ingrained in Canadians that little prompting was needed to get citizens to answer the call. On the home front, *matériel* was manufactured at unprecedented rates, and the result was an economic boom for the nation.

More importantly, Canada gained a great reputation and earned respect, honour, and friendship that would last forever. In the war for democracy and freedom, Canada found a place among the world powers. Sacrifices were willingly made in the quest for the good of humanity.

Because of its role in the Second World War, Canada became a founding member of the United Nations. On April 14, 1949, the Netherlands joined Canada as a member of NATO, thereby solidifying a bond that guaranteed that the two nations would support and protect each other. It was a bond between friends.

The Second World War took an incredible toll on the Netherlands in lives and suffering. It was a neutral country that was invaded, occupied, and dragged into a war. The suffering of the Dutch was unparalleled in their history. Seventy-five percent of Dutch Jews had been exterminated — the largest percentage of any country, with the exception of Poland. Yet the plight of the Jews was not due to anti-Semitism in the Netherlands. More Dutch have been honoured as "righteous Gentiles" by the Yad Vashem (the Holocaust Martyrs' and Heroes' Remembrance Authority in Israel) than any other people during the Second World War. The Netherlands actively protected Jews and was the only Nazi-occupied country to have a general strike to protest the pogroms.

Ada Wynston

I think those who hid me are heroes, I'm still in touch with the kids and they're all from seventy on down, and I have lost three of my war sisters and brothers, they have died. I arranged for them to get the gold medal of Israel, the Yad Vashem medal. It took me five years, but I thought it was very important that you step up and say, "I know what you did, it could have cost you your family," and unfortunately the parents died before Israel decided to say yes. I was asked by the state of Israel to come to Holland, to go to the synagogue where it would happen and thank all these people who saved our lives when we were children. So I was there when the kids got the medals and when my rescuer, who was in the armed forces, got his, and he won't talk about anything. He and I talk. He hadn't seen

TOP LEFT: *Westerbork: the memorial to those who died. Each block represents a precious life lost in the Holocaust in the Netherlands.* TOP RIGHT: *Westerbork: the impact of the loss to the Netherlands.* LEFT: *The victims of Westerbork.* RIGHT: *Monument to the victims of the Holocaust erected by Israel at Westerbork.*

me in forty-eight years and he picked me out of the crowd. He was eighteen at that time. He received a gold medal, and he thanked the state of Israel on behalf of all the rescuers. These people took a risk, whether they knew it or not. It was mostly because their religion had taught them to help your neighbour, whatever the consequences.

Henry Schogt

At the end of the war people didn't have many illusions about the fate of the Jews. Whereas the non-Jews had a much greater chance of survival, even when they were in Germany, even when they were in a concentration camp.

Corrie Schogt

There were people who knew more, and other people who didn't believe it or didn't want to hear it. I think Henry's family was very aware of the great dangers and the horrific things that happened. I was young and hopeful — those years were very grim, I was always waiting for the moment it would be over and the family would be reunited and we would live happily ever after. Well, that didn't materialize. I was still in school at the end of June, and I would go to all the Red Cross lists that came out, but only the people who had survived were on those lists. Slowly my sisters and I realized that they [her parents] had not survived, and slowly we heard, of course, from our relatives who had seen them off on one of the last trains from Theresienstadt to Auschwitz.

ABOVE: *The wall of names of those who passed through Westerbork. The thousands of names are a staggering reminder of what happened there.* LEFT: *Memorial at Westerbork museum.*

Henry Schogt

They were on one of the last trains from Theresienstadt, and one of the last gassings at Auschwitz. They stopped gassing in early November and they went in late October — it was maybe a difference of ten days. We knew and we didn't know. This is one of the problems that nobody came back. It was obvious what was happening when they started raiding an old people's home and there were people from that home in their eighties or nineties or I think even the oldest was 102 — and sent for work in Germany, and the same with babies.

Corrie Schogt

I don't remember what we thought at the time.

Henry Schogt

I remember what I thought but I also remember that I always hoped that …

Corrie Schogt

… that they would come back.

Henry Schogt

I had a friend, and until the moment that I saw his name in an enormous book that was published in '95 with all the names of the victims of the Holocaust in Holland, I still hoped. Corrie's parents are also in that book. You see it in print, and that is the definitive end.

Al Armstrong, 14th Canadian Hussars

When we go into the schools as speakers I always take the Anne Frank story with me, especially when I'm speaking on Holland. Everybody should know about the Anne Frank story. Anne Frank died in March 1945 — if we had been any quicker maybe we could have done something for her and people like Anne Frank. Anne Frank is not an isolated story, there's a lot of Anne Franks, and there's a lot of the Dutch that hid the Jewish people — a lot of them, more than people realize.

The Netherlands was a nation that resisted, sometimes passively with non-violence, sometimes through underground military action. Unwilling to submit to the oppressive Nazi regime, the Dutch organized one of the most effective resistance movements of the war. Despite the dangers, they retained their identity and would not be coerced into accepting an ideology that was at odds with their morals. They may have been powerless to stop the atrocities around them, but they did speak out against them. Refusal to remain quiet says a great deal about their character and bravery — two things that the Dutch people were glowing examples of in the darkest of eras.

For two countries that did not have close ties prior to the Second World War, Canada and the Netherlands did have a lot in common. Quiet and reserved, both were liberal-minded and peaceful, yet in the face of injustice they stood up for their convictions and showed a level of strength that is rarely exhibited — characteristics clearly exhibited by the

Dutch in how they handled their hardships during the war and also made evident by Canadians as they came to the aid of an oppressed nation.

The bonds between Canada and the Netherlands began early in the war, when the Dutch royal family was given safe haven in Canada. The welcome they received warmed their hearts. The Canadian public was moved by the family's plight and was charmed by the young Dutch princesses. These were friends in need, and Canada was a friend in deed.

Wedding of Captain R.B. Menzies (Highland Light Infantry) and Miss Pamela Manus Van Der Jagt in Vaarden.

The other key factor in their bond was the central role that Canada played in De Bevrijding. Most Dutch cities and towns were liberated by Canadian forces during the final nine months of the Second World War. More than seventy-six hundred Canadians gave their lives for Dutch freedom. Many more sacrificed their bodies to wounds in the quest for liberation from the Nazi oppression that enveloped Europe. Such sacrifice earned the gratitude of the Dutch people, as did the airlifts and convoys of food to the starving, the rebuilding of the country after the war, and, most importantly, the delivery of freedom, the most precious of all gifts. It is comforting to note that out of horror and despair such a friendship could blossom.

The union of Canadian servicemen with Dutch war brides forever entwined the lineage of the two nations. So great was the impact of Canada's role in determining the destiny of the Netherlands that immigration to Canada grew, and vibrant Dutch-Canadian communities appeared all across the country.

Gert van't Holt

I think no two countries share the magnificent love that is so evident between Canada and the Netherlands. It is because after five years of occupation the Canadian soldiers gave back our liberty, our freedom, and the bonds were stronger because the Canadian soldiers stayed in the Netherlands after the war. That is why the Canadian veterans have such big bonds with Holland and not with France or Italy. They were moving through those countries, but in Holland came the liberation, and the soldiers stayed for a longer time. So they had the possibility to get in touch with the people, and I think this bond of friendship is still there.

Jack Heidema

The friendship started in the fall of 1944 when the south was liberated by the Canadian troops, and that grew stronger and stronger, and it will never go away. It's been sixty years, and that friendship is strong and deep. It has deep roots, and the roots go back to all the suffering, and the suffering was ended by the Canadians. They were the liberators. It will never go away. Talk to any Dutch child eight years and up, ask them, "Tell me about the Canadians." They go, "Canadians liberated my grandpa and my grandma." They know. As a matter of fact, the national anthem "O Canada" is taught in Holland, it's part of the curriculum in the Dutch schools.

Al Armstrong, 14th Canadian Hussars

It's been sixty years, and I find it very difficult to believe that the Dutch still feel the same about us as they did then. I've been back to France, back to Belgium, back to Holland, and in Holland if you're wearing a maple leaf on your lapel as a civilian, they still can't do enough for you. The first time I went back to Holland in 1972 I was with a branch colour guard, we were a veteran colour guard. We did a parade into a cemetery, and where they stopped us there, the chap who was with me saw that the first nine rows were men of his company. It was a very devastating effect. So we went back into town, we were sitting in an outdoor beer garden quietly talking. I know he was very upset. And there's a Dutch couple standing at the entrance of the beer garden, and they had a little girl. Len and I were sitting there talking and the first thing I know this little girl was tapping me on the shoulder. I look around and she's got a huge bouquet of flowers and in good English she said, "My mother and dad want you to know that they thank you for what you did for us." That is very emotional. That's the way the Hollanders are.

Martin van Denzen

After the war there were no houses in Holland, living quarters were very scarce, there was no work. So that's when the great influx of people that started to move away, and a lot of them went to Canada. Professionals and non-professionals, they built a life in Canada. Princess Margriet was born in Canada, and she is known as the Canadian princess, more so by the early immigrants than by the newer ones.

Pierre Faribault, Fusiliers Mont-Royal

The Dutch have a great recognition for the Canadians. In 2000 I went over for the big party they had there, and it was amazing to see that the majority of those people weren't even born then and they still have a great recognition for the Canadians.

I remember after that I rented a car because I went to France, and when I came back with the car to return the car in Amsterdam, I was stopped by a cop. He came over, and I said, "I am a Canadian and I'm lost." He said, "You're a Canadian, what can I do for you?" He forgot about the thing that I did completely. I asked him what did I do, and he said I was in a bus section. I can't speak the Dutch language, so I couldn't read the road sign, but he changed his mind the minute I said I was a Canadian, no matter if I was a veteran or not. I was a Canadian period. To me Holland is my second country.

Charles Barrett, Highland Light Infantry

I hadn't been to any reunions, I avoided them because when the war was over I closed the book. I came back to a daughter and a wife, a daughter I had never seen. I was busy getting adjusted to having a family and getting back into work again, and I concentrated on that. I put the war to one side, and I really didn't follow up on the reunions or anything to any extent. I didn't want to talk about the war; I lived in the present and planned for the future. I did go over to Holland for the fiftieth anniversary, and it was the most rewarding experience I've ever had. To see the gratitude and the kindness and the friendliness of the Dutch people was really remarkable. I stayed with a gracious, friendly family that I had never met before, and I felt very much at home. Now the one thing that I realized while I was there was how they revere the dead that we left behind us. Every child at some time in the school year is given a grave to look after. It's too bad that we in Canada have never got that sense of respect for what was done for this country.

John Drummond, Regina Rifle Regiment/Saskatoon Light Infantry

I was back in Holland on three different occasions. Two of them — 1995 and the year 2000 — a lot of it came back to me then. I still have contacts there, I keep in contact with some of the people. This one lady, she was only ten years old when the war ended. I was in this small town at the end of the war, and we were involved with the Underground, and they took pictures of us and got names and addresses. I can remember we were there possibly a couple of weeks in that town. Across the street from where we were staying the father of this family came to our place, and they wanted several of us to go over and meet his family. I think that three or four of us went over, and I just received some mail a few days before and I had a parcel of chocolate bars from my mother. This fellow said he had three girls in the family, three young girls, so I took three chocolate bars and I gave them to these kids. They may be eight, ten, and twelve, and it was the first chocolate that they had remembered seeing. That was quite a treat for them. When I went back there in '95 I had a letter from the mayor, and he wanted me to lay a wreath at their celebration. They have two days of celebration — the first day is the liberation and the next day is remembrance. They were having a function in the library, and I was invited to go to that, and this woman came over to me and she had an album with her, and she said to me, "You're Mr. Drummond," and I said yes. She said, "You wouldn't remember me, but I was the little girl you gave a chocolate bar to," and she told about living across the road and she remembered me coming over, and so I had a little visit with her. She had this album and she was showing me pictures that the Underground people had taken at that time and here she had the three wrappers of these chocolate

LEFT: De man met de twee hoeden (The man with two hats) *was sculpted by Dutch artist Henk Visch. The statue celebrates the bond between Canada and the Netherlands. A second statue was erected in Ottawa. Located near Het Loo Palace in Apeldoorn, the National Monument is located in the city that celebrates De Bevrijding with the May 5th parade every year.* ABOVE: *The imprint of Canada on the Netherlands (detail of the National Monument in Apeldoorn).*

bars in the album. After all that time, for fifty years! So I've kept in contact with her and she has a lot of memories about the liberation. A lot of those people still have quite a hatred for the Germans. They've never forgotten it.

The evidence of these bonds can be seen in the Netherlands to this day. The Dutch town of Diever incorporated the maple leaf into their coat of arms. Memorials and military plaques commemorating Canadian actions and deeds during the war are found all over the Netherlands. Dutch schools teach about Canada and the role Canadians played in their history. That ongoing education has created an atmosphere of warm hospitality for Canadian visitors to the Netherlands.

Al Armstrong, 14th Canadian Hussars

Some of our men have talked to the children of Holland when they go back on reunions and so forth, and they usually have twenty or twenty-five questions they have to ask, and I'm ashamed to admit it, but the questions they ask can make some of our Canadian school sessions look really bad. These kids knew more about what we were doing there than our people do.

Douglas Lavoie, Fort Garry Horse

You can't go anywhere in Holland and the children not know about what Canada did during the war. They weren't there, they weren't born, they weren't even thought of, but their parents and their grandparents kept it alive. That goes for Normandy too. Of course there was lots of France that hardly even knew that the war was on. But the parents and grandparents, their children all know what the Canadians did. Why our children don't know what they know over there — I suppose it's always been said that Canada's not a warlike nation. Whether we were warlike or not shouldn't be an excuse that our children are not taught what the war was all about, what the veterans did, and what other people think of Canada over in Europe. There's something planted there, and it's not going to leave overnight.

Every May 5 when the Dutch celebrate De Bevrijding, they pay tribute to Canadian veterans who liberated their country. The parades in honour of Canadian veterans are now legendary for their magnitude and the warmth towards the Canadian men who came to the Netherlands as liberators and left as lifelong friends.

Sydney Frost (Princess Patricia's Canadian Light Infantry) at the May 1990 celebration of the crossing of the Ijssel River (with the 48th Highlanders).

George Mummery, Highland Light Infantry

You've heard of the parade at Apeldoorn? I don't call Apeldoorn a parade, I think it's one of the biggest love-ins that I've ever been to in my life. You're walking down, and all the grey-haired women, they're all the age that you would have been there, so you go over and you kiss them and that's fine. And then the following year when we get home and I went to the Warrior's Day Parade at the Exhibition and my regiment doesn't have a big group here, so I was marching in with the 48th Highlanders, and we just got through the Princes' Gates and out of the people from the sidewalk about twenty-odd feet away this woman, I guess would be mid-forties, came running out and threw her arms around me and says, "I remember you." I said, "Sorry, I don't," and she said, "I'm from Apeldoorn" — she was here on a holiday. She said, "I remember you from the Apeldoorn parade!"

Elly Dull

It is a love affair. The Canadians were so prominent in Holland, and it really struck me again when I was there at the fiftieth Liberation festivities. I had been in Canada for many years, but it was very important for me to go back to Amsterdam in May 1995 when I was standing on the very same stone that I stood on fifty years earlier as a child to see these vintage war trucks and jeeps and everything coming back over the very same bridge, down the same boulevard. When the fiftieth Liberation festivities were there in 1995, I think six thousand veterans came over, and to me it was really reliving what we saw then, and just how deeply grateful, how enormously joyous, how unbelievable people were that this was actually happening — how friendly these boys were. We didn't realize these were boys from farms, from Newfoundland, we couldn't even pronounce the name Saskatchewan, we didn't have a clue about the geography; they were from far away, they spoke English, and they had a maple leaf, and they were very friendly.

Jim Parks, Royal Winnipeg Rifles

The people start clapping and that feeling you get that goes through you, you can't control your emotions. In order to control mine I walked over to start shaking hands instead of staying in the ranks. I figured to hell with this, why should I stay in the ranks? I started shaking hands. A couple of other guys did the same thing, and it spread right along the parade. People were shaking hands and hugging you and all that, it was quite an experience. You say, "Why me?" You soak it up and you still can't say, "Why is it I'm doing it, why am I getting this?" You don't know how to react to it. Well, if the tears come, well, let them come. I used to worry about that, but not anymore. But if a tear comes, let them come.

Ada Wynston

I have been active with the veterans since 1980. I go back every five years when they go to Holland to celebrate. I work closely with the Thank You Canada committee, with the parade people in Apeldoorn. I do anything I can to help them at least to relive some of the good things, they don't want to talk about the bad things. When they go to Holland they feel at home, and for me it is so important — especially now that they're aging rapidly — to give them the chance to be treated royally, and they get that when they go to Holland. In a city like Apeldoorn, which was first liberated by the 48th Highlanders, three hundred thousand people show up for a parade of Canadians — that's a lot. And they're overwhelmed by this, and I say don't be, it's normal. They get flowers or they sit on tanks and I talk to them and they say, "We don't get this treatment in Canada," and I said, "That's not my fault. You have to speak up, you don't talk about what you've done. Speak to the children in the schools, they don't know what you did." And this is what Holland does, they won't forget. In '95 we set up a foundation, five hundred indigent veterans threw all their names in a hat and pulled out fifty-five because we didn't have any more money, we couldn't get anything out of [the government of] Canada, and those fifty-five went over in '95 and we had billets for them, all of the vets travelled free. Nobody had to pay a cent when they were there. Now it is up to us in 2005 to give them one more chance to go for the sixtieth anniversary.

Elly Dull

It is immensely important, and it lives through the next generation and the generation after that. Going back to 1995 the fiftieth Liberation celebration in Holland, and it has been noted every year, but certainly every five years and massively so in 1995. There were planeloads of veterans going over, I think six thousand in total plus their caregivers. We went in April to be there in May, and I made sure that my children were there because they were really brought up with this story, and I remembered being moved, and there were some veterans ahead of me in Schipol airport and as they went through the passport check the veteran presented his passport, and the custom official said, "Sir, we didn't ask for your passport when you entered here fifty years ago, and we don't ask for it now. Please be welcome."

> The evidence is apparent in Canada as well. Every spring the tulips bloom in Ottawa and across the country. As a gesture of gratitude, Queen Juliana presented Ottawa with one hundred thousand tulip bulbs in 1945. The annual bloom became a tourist attraction, and in 1953 the Tulip Festival was started. Today the festival has grown nation-wide, with over 2 million tulip blooms reminding Canadians of the friendship that has blossomed between the two countries.

Al Sellers, Governor General's Horse Guards

Because Canada gave refuge to the Dutch monarchy in Ottawa during the war, I think that struck home with the Dutch too. They had a little bit of Holland in Canada. I guess we'll never be able to explain what keeps us so darn closely attached. I can't — it's just a natural thing.

Al Armstrong, 14th Canadian Hussars

When Margriet was born here in Ottawa, they made that little part of where they were a part of Holland. I think that was great, it was another connection between our two countries. If you've ever been to Ottawa, just look at the tulips as proof of our ties.

John Honsberger, 4th Canadian Armoured Division

We have the connection with the Tulip Festival in Ottawa and so on. The Dutch developed a special relationship.

> Perhaps the most poignant and lasting evidence of the bond between the Netherlands and Canada is the Canadian War Cemeteries in the Netherlands. These monuments exemplify the personal sacrifice of each Canadian soldier who fell fighting for De

LEFT: *The Canadian War Cemetery at Bergen op Zoom.* CENTRE: *The Canadian War Cemetery at Holten.* RIGHT: T*he Canadian War Cemetery at Groesbeek.*

Bevrijding. Every name places a human face on the conflict. Every age shows how young the men were and how much of a lifetime was forfeited for others to live in freedom. Each a Canadian who would never return to his homeland again, permanent guests on Dutch soil — soil that they died making free.

Gert van't Holt

When I walk around [the Holten Canadian War Cemetery] I always get sad when I read the ages of the young men who are buried here — eighteen, nineteen, twenty years old. They came over to a strange land far from home and gave their lives for people they didn't know. We don't know the men who are buried here, we don't know their faces, but we know that they came to sacrifice their life for freedom. In one way or another they are our friends, and we will always take care of this cemetery to thank the people who came over to liberate us.

George Mummery, Highland Light Infantry

I lost a lot of buddies. There are eight cemeteries where our guys are buried. Most of the last group are buried at Groesbeek. We lost five hundred and some-odd — which is quite a bit. We went through a lot of guys. There were more wounded than there are killed.

It's quite emotional really because you're reading the names of the guys you knew. Like here you go through a cemetery and you see Mr. Jones or Mr.... but now you're looking at Private so-and-so eighteen, Sergeant so-and-so twenty-one, Lieutenant so-and-so twenty-four, and they never got a chance.

ABOVE: *The monument at the Canadian War Cemetery at Holten.* CENTRE: *Inscription at the entrance to the Canadian War Cemetery at Groesbeek.* RIGHT: *The monument with wreaths at the Canadian War Cemetery in Bergen op Zoom.*

Ed Newman, Royal Hamilton Light Infantry

They do a marvellous job of tending the Canadian graves. They have a system in Holland where once the child is four years old they take them out to the cemeteries and this is an annual thing — my understanding is three times a year— including their liberation day and of course the eleventh of November. They go around and they place a tulip on every Canadian's grave, and this is done by the children from the ages of four until they're twelve. Each year there's a new group of four-year-olds and it's an ongoing thing, and it's been that way ever since the war ended. This is how they introduce them and they're in this program for eight years. It's just an absolute ongoing tribute, there's no two ways about it. And it's marvellous.

Lini Grol

Oh, you should see the war cemetery in Nijmegen! It is just impeccable, and the beauty is our Dutch children are quite rambunctious, they're little devils. The teacher comes there with them and they each have their own grave and they quietly go to their own grave, they have adopted their own grave. They put a little flower in. I took my parents there one day, now my parents knew how these little rascals were and, oh, that teacher coming there, she is going to have it. And they were amazed how good they were at the cemetery, no noise, they were all quietly going about their business, then they lined up and prayed and they went again. They are still there, they still come there a few times a year, the teacher comes and they tell them about the war and how much we owe the Canadians and the Americans. Canadian boys were seventeen years old if you please, mere children. To be frank the Germans were worse, they had children who were fourteen years old.

Gert van't Holt

Because a lot of Canadians came to Holland to visit the graves, we had in the fifties and sixties a program that was called a hosting program. The families of the fallen soldiers came to the Netherlands and we put them up with host families — so

Group of victorious Canadians holding up a captured Nazi flag.

there was growing a bond between Dutch people and the families of the fallen soldiers. We called it the pilgrimage, and every year hundreds of them came over to Holland, were invited to visit the graves, and we had a ceremony. Especially in Holten where the cemetery is located, there are very strong bonds with families in Canada because of that.

I am the chairman of the committee Welcome Again Veterans. This committee is in Holten. In the eighties there came a question from Canada from the veterans of the world war to visit Holten in the same way as the families did in the fifties and the sixties. We invited the veterans to come over to Holten, they were hosted by local families, and we had a ceremony here. In 1980 we had hundreds, in 1985 about two hundred, in 1990 we had seven hundred, and in 1995 we had four thousand of them to host in this area. We made a program for them of sightseeing, visiting, but the main thing is the ceremony here at the cemetery.

Why we fought: Canadian soldiers with Dutch children at Marken Island in July 1945. Left to right: J.Dolan, E.R. Hancock, H.S. Neely.

The Canadian War Cemeteries are kept immaculate. The care of the Dutch people ensures that the memory of these men will be honoured forever. In southwest Netherlands is Bergen op Zoom Canadian War Cemetery, where 968 Canadians are buried, casualties of the Battle of the Scheldt. Near Nijmegen in eastern Netherlands is Groesbeek Canadian War Cemetery, where 2,300 Canadians rest and another 103 are memorialized since they have no known graves. North of the city of Holten in northeast Netherlands is the Holten Canadian War Cemetery, where 1,355 Canadians are buried, most of whom were killed in the later stages of the war.

Canadians who died in the Netherlands are also buried at the Reichwald Forest Cemetery in Germany (706 RCAF and 1 soldier), the Rheinberg War Cemetery in Germany (516), and the Adegem Canadian War Cemetery in Belgium (848, mostly from the Battle of the Scheldt).

The cost of De Bevrijding was high. Canadians are proud of their role. The Dutch will never forget. It can be summed up by the inscription on the memorial at Groesbeek Canadian War Cemetery: *Pro amicis mortui amicis vivimus*, "We live in the hearts of friends for whom we died."

Lest we forget.

The Canadian War Cemetery at Holten.

Janice Summerby — Veterans Affairs Canada

Jean and Calvin Wilson — Black Watch Association

Jack van der Laan — The Canada Netherlands Friendship Association

Captain Tim Fletcher — The Royal Hamilton Light Infantry

Martin van Denzen — President, Dutch Canadian Association of Greater Toronto

Andrew Irwin — Royal Canadian Navy

Elizabeth Delbello

Baldwin Verstraete — Verstraete Travel & Tours

BIBLIOGRAPHY

ARCHIVAL SOURCES

Association of Liberation Children

Black Watch War Diary

Canadian Heroes

Confederation Remembers Archives

Department of National Defence Canada

Department of Veterans Affairs Canada

Dutch Consulate Toronto

Dutch-Canadian Association

Estevan Saskatchewan Library On-Line SSR Resources

Government of Canada Privy Council Office

Highland Light Infantry War Diary

Horton Journal of Canadian History

Humboldt State University digital archives

Jewish Virtual Library

Juno Beach Centre

National Archives of Canada

Radio Netherlands Wereldomroep

Rijksinstituut voor Oorlogsdocumentatie

Royal Winnipeg Rifles War Diary

Simon Wiesenthal Centre

Thank You Canada

The Anne Frank Centre

The Dominion Institute

The Holland Ring

U.S. Army Centre of Military History

University of Oklahoma Law Centre digital archives

War Amps of Canada

Webster University digital archives

Welcome Again Veterans

BOOKS

Amsterdam tijdens den hongerwinter. Nederland-Archief: 1947.

Fowler, T. Robert. *Valour in the Victory Campaign.* General Store Publishing House, 1995.

Frank, Anne. *The Diary Of A Young Girl.* Bantam Books, 1991.

BIBLIOGRAPHY

Green Route Up: A Canadian Armoured Division. Netherlands: Mouton & Cy Ltd, 1945.

Michelin Benelux 2004.

Reader's Digest Great World Atlas.

Schogt, Henry. *The Curtain: Witness and Memory in Wartime Holland.* Waterloo: Wilfrid Laurier University Press, 2003.

Willes, John. *Out of the Clouds.* Port Perry Printing Ltd., 1981.

INTERNET SOURCES

www.auschwitz.dk

www.blackwatchcanada.com

www.godutch.com

www.koninklijkhuis.nl

www.thefreedictionary.com

www.warmuseum.ca

www.worldwar-2.net

MAGAZINES AND NEWSPAPERS

Airforce Magazine

The Globe & Mail

The Hamilton Spectator

PHOTOGRAPHIC SOURCES

1st Canadian Parachute Battalion Association

Charles Barrett Highland Light Infantry

Department of National Defence Canada

Elizabeth Delbello

Imperial War Museum (U.K.)

Jim Parks Royal Winnipeg Rifles

National Archives Of Canada

Nederland-Archief

Rijksinstituut voor Oorlogsdocumentatie

Sydney Frost Princess Patricia's Canadian Light Infantry

U.S. Department of Defence

War Amps of Canada

Welcome Again Veterans

TRAVEL SPONSOR

Joel Matlin, President, AlarmForce

RECOMMENDED READING

Sydney Frost. *Once A Patricia.* Vanwell Publishing, 1988.

Sydney Frost. *Always A Patricia.* Borealis Press, 2004.

Lini Grol. *A Matter of the Heart.* Essence Publishing, 1997.

John Honsberger. *Osgoode Hall: An Illustrated History.* Toronto: Dundurn Press, 2004.

Richard Rohmer. *Generally Speaking: The Memoirs of Major-General Richard Rohmer.* Toronto: Dundurn Press, 2004.